KIND
THANK
FOR ALL YOU
HELP I SO HAPPY
TO KNOW YOU
& LOOK FORWARD
TO KNOWING
MORE !!

State of Mind

The Man Who Knows Reveals
The Secrets of Mind Over Matter

Alain Nu

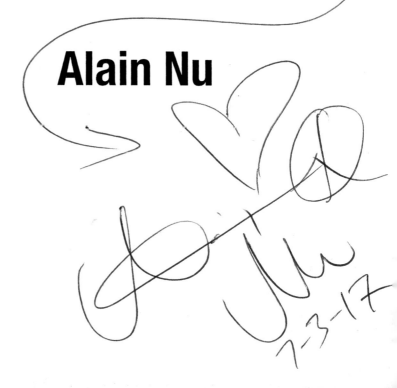

7-3-17

Library of Congress Cataloging-in-Publication Data

Library of Congress Catalog Number: 2015954450

Copyright © 2015 Alain Nu
ISBN-10: 0-9842085-6-9
ISBN-13: 978-0-9842085-6-2

Publisher: CFBP Bestsellers
An imprint of CFB Productions Inc.
P. O. Box 50008, Henderson, NV 89016
www.CFBPBestsellers.com

Typeset in 11/18/24 Helvetica Neue and 11/14 pt Hoefler Text.
Cover illustration and design by Stuart Palm.
Photographs by Fredde Lieberman.

DEDICATION

I dedicate this book to Nicolette Anika Nu. The world will be so exciting for someone who is as creatively energetic as you. I know it will be filled with laughter, ideas and dreams.

It will also, at times, be quite challenging and filled with lessons. Pay close attention to the lessons... you always somehow come up with a way to understand things. Your wisdom is beyond your years. I'm not sure how you do it, but whatever you are doing, just keep on doing it, because it's working! You are so charming and bright; I don't need to be a mind reader to know that yours will be a joy-filled, adventurous, and incredible life.

I am always there for you. I hope that one day you will read this book, and it will intrigue you, and make you laugh.

I will love you until the end of time.

ACKNOWLEDGEMENTS

I want to thank the universe for granting me this experience here on Earth. I also thank every one of the following for their special contribution to my life: Tanya Thielke, Douglas Moors, Katherine Rettke, John B. Alexander, Victoria Alexander, Lloyd Auerbach, Sir Richard Branson, Bill Brunelle, Joey Burton, Oso Mfundishi Tayari Casel, Laurel Chiatt, David Chorvinsky, Scott Deming, Bill Duggan, Brenda Dunne, Deborah Enten, Jerome Finley, Chris Fleming, Paul Foster, James Fox, Lorne and Emily Greene, Bill Hayes, Steve Heston, Richard Garriott, Uri Geller, Scott Grossberg, Patrick Hull, Robert Jahn, Ryan Katz, Diane Keane, Eileane Keane, Matthew Lesko, Wendy Lesko, Chris Moon, Marcia Proctor, James Randi, Deborah and John Rogers, Ken Trombly, Richard Webster, Andy and Linda Weintraub, Aaron Alexander, Scott and Jenny Alexander, Kara Allen, Lee Asher, Steve Banachek, Nick Belleas, Leo Boudreau, Joel Braverman, Craig Browning, Bob Cassidy, Linda Cator, Christian Chelman, Christopher Davy, Joan DuKore, Kevin Dunn, Enrique Enriquez, Jeff and Tessa Evason, Rebecca Fried, Joel Givens, Gary and Junko Goldberg, Denny Haney, Will Hardyman, Clay Harris, Chis Hatfield, Mike High, Scott Hitchcock, Ken Horsman, Spencer Horsman, Wanda Jacobsen, Mikey Johnson, Ross Johnson, Michael Jons, Brandon Kent, Jerome Lim, David London, Millard Longman, Dirk Losander, Sheila Lyon, Dan Marx, Rick Maue, Max Maven, Jack Maxwell, Mike Meadows, Jeff McBride, Larry Miesse, Bill Montana, Janet and Hoa Nguyen, Carla and Steve Phillips, Christopher Real, John Riggs, Cynthia Roebuck, Michael Rosman, John Ross, Alex Saltz, Irvey Saltz, Warren Saltz, Nate Sangsland, Sue Schulze, Neale Scryer, Luna Shimada, Lattie Smart, Faith Leahy Thielke, John Thielke, Christopher Thisse, Steve Thomas, Desiree Velez, Sandy and Danny Vogelman, and finally, my dogs Gypsy and Juji, and my cats, Clover, Jinx and Saki.

Special thanks goes to my executive editor and personal manager extraordinaire, Clinton Ford Billups, Jr., my valued literary consutant Dr. Richard Restak, as well as my proof-reading squad: Erik Bisanz, Elly Brown, Bill Cushman, Gregory Edmonds, Stuart Palm, Daniel Ulin and Mike Vance. Where would I be without someone to proofread my book? A huge thank you goes to my friend Stuart Palm, who is an extremely talented artist and a very gifted psychic entertainer and speaker from Hong Kong. Finally, thank you, Fredde Lieberman, for making me look good in your photographs.

CONTENTS

INTRODUCTION

My name is Alain Nu, but as *The Man Who Knows*, I am getting a very strong impression that you bought this book right after having experienced seeing me perform somewhere, be it on TV, the Internet, or a cruise ship; watching my show at a theater, casino, university or company event; or hearing me on the radio.

How am I doing so far? If you've never seen me in performance, then I stand corrected. After all, this stuff is not an exact science! But let me continue to read your mind... I am sensing that you are interested in learning something amazing to show your friends and associates at your next business association networking event, family reunion or local pub... Am I getting better?

Still, there is something more about you than all that obvious stuff. It's quite possible, if you can remember, that you had a strange dream or premonition that meant something more to you later. If not a dream, I feel it was triggered by some other experience of something you cannot understand that occurred at some point in your life, which made you wonder about the possibilities of another world or another dimension. You were wondering if this book might be able to provide scientific answers to you that might settle the confusion or awe that you felt.

You may have had these experiences recur throughout your life at different times. Try to remember those moments. I feel like there might have even been an encounter that happened to you that involved some kind of entity or spirit that you became aware of, and still possibly, to this day, are a little creeped-out about. If this is not true, then this book was probably a gift, given to you by a strange friend to whom something like this did happen!

There is no doubt in my mind, though, that you are a bit skeptical by nature. You enjoy analyzing. You are not gullible, but you have insecurity about being thought of as gullible. This may have turned you into a bit of a practical rationalist—later in life, you have become a quick-search "Internet wizard," of sorts. You have become an independent spirit of your own learning and your knowledge comes to you from many sources. You are modest about your sources of learning, though you have every reason to not be. You are interested in different aspects about life and how to go about it in a way that is fruitful and productive, not just for yourself, but also for those around you. You tend to look for affirmation from the cosmos more often than you think. To this end, you have a tendency to also cast your luck to the wind, and yet, sometimes it feels to you as if things could still be a bit better.

No, you are not that predictable. I strongly believe that you picked up this book for a reason that will come clear to you. As you looked at the front cover of this book, you were probably a bit skeptical, which caused you to begin flipping through a few of the pages in the middle of the book, just to make sure that this would be something that you were truly interested in. There are only certain books that can really grab you. In this case, a thought crossed your mind that this could be a book about brain games and psychological tricks that you can learn with which to amaze your friends and colleagues. Another thought crossed your mind that possibly, if there could be something, this book might offer you in the way of principles, techniques and clues of how one might learn to really read other people's minds telepathically. You became curious about whether this book might enable you to activate something within yourself that will improve your own telepathic and intuitive mind power with concepts and exercises from which you can try and get instant feedback.

If any of what I mentioned above is true, then not only am I good, I'm also pretty sure you made the right choice. This book is divided into five sections. Part One will offer some rarely-openly-discussed insights regarding the fascinating world of mentalism. It will also teach you some of the "effects" of how mentalists can entertain people. You will learn a few clever psychological "routines" in order to amaze and delight your friends and colleagues. And with just a little bit of practice, they really do work!

There is always an easy and practical explanation to creatively solving the most mysterious things. But not everything in this book will necessarily have an explanation. This is, in fact, where my true interest lies, in the never-ceasing and constantly growing collection of strange and inexplicable things that people have continued to document and spread rumors about. So long as you are aware of enough of the things that happen around you, you are bound to come across certain things that happen in your life that you don't truly understand and that don't make logical sense at all. Usually these moments are so insignificant that it is hard to even notice that they happened. Or perhaps, could it be that we convince ourselves that there is some other logical reason for it happening, so we ignore it? Sometimes, the moment is so strange and so strong that it sticks out, making it completely impossible to ignore.

There are usually the weirder stories of spirit-encounters and psychic impressions that you hear about. If you are hearing such stories second or third-hand, you usually feel that you must be missing an important ingredient that would explain that the whole thing was not really what those people said or thought it was. However, if your experience is first-hand, and especially if there were other people who were there, who were able to verify your claim as having truly happened, you never are really able to solve the mystery except to say, "something must have happened." So it just sits there, and you don't ever really know what to do with it except to just sometimes remember that it happened. Much of the time, you will even force it out of your brain, and forget that the entire incident happened at all, just to make proper sense of reality. If you do that, however, it still remains a part of your subconscious.

In Part Two, I will be recalling some of my own true stories, aspects of my life, as well as the stories of different people, some who are friends of mine, and some people who I have met and become friends with during my research and travels. Some of these people are experts in their own unusual studies. Some are showbiz folks, since that is my immediate community, then again, some are just ordinary, educated people, but who just happened to experience something uncanny that could not be ignored.

Part Three will begin by introducing you to the amazing and enigmatic Uri Geller, who built an extremely successful life around being the man of mystery that he is. From there, we will begin a discussion on many of the more recent scientific studies that will likely, shift our human understanding of all things into an entirely new era of how we think of ourselves. Serious scientists, some at prestigious Ivy League universities, were involved in many of the studies. After years of research, we can now experiment on our own thoughts using basic electronic methods and principles that enable you to test your own personal mental abilities over the laws of chance and expectation. One may also, using the same apparatus, experiment on one's own ability to direct the laws of certainty by using the power of one's will. It is the hope of those scientists who have invested so much time, money and research into this field that eventually it will become possible to see, without a doubt, that there is a part of your mind which can do something that you didn't originally know you could do. Those who have bothered to put to the test any of the Random Event Generator (REG) experiments will have, most likely, surprised themselves by the strange connections that they witnessed. This includes me.

Part Four will crack open the door to some ancient mystical knowledge and may introduce you to a whole other form of understanding. Many of you might already have a basic understanding of the Chakras and Numerology, but do not understand it enough to see how easy it is to integrate them in useful ways. Neither affects any other core belief system or religion negatively, although interpretations may vary between cultures. While visualizing the Chakras (for the body) or the secret messages embedded in Numerology (for the mind), there are easy ways to use these systems as a profound guide filled with ancient teachings and wisdoms that can help direct the energy of your spirit. You will also be invited to experience the mystical effects of these ancient but practical ideals. They are, after all, based on the oldest and most powerful secret systems of understanding known in human history. Normally, this realm of understanding and appreciation of such mysteries is conducted completely outside of the realm that occupies the world of performing or capital gain. When one looks at some of the more mysterious characters throughout history, it's interesting to note that many of the most-gifted individuals were not at all looking to do anything other than to explore the infinite limits of their own selves. Many them, like Edgar Cayce, were not performers. Some have become world-renowned people of mysterious powers. In most cases, however, it is not the money that drives them. It is their practice of such unusual teachings and its wisdoms that is (in most cases) the practitioner's true passion.

Part Five will take a moment to consider everything that we've experienced in the previous four parts. It will then offer ways for you to prove to yourself the possibilities of an invisible cosmic connection, by offering suggestions on what you can do to test yourself day to day, so you can practice throughout life. In this last section of the book, these tests and experiments will not be methods manifested by any form of mentalism or overt deception of any kind. You will be offered a chance to test your own actual "psychic awareness" by literally sensing the energy within you and around you. You will be shown how to test your own ability to project or predict the future, or even to truly read people's minds while fluidly connecting with mathematic interpretations and the energetic movements of other-worldly cosmic dimensions!

Impossible, you say? Well, prepare to open your mind. Read on, and experience for yourself, the impossible made possible!

Enjoy,

Alain Nu
The Man Who Knows™
Washington, DC

PART ONE

REFLECTIONS OF FORGOTTEN POWERS

Just what is mentalism? Is it a power? Is it a trick? Or could it be both? It seems odd that this paradox still exists today. I call it the Mentalism Paradox. You are now about to witness, as I try to explain everything that I know about how to make sense of it all. And after we uncover as much as I can on this subject, we will try to break into other paradoxes as well. These days, mentalism is seen as a discipline within the performing arts. So to begin, calling oneself a mentalist, is similar to calling oneself an actor, or a producer, or a writer. The art form, in other words, does not embody the entire person. So the fact that one might dedicate oneself to a specific practice does not mean entirely that one ought to be perceived as a practitioner of only that one thing.

Many "paranormal people" who have embodied the role of urban shaman, or mysterious enigmas, will use mentalism within their repertoire, but that does not account for everything that they do or all the disciplines that they know. Mentalism is certainly not even the most mysterious art form among the other mystery arts. Oracle readings (like cards, palms, runes, and numerology) have been taught since ancient times and can be quite mysteriously revealing of yourself or others around you. Hypnosis is not only uncanny but quite helpful in many different ways, yet it relies on nothing but pure mental suggestion. Ghost hunting also has its own methods of being sensitive to interpreting unstable fluctuations in otherwise random signal patterns and can produce quite amazing phenomena without any use of trickery.

In many ways, there is a good possibility that mentalism routines were first used as a "theatrical support-system" for other mystery art forms like spiritualism, séance rituals, and even tribal shamanic ritual presentations. Mentalism was also most likely used to "sprinkle lightly" over more in-depth mystery presentations of spirit mediums to help punctuate or flavor early spiritualist parties and gatherings in the late 1800's to early 1900's with something that came across as both topic-related as well as enchanting to share. It was during this time that the art of mentalism formed one basic underlying philosophy. It is important to know that, otherwise, mentalism does not rule out any method, principle, or design, to support its own existence. Because it has been viewed upon as an "entertainment" throughout history, there was never anything that prevented it from using anything at all, which it had at its disposal, to support both its purpose and success.

CHAPTER 1

FACT OR FICTION?

To offer the most precise definition for the presentation of mentalism, whether such a demonstration is seen executed using scientific, psychological, oracular, mathematical, hypnotic or illusionary means, it will be perceived as "mentalism" so long as it supports the idea of evoking genuine mystery and amazement into its overall concept. Therefore:

Mentalism is ANY kind of demonstration that is designed to amaze, baffle or surprise, and which refers to any aspect of the mind, the way we think, or the human cosmic potential.

I believe I am quite accurate to boil this definition down to the above statement. In the following chapters, I will supply you with some beginner mentalism routines, which you can learn and practice to amaze your friends with. All of the routines are based on clever ideas that I have taken the liberty to update, evolve and improve upon. For now, however, allow me to introduce you to the thought process in the most objective way I can. Mentalism is shrouded in many mysteries as well as mysterious lessons based on its philosophies. What exactly is it, and how relevant is it to the world of unexplained phenomena?

When watching television specials or special events which spotlight a mind reading performance, or seeing someone doing this on stage, it is much of the time the goal of the performer to offer the experience of the most genuine inexplicable phenomena, either for real, or, if not, as if it were happening for real. So a mentalist can also be any mystery artist who might use a back-up plan in case their attempt at real mindreading starts to feel like it is not working or perhaps just make use of a "novel aside" while providing their evening's worth of entertainments. Many professional mind readers today, in fact, do try to interact with their observers so that a genuinely mysterious connection somehow forms, but will also be prepared to include, within their program, a small repertoire of more theatrical routines or illusions to add more mystery, texture and flavor to their program. These days, there are performers who perform only mentalism, as it has now become its own discipline within the broader genre of what would be best called the "mystery arts." Occasionally, you will run into university professors, lecturing physicians, priests, rabbis, corporate speakers, hypnotists and people of all trades and professions, interested in mentalism. Even Seinfeld actor, Jason Alexander, designed his own show in 2006 that he premiered at the famously renowned Magic Castle, in Hollywood, CA, in which he played his own role as a mentalist.

The main purpose for mentalism is primarily entertainment, yet it is so close to being perceived as genuine that it is often confused by any live witnesses that what they are seeing must be real. Performers who follow a mentalism format generally will try to control the audience's experience so the effects are theatrically displayed in an entertaining but amazing paranormal way. So how is mentalism different from being a magician? Some believe that there really is hardly any difference. That since it is mostly a deception, and a deception is a deception... then it must be just all about fakery and hoaxing. But between the performance of magic and mentalism, what mentalism recognizes is that it is generally better at invoking a genuine feeling that supports the belief or contemplation in the uncanny powers of our minds and other human potentials. Magic, on the other hand, is generally more about entertaining people with visual surprises, illusions, intellectual curiosities and absurd premises that defy logic and our senses, but in a way that usually does not provoke belief systems.

So whereas the intent of magic seems to center itself on impossibilities, mentalism's contribution to the mystery arts is seen to more center itself on our mind's amazing *possibilities*.

ACTS OF MENTALISM

Mentalism can be a genuinely real demonstration of mind power, focus or exceptional human control. An example of such would be as follows:

You show an ordinary straw and a potato and then proclaim that you will use the power of your own focused energy to literally push the straw directly through the potato. This would be an act of solid through solid. By knowing how to hold the straw, how small and soft the potato should be and how much force to exert in which direction, you can do exactly what you proclaim in a most impressive manner! Since you state that something amazing is about to happen, until your audience sees it with their own eyes, unless they have seen anything like this before, no one will realize until then that it could ever be done. The effect is not only amazing, but what you say will happen is exactly the thing that does actually happen (when done correctly). So, in this case, the mentalist presents a demonstration of physics that is both *genuinely real and really impressive.*

Mentalism effects can also employ mathematical or psychological principles that are used to guide one's line of thinking into believing that some extraordinary mind reading feat has taken place, when in fact it is actually a well-done hoax that only refers to that alleged human potential without actually being it.

To a more extreme degree, one could pretend to put a coin in one hand, while concealing it in the other. After which, if one closes both hands into fists and then has the audience imagine that the coin is actually a subatomic particle that occupies no determinate time or space (as in the laws of quantum physics), it could be experienced by an audience to mysteriously (albeit, deceptively) travel, from one hand to the other, by means of *conscious intention.* Done well *technically,* that could be defined as a mentalism effect. A mental metaphor, which more precisely, uses the coin (and the mystery) as an example. The magic principle which one uses to make the audience believe that the coin is being placed into one hand (when it actually isn't) becomes the analogy to the indeterminate state of the atomic particle you are asking your audience to imagine it to be. Any profound or amazing demonstration that refers to the mind and how we think is technically an act of mentalism.

The most common perceptions of how mentalism is thought of, however, come from a more psychological perspective. Here, one uses the very skills that one expects a mentalist to use in order to exhibit some very successful (and clever) demonstrations. Skills in face-reading, perceptual manipulation, lie-detection, and subliminal suggestions among other principles are all used to give the presenter an edge.

So as for the question of whether or not mentalism is fact or fiction, the truest answer is that it really does explore both, and does so in a way that cultivates deep fascination. It is most concerned with creating an ultimate sense of intrigue above all else. Throughout ancient history, mysterious practitioners have used the secret theatrical principles of mentalism in shamanism, spiritualism, psychic readings, and nowadays, to just simply break the ice with people you don't know in order to create a unique connection to those around you.

CAN SUCH POWERS BE USED FOR EVIL?

Philosophically, in its most positive light, mentalism can be seen as a way to open up one's curiosity and fascination for how we think or see things. It might give us the confidence to investigate further how powerful our minds actually are, how sensitive we can be to our surroundings, or more simply, how much the concept of "fortune" plays into our lives.

One wonders, if corrupt people were to practice such secrets, how they might use them reprehensibly. By and large, the more influential artists who teach such skills try to keep an eye out to notify others when this kind of corrupted thinking is spotted in someone they come across. It is obviously morally unacceptable to use such disciplines for anything nefarious, and it is difficult to learn from others if the respect you have for such knowledge can be spotted as faulty or corrupt. Of course, that is not to say that mentalists are guaranteed to be honorable people either. Mentalism is only a discipline taught within the mystery arts that is used by practitioners in a vast assortment of way. Its primary purpose, though, is to entertain.

THE MYSTERY ARTS AND MYSTERIOUS ENIGMAS

The "mystery arts" is a tiny subset of the arts and entertainment world that would include such disciplines as fortune telling, stage hypnosis, sideshow, magic, mentalism, séances, etc. Though each is considered a mystery art form that may borrow or apply an aspect of another's techniques, each is also its own separate discipline.

Because the concept of mentalism allows it to embody any demonstration, effect or trick that is designed to amaze one about our minds or how we think, (as mentioned before), mentalists, usually more so than other practitioners, will tend to use outside principles that are applied from other "mystery art" disciplines. One may explore genuine ESP, hypnosis, oracle reading, sideshow feats, parlor magic, and/or séances. In many ways, mentalism has produced many world-famous mysterious enigmas and men of mystery. The most well-known and influential public figures who have taken on this role over the past fifty years would include The Great Dunninger, The Amazing Kreskin, Uri Geller, and more recently, David Blaine and the UK's Derren Brown, among a few others. However, if you examine each individual's personality, audience and repertoire, it becomes easy to notice that each artist is very different from one another with regards to how they combine, express and apply themselves and their presentations to fit their specialized *brand.*

One must note that these performance artists are not just mentalists, since it appears all of these mysterious public figures are/were also masters of multiple unusual disciplines. So the characters mentioned above no longer are just mentalists, illusionists, hypnotists or psychics. When they begin to start pulling ideas and concepts from other disciplines, it becomes harder to tell exactly what these people are. I see these people as "men of mystery" or "mysterious enigmas." They may use multiple applications of many different disciplines within the mystery arts to convey a specialized style, but what they are doing is just as easily seen as *secondary to who they are and what they are conveying.* It is ultimately the *message* they deliver as public figures about honoring the way we think and how we make choices in our lives that is what they represent and communicate. The demonstrations themselves are *only* presented to engage, exemplify, and punctuate the overall message with elements of theatricality and amazement. Thus, as in all things, it is not about the art, as it is about the artist.

LIFTING SPIRITS USING DEVICES OF DECEPTION

It seems easy to realize that the very nature of mentalism, as mentioned above, supports the idea of our minds having incredible untapped powers. So if one were to try to take stock in such a practice, one might begin by contemplating:

1)   What came first, the illusion or the reality?

2) Might the performance of such mysteries simulate a true mystery that might have actually happened, or a power that we once had which might have been forgotten in history?

3) Can some mystery arts (like mentalism) be seen as a curious vision of things to come?

Perhaps a vision of something that we may all one day comprehend, much like many science fiction authors have written about devices, evolutions and conceptual thinking even before they were brought into existence? For instance, will there ever come a day that we will actually be able to genuinely materialize a live rabbit from within a hat? You may laugh now, but wait another thirty years, and see what happens.

My personal feeling is that ancient ceremonies, mantras, meditations, blessings of all kinds, and even the use of fire and visual theatrics were designed to be symbolic of one's personal spiritual evolution and journey; to rise above the feeling of having limitations and realize our limitless scope to manifest whatever we want in the most profound ways. All of this can be done with just whatever personal resources we have and mental focus. There are those who give in to their humanity, and there are those who try to rise above. At its most base level, our ability to believe is the beginning to everything we have been able to manifest throughout history. Each ceremony, blessing, and incantation is simply there to magnify one's power to believe. Can belief be the beginning of cosmic manifestation? Perhaps it is.

LIES? OR, EXPRESSIONS OF OUR LIMITLESS MIND?

There have recently sprung up a new breed of performance artists who study mentalism techniques, but whose agendas are to demonstrate the *nonexistence* of supernatural powers. The rationale being that since it is possible to create the experience of paranormal phenomena which is only produced by theatrical means, that there must be a greater possibility that *all experienced phenomena* can be broken down to being seen as an elaborate combination of convincing things that lead to a *false belief.* Furthermore, it is rational to think that a false belief spun in the wrong way can be harmful to those who are misled. As a life-long career practitioner and student of mentalism, I have thought and contemplated a lot about this.

Certainly, debunking phony alleged powers has proven to be effective at making one wary of being made gullible. Aesthetically speaking, however, I don't personally believe it is the most effective way of using the art of mentalism. Firstly, the notion that performing mentalism can produce harmful consequences by advocating a belief in something that isn't real, or that it can be used in other unethical ways, is actually not as likely to happen as one might imagine. It takes a great deal of knowledge and years of professional training to become skilled at the many disciplines one would need to master in order to actually blame the entire art of mentalism for such crimes. It would be similar to blaming all clowns for being like serial killer and professional clown, John Wayne Gacy, or blaming the entire art of magic for all the petty to larcenous crimes that magicians have committed over the course of its history.

But it is easy to see that the techniques of mentalism, much like all other art forms, can be used to communicate or manipulate any type of thought, given some cleverly applied creativity. Therefore, one can easily see how mentalism can also inspire one's belief, and communicate insightful messages using its ability to impact its audiences. Many have used their abilities with wisdom and respect throughout the ages.

As it appears, from examining the intentions of early shamanism to modern spiritualism, there is an element that can be seen more from the standpoint that its intention is to use the illusion it creates to magnify the majesty of inspiration and internal transformation in others. In many ways, the art and the very architecture of churches old and new are also designed with great care to aspire towards and/or impress the gods that watch over us. Therefore, just as the stunning beauty of such artwork encourages the churchgoers to be moved to enlightenment, the realization that the act of *beautifying* is also a form of deception might then bring up again the question of both good and bad intentions. As much as it appears that deception on this level can have manipulative intentions that are designed to influence public decisions to its favor, a more sophisticated agenda can be said about its positive intentions. Through such ritualistic intensifying as in the theatrics of priests and shaman, healing processes have also been witnessed to inexplicably manifest. Of course, whether such manifested healing has any connection with the blessings offered from delivering such rituals and incantations remains a controversial mystery.

So might there be something to these ritual devices of theatrics and deceptions that give us something that is more a blessing than just a "lie?" Oddly, there may actually be. Thus Santa Claus is still safe in the minds of children, and mentalism will continue to be a perplexing expression of amazing human potential and of the limitless mind.

CHAPTER 2

TRY MENTALISM

As mentioned in the previous chapter, mentalism, mediumship, psychic detective work, fortune telling, and hypnosis are only five interrelated disciplines among many other practiced "mystery arts." To give you a few examples of the clever methods that one may stumble across while researching the topic of mentalism, however, one must realize that here, you will find mostly methodically-based theatrics that nonetheless deliver quite clever and baffling results.

Such demonstrations are simple examples of the theatrical deceptions that mystery performers and practitioners sprinkle into their programs and presentations to enchant and entertain the notion of superpowers that we may one day realize that we have had access to all along. Or perhaps, could it be an ability which we might have once possessed, but somehow forgot about at the dawn of civilization? As far as the theatrical effects of mentalism refer to specific alleged human potentials or synchronistic scenarios, the act of such a demonstration is generally not the phenomenon itself. Of course, the purpose of this is only to illustrate theatrically an amazing property of the mind while producing an entertaining, baffling and successful result. To use actual ESP, telekinetic healing, or to contact genuine spirits is obviously not always certain, thus performers have, throughout the ages, fallen back on a few mentalism effects, by using other mystery art disciplines as a way to support their own practices. In more recent times, however, this has turned into a "performance mystery art" unto itself.

Mentalism, even if only theatrical in its methods, nonetheless, seems to possess a mysterious effect on the mind. Oddly, the experience of such presentations has been seen to activate motivation, inspiration and change, if not something far deeper and spiritual. As this begins to fold back into properties of hypnosis (which is mostly used for shifting mental patterns and self-transformation) it becomes more evident that mentalism can be used as an *experiential aid* to support the notion of achieving higher mental states and vibrational levels, in the same way that understanding effective communication techniques (like Neuro Linguistic Programming) can guide people effortlessly into trance. Faith healing, as taboo a subject as it is in western society today, has become very popular among certain celebrities, and people in more affluent circles who will travel vast distances to connect with the divine energy that surrounds such people and their customs. Are we only talking about eccentrics here, or is there a more relevant connection?

Most of the time, we tend to see mentalism on viral videos and on television programs. In many ways, this utilizes mentalism in its most effective way, for it is actually more powerful to use mentalism in small doses so that it most effectively leaves people in a state of awe. This state of mind, *created by the illusion* becomes the conduit to hypnosis or a temporary trance state. It is the deception created by mentalism (though scorned by many) that ultimately inspires the mind with a greater awareness or sense of human potentials and possibilities, which are achievable even if against all odds. Despite condemnation from those who warn others that mentalism can lead someone unwary to believe in a false reality, perhaps it should still be permitted as an exploration of what essential positive attributes, besides basic entertainment, it might also possess?

The characteristics of the modern *urban shaman* or *mysterious enigma* can be ultimately summed up as being a combination of:

1) Acquired specialized knowledge and/or alternative disciplines (which may or may not include a theatrical understanding of mentalism): Usually, this is knowledge that is passed down from teacher to student and done so with a sense of respect and loyalty to the message.

2) A strong, charismatic communicator: In urban environments, being a strong communicator helps to connect with the vast and diverse cultures that share the same region. Powerful abilities and talents of such mysterious enigmas will also demonstrate the strength of his/her ability to communicate, since communication can be felt non-verbally, and on vibrational levels as well

3) A benevolent interest in using all personal knowledge and wisdom to empower, inspire and resonate strongly with the

individuals who experience meeting them.

In this chapter, I will introduce you to a few simple methods for effects that will give you a good "starter collection" of fun and original presentations to learn and practice. The purpose of this chapter will be to give you an appreciation for some of the psychological tricks that a mentalist may use, but it will not be, by any means, representative of the entire world of clever ideas and techniques that are out there for you to learn at your leisure. I believe I have laid out a good introductory course that will hopefully, if anything, show you just how intriguing and fun these demonstrations can be to try yourself. If you would rather not spend time on learning every idea from the next few chapters, simply skip ahead to Part Two, and then come back to these beginning chapters when you have more time to dedicate.

Of course, with great power comes great responsibility. So before trying any of the following routines, meditate on how you will deliver it with your own style and subtlety at your next luncheon.

THE CAMPAIGN THAT NEVER WAS

Before we get started, it's probably best that you Google the list of American Presidents, because what I am about to create with you in your mind is a "campaign that never was." We will begin our mental journey by having you first imagine that you are in outer space staring down at the Earth. As you imagine this, find a specific continent on the planet to focus on."

Not a country, mind you, but a more general continent, like 'Europe.' So choose any continent, except Europe, since that was what I just mentioned, okay? You should now have a continent in your mind. Spell it in your thoughts, without writing anything down. Once you've done that let me know. Thank you!"

"Now focus only on the last letter of the continent you have spelled out. If you can, transform that LAST LETTER, so that it now will become the FIRST LETTER of the last name of one of the Presidents of the United States (living or dead)—so, for example, if it's the letter 'L,' think of Lincoln. Go through your list if you have to, but be quick about it. Once you have corresponded the *last letter of the continent* you are thinking of with the *last name of an American president*, what I am now going to do is install a weird image in your mind. I will try to make what you are thinking of now, unlike anything you have ever thought of before. This will be done to make your thought easier to pick up on. So we will continue my mysterious spell as follows..."

"I want you to try to visualize yourself wearing a campaign shirt that has the president's LAST NAME in big letters spelled out across it. You have gone back in time and found yourself during an election time, and you are proudly wearing this candidate's campaign T-shirt while waving an American flag. Now focus on the *second letter* of the president's last name for a moment...

Tell me if you can make that SECOND LETTER become the FIRST LETTER of one of the fifty American states that you can think of. If you can think of a state that begins with the second letter of the President's last name, imagine the president that you are thinking of as representing the state you are now thinking of.

"All American states can be reduced to a two-letter abbreviation. Tell me, could the SECOND LETTER of your state's abbreviation be used as the FIRST LETTER of a WILD ANIMAL that you might see while on a jungle safari? If so, I want you now to imagine yourself wearing your campaign shirt, with the president's name on the front, the two-letter abbreviation of the state you are thinking of on the back, while taking this wild animal, as a pet, out for a walk on a leash to the next local town hall meeting."

"You must admit, you have never thought of this image before in your mind, so this is a completely fresh thought, unfettered by anyone else's influence but your own? Please spend a few more seconds, visualizing exactly the spelling of the President's name printed across your shirt, the state he now represents printed across the back, and while walking your new pet wild animal to the next town hall meeting.

"Wait! I see something! You are representing the state of Delaware, your shirt says VOTE FOR ADAMS, and you have a very large ELEPHANT at the end of your leash—Am I right?"

INSTANT A

That was fun, right? I'm pretty sure it worked, because so long as you

14

followed my instructions as most people would, you would have had
limited choice from the very start. In mentalism, this technique is
known as a "force," because although it appears that your choices
were determined by your own free will, there were actually a couple
of subtle ruses at play that made it so that one's outcome is cleverly
forced each time. What makes this a devilishly fun piece of
mentalism, is how it uses the psychological technique of *process
misdirection* to lead away from the obviousness of its own method,
while simultaneously creating a bizarre picture in your spectator's
mind that becomes surprisingly accurate when revealed.

The first, and most important ruse, is what I will refer to as, my
"Instant A" technique. The goal here is to simply get them to think
of the letter A without realizing that it will be the only letter that
they can think of. The way you instruct them should feel nonchalant;
but at the same time, be assertive with your directions as you say:

Before we get started, it's probably best that you Google the list of
American Presidents, because what I am about to create with you in
your mind, is a "campaign that never was." We will begin our mental
journey by having you first imagine that you are in outer space
staring down at the Earth. As you imagine this, find a specific
continent on the planet to focus on. Not a country, mind you, but a
more general continent, like 'Europe.' So choose any continent
except this time don't choose Europe, since that was what I just
mentioned, okay? You should now have a continent in your mind.
Spell it in your thoughts, without writing anything down. The act of
spelling creates a "mysterious spell."

Although you don't have to recite the above lines like a script, by
doing so, you would be justifying the reason for your spectator to be
focused on the spelling of the names, while making the play on
words with the sort of spell that one would magically cast. We also
begin the process with the thought of our planet and the continents
on the planet, so the mental feeling conveyed is that of moving from
a very broad to a very specific image.

Yet, because you want to be specific about them thinking of a
continent and not just a country, you give them the example by
saying, *"like Europe. But since I said that already, any continent except
Europe, okay?"* What has happened here is, by eliminating Europe,
you have just made it so that your spectator cannot think of any

other continent that does not end with the letter A! You now have your Instant A.

At this point, it's an interesting force, but it is not very deceptive just by itself. If one were to backtrack, it might be easy to reconstruct that the choices immediately became limited once the continent of Europe was eliminated. So in order to be a convincing mentalism effect, it must use a form of *process misdirection* to direct the audience's mind on something that legitimizes the process that is being used on them while maximizing on the impact of the effect.

"Now focus only on the LAST LETTER of the continent you have spelled out. If you can, make that LAST LETTER, now become the FIRST LETTER of the LAST NAME of one of the Presidents of the United States (living or dead). So if you were thinking of the letter 'L', you would think of Lincoln, and so on. What I will now try to do is install a weird image in your mind that I will try to make unlike anything you have ever thought of before. This will be done to make your thought easier to pick up on. "

This is why diverting their attention by causing them to think of the last name of an American president that begins with the letter they are thinking of is so subtly deceptive. Because there are only three *famous* American presidents whose last names begin with the letter A and two of the three of those presidents are named Adams; you have now given a more specific visual image for your spectator to focus on (themselves in an Adams campaign shirt), while simultaneously misdirecting them from their original choice of "continent." You have now more specifically forced your spectators to think of themselves wearing a Vote for Adams campaign shirt.

In truth, there is a slight chance that the president that they will be thinking of will be President Chester Arthur. However, seriously, who ever thinks of him? Interesting here, is how few people will think of this example compared to Adams. In fact, it will so rarely occur, that you can even use it to further convince your audience of your powers by saying. "Well, you *could* have thought of Chester Arthur..."

Everything that you say, and how you say it, becomes of the utmost importance when delivering such a demonstration. The above mention of the Lincoln example also makes it so that someone doesn't unthinkingly go for the first name of "Abraham" if they can't immediately come up with a president. In fact, if they cannot think of any names for a president, quickly resort to one of the other effects in this chapter. It's always important to know just the right time to bail out of an attempt to create an astonishing moment. This effect requires both a person's ability to know American presidents and states, as well as an ability to spell. Finding someone with all three of those qualities can sometimes be more challenging than we would like to think.

All your justifications should appear sound, regarding how (in order to make your spectator's thoughts easier to pick up on) you will give them something specifically absurd for them to visualize. It stands to reason that a specifically absurd image might be easier to psychically connect with than something that might get confused with other more common thought patterns in one's brain. Also, memory artists use *mnemonics* to form strange visual images in their brain that make our memory function with a larger and more organized capacity (for more on this, see *Presidential Memory, later in this section*), so it oddly makes sense that part of the process would be to make your spectator visualize something they have never thought of before... like visualizing themselves wearing an absurdly outdated campaign shirt!

After they have confirmed that they have a president's last name printed on a campaign shirt in mind, your goal is to now create even more psychological deflection. So what you will do is continue to lead your spectator's attention away from the initial "Instant A" force by drawing them deeper into its own process. As you have them spell their president's last name, you focus now on the SECOND LETTER in the spelling of that name and ask them if it can become the first letter of one of the fifty American states that they can think of. Just as Adams is usually the only conceivable answer for a president, DELAWARE will be the only conceivable answer as they try to associate the letter D with an American state. If you notice that they have trouble coming up with something here, this is a good signal to know that something went wrong. It's ok, since mentalism isn't an exact science, but the chances are high that they will have stumbled right down the path you chose for them.

Finally, since everything works nicely in threes, you will now triple the power of your prediction by having them concentrate on, first, abbreviating the state they are thinking of into two letters, then taking the second LETTER of the state they are thinking of, and asking them if that letter can somehow become the FIRST LETTER of a wild animal that they might visualize seeing while on a jungle safari. Here, the letter E (of DE) can only lead you to one great big obvious answer, and that would be an ELEPHANT.

A final element of distraction can now be applied here by having them shift (again) their entire focus on this absurd image of them wearing a campaign T-shirt, with "Vote for Adams" on the front, the letters "DE" on the back and while walking an ELEPHANT to the next town hall meeting. The nice thing that happens here is that the absurd image that is created overshadows the *Instant A* force, making it more difficult to backtrack. The process appears so plausible that it will even make some people forget that a continent was initially chosen in the first place. With just a little extra dramatic acting you can now be seen as a mind reader who can improvise picking up on another person's thoughts, or at the very least, offer an entertaining icebreaker at your next party, association mixer or public speaking presentation.

BACKGROUND

Some of you who are reading this are most likely marveling at the ingenuity behind such an effect. Where does this come from? Researching such techniques will bring you to such mystery creators as Al Baker, Karl Fulves, Matin Gardener, Stewart James, and a host of others. The original source for this particular technique is not known. Many recent creators, including H. Arcana, Atlas Brookings, Joshua Quinn, and Neale Scryer, have used this technique of using a single letter to offer up a limited range of choices within a subject category.

H. Arcana and Joshua Quinn were the first to recognize that essentially every letter in the alphabet has certain categories that one can offer a range of items for, but in which there are only one or two conceivable choices. H. Arcana published it as *The Inception Principle* in 2012. Quinn published this concept in his book, *Paralies*, in 2008. I developed this particular presentation specifically for this book, so it is entirely possible, in case you are not from the United States to use a similar format to develop your own presentation based on this principle.

MENTAL ZOOM LENS

The Instant A idea of starting the pseudo "mind reading process" by having them visualize our planet and then a continent (besides Europe) is a fun and subtle process, as it starts from a very broad extraterrestrial perspective and flows nicely into the decision to focus on a continent. But not everyone is satisfied with the idea of having people concentrate on an American President, as not everyone will be able to think of one. I like to always try it, because if they can think of one, there are over 44 presidents, and that's enough to make the selection of possibilities appear impressive. But there are obvious concerns when asking someone to think of an American president. For instance, in case you don't happen to come from America.

Here is an alternative effect that is only slightly different. It would best not be done alongside the first effect, as it uses the same Instant A principle, but once you get them to think of a continent, continue by saying:

"Now focus only on the LAST LETTER of the continent you have spelled out. Try to make that LAST LETTER of the continent you are thinking of, now become the FIRST LETTER of the first INSECT you can imagine, if that is possible. Do you have one in mind? Perfect."

"So first we began from a large perspective of our planet, but now we will quickly zoom your mental lens closer into what you are thinking of now as a small INSECT. Visualize the appearance of that one insect for a moment, and now, spell the insect singularly in your mind. Take the LAST LETTER of the spelling of the insect and now have it become the FIRST LETTER of the first VEGETABLE that you might find in a tossed salad or on a pizza, if you can imagine one. Take your time to think of something easy to visualize if possible."

"So you've moved from visualizing an insect to thinking of a vegetable. Imagine that vegetable in your mind, growing in a garden with the insect that you have also chosen, standing on it."

"Let's widen our lens again, so that we are back in space, and now let us form a month and season around our little specimens. Spell the vegetable you are thinking of. Can you make its LAST LETTER now become the FIRST LETTER spelled in one of the twelve months of the year?"

"Let's now use this simple image to create a specific feeling. Imagine what the weather feels like for it to be the month you have selected. Now imagine a garden of vegetables and a basket filled with the specific vegetable that you thought of.

Now zoom in your mental lens and imagine the insect you imagined to be on one of them. Perfect. My impression is that it's breezy day... it's October! And you are thinking of a basket... full of tomatoes! And the insect is you are thinking of... is an ant!"

 The idea of visualizing a mental lens that is in the act of zooming in and out also helps to distract the spectator's analytical deconstruction by using the *process misdirection* that I mentioned earlier. This is a very economical way of subtly concealing the method of the mental force.

Obviously, the only insect that can be selected is an ANT. There is a possibility that they might be thinking of an APHID. If that is the case, they will have a hell of a time trying to think of a vegetable that begins with the letter 'D.' If you notice this, it is because they chose APHID as their insect. If that particular insect was chosen, it is probably because they are into gardening. That, just by itself, could give you an altogether different effect!

Likewise, if they chose ANT, by using the words *salad* and *pizza* to help them with their decision for a vegetable, you will be more likely to have someone choose TOMATO than if you didn't include those two key words. Obviously, the choice of the month of OCTOBER is the only option available for the letter 'O.'

SCRIPTOZOOLOGY

There is a multitude of ways to explore this principle by discovering how each item that you might force can equate to one another in a clever presentation. It's possible, for instance to play with the idea of not just offering the earth's continents. By limiting the selected group to only those that begin with a single letter, different variations can be applied:

"First, imagine you are in outer space, and you are looking down at our planet.

"Focus on the land masses, and imagine any country in the world that you can think of... Let's say any country or continent in the world that begins with the letter A, (you know, like Afghanistan, -- but think of something different from that since I just put that one in your mind). If you think about it, there is actually a fair amount you can choose from... So, do you have one? Excellent.

"... Now, SPELL it in your mind. Don't say anything out loud-- just imagine SPELLING it in your mind... by doing this, I will now weave a mysterious SPELL!

"Imagine going to the last letter of the country or continent you just spelled... and *erase* all the other letters but the LAST LETTER, and now make that *last letter* become the *first letter* of ANY INSECT that you can think of.

"So now we are moving from VERY LARGE to VERY SMALL... ANY INSECT that you can think of which begins with the last letter of the country or continent you started out with.

"Make sure you can spell the insect in your mind as well, because we will continue this 'spell' by having you now go to the LAST LETTER of the INSECT you are now spelling in your thoughts, and imagine that you are on a jungle safari, as you will now see if you can make the *last letter* of the insect become the *first letter* of the FIRST WILD ANIMAL that you can think of that begins with that letter... OK, do you have one? I sense some of you are still with me... so let's continue...

"Spell the name of the wild animal that you can imagine seeing on that jungle safari... spell from the first letter to the last letter... but as soon as you get to that last letter, you are going to give that wild animal 'wings.'

"Take that *last letter* of the wild animal you ended up with and make that become the *first letter* of the first BIRD that you can think of that begins with that letter.

"Now concentrate... The bird... Is it a black bird?

"I was going to say ROBIN, but was it a RAVEN? YES? Well then,

21

go Ravens! Wait... concentrate again... were you also thinking of an ANT and a TIGER? It must be my animal magnetism.

THREE COURSE MEAL

What you have learned thus far, are three ploys that, when applied to my *Instant A* force, disguises it nicely and offers three different outcomes. You will see that a similar effect is played out in this effect as well, but the method that is applied in this case is slightly different. The technique used, though far older than the Internet, has an ever-continuing cycle of viral play even to this day. But the manner in which it will be used here will "up the ante" on its effectiveness.

Let's begin by having you clear your mind as you prepare to do some simple math equations. Are you ready?

$$3 + 3 =$$

$$2 + 4 =$$

$$1 + 5 =$$

$$0 + 6 =$$

"That's very good! Now say 'six' three more times in your head, and then quickly think of the first vegetable that comes to your mind. Do you have one? That's excellent!"

"Spell it out in your mind, and then tell me if the SECOND LETTER in the spelling of the vegetable you are thinking of can also become the FIRST LETTER of a fruit that might come to your mind. It does? Great! I can tell already that this is going to be delicious!

"So right now, you are freely thinking of a VEGETABLE, we'll say, baked, as a side dish, okay? You are also thinking of a FRUIT selection. Let us imagine that fruit baked into a pie... Is that something that you can visualize? Great! Now, can you imagine yourself feasting your eyes on the dish and smelling it in front of you? Excellent. Now concentrate on the spelling of your fruit. Imagine spelling it all the way to the last letter. Wait, hold on. Go back one, to the *second letter from the last*. Can you now make that second letter

22

before the last become the first letter of a seafood main course that you can think of? Like a salmon, flounder, trout, Mahi Mahi, shrimp..."

Most people, after undergoing the above process, will be forced into thinking of LOBSTER main course, with baked CARROTS on the side and an APPLE pie for dessert! Though, I am certain, you understand most of what is going on here already, you are probably wondering why you thought of a *carrot?* Well, it's interesting. I have known about this since I was a teenager, and it was always done by first adding up numbers that equate to six.

It never made sense to me why someone would be psychologically forced into thinking of a carrot after being told to add up numbers that resulted in the number six. I even read somewhere at some point that perhaps it's because there are six letters in the word carrot. There is also the distinct possibility that it's because the number SIX rhymes with STICKS, and associatively, one might make a sideways connection of visualizing or thinking of carrot sticks. Some have conjectured that it might be because the spectator is made to visualize a vegetable that might be imagined in small bunches, of say, six at a time.

My personal feeling is that it's entirely possible that so much psychic energy has been placed in this bizarre act of summoning it forth throughout the ages (not to mention the Internet) that it will produce staggering results against all odds *just because.* No need to analyze it, so long as it works. Whereas some may feel that the *carrot force* may be done just as well by eliminating the math part, and by just straight-out asking the spectator to think of a vegetable, my personal feeling is to go ahead and make them do the math. It'll exercise their minds and nevertheless makes no true sense to the process anyway.

DO I KNOW YOU?

"What is your name? Why, that is correct! Of course, I am just kidding. Would you mind coming up here and helping me make a few decisions? Let's give this young lady a round of applause! Now you are up here only to make a few spontaneous choices, is that okay? Would you say that you are a spontaneous person? You'll do just fine! As you can see, I have a flip chart here, so I can write down a few impressions that I am about to have about you. Now I haven't written down anything yet, but I will write down a total of three impressions about you (performer now draws three lines across the front page), and as I am so confident that this will go well, I am going to sign my name on this page right here at the very bottom... if, for no other reason than to believe that *you will want it* by the time this is all over.

"Let me also turn this easel away, so we can reveal it all later, but I will now write here at the top, my first impression... So tell me, if a color that depicted your current state of mind could pop into your thoughts right now, what color would that be? (Orange?) Okay, this is going to be good, I will now write my second impression right here underneath my first one... this will hopefully work out as I am planning it. Now, tell me, if you were to describe yourself in a single word, what word would you use to describe yourself?" (Independent?)

"This is going to be very interesting! I will now write down my third and final impression... FINALLY, please tell me, *what part of your body do you think is your most valuable physical asset?*" (Eyes?)

"So you have chosen the color 'ORANGE' to describe your mood, the word 'INDEPENDENT' to describe yourself, and your 'EYES' as your most valuable physical asset... Interesting, as this test was to see how much of a connection we could make, and though we have really only just met, look at how close this came!" The flip chart easel is now turned around for the first time, and written across the three lines previously drawn are the words, "ORANGE, INDEPENDENT AND EYES" which you can quickly give away, especially since it has been pre-autographed.

The above description is one way that this effect can work. It doesn't have to be done on stage with a flip chart and can just as easily be performed as a one-on-one effect using a business card. The idea is based on one of the oldest mentalism techniques known, called the "one-ahead" principle. In order to get one-ahead, what you will first do is draw three lines across the middle of the card or flip chart, and then as you spin it out of view, you will make your remark about how you are so confident that this will be successful, that you will give them your autograph in advance of making your psychic impressions. Of course, this is all said as a joke, but it is also part of the ruse. Quickly sign your name at the very bottom of the page, but then also quickly write the word "eyes" on the *third line*. Now *pretend* to write something on the first line, but do not writing anything down at all. Step back and ask her to name a color that represents how she feels or wants to feel. When she calls it out, say, "Perfect! Let's try another one."

Ask her to now try and describe herself in a single word (and within ten seconds, so it doesn't take too much time). Tell her to think about it, but not say it out-loud. Look into her eyes as if trying to discern her thoughts... Then smile.

Quickly, write down your second impression as whatever color she just mentioned on the very *top line*, whilst pretending that you have just written what she was just now thinking. It is crucial that she (and everyone) believes that, indeed, all you did just now, was jot down your second prediction and nothing more.

Now step away again from the easel (or lay your card down) and say, "Ok, what word did you choose to describe yourself?" Take note of what she says. As soon as she tells you, however, act excited yourself and tell her that she is doing is perfectly great and that this game might be too easy. So spend some time pretending as if you are trying to decide what to finally make her choose. Walk over to the flip chart for the final time and boldly write on *the second* and remaining empty line (either exactly the word she chose to describe herself or something *close to it*), and set the card down or move the easel up to a more prominent position ready to reveal.

The impressions are now all set to reveal. All that you must do is hope for the best as you ask her for your final piece of information: *"If you were to choose yourself, what part of your body would you say is your most valuable physical asset?"* The interesting thing here is that it doesn't even matter if you get it wrong. The demonstration will appear successful regardless as two out of three still beats the odds nicely. Also the chances are extraordinarily high when one asks a woman a question of that nature that, she will fall into the trap of freely choosing her EYES without even realizing it. It is a simple matter of revealing your impressions, to prove just how well you know her regardless of your having never met before!

Context is everything when presenting a mentalism effect. The effect here is obviously one in which you are showing your ability to anticipate a person's characteristics without previously knowing her. So if you had the foresight to choose a woman who seemed to already have a confident look in her face and eyes, the chances would be higher that she would make such a choice for herself.

CHAPTER **3**

USING MINIMAL PROPS

THE RING, WATCH & KEY

"On the subject of being psychic, it is never 100% surefire with its results. So it's a bit like the world of gaming in that sometimes you win and sometimes you lose. And you have to learn to be a good sport when you lose, which is hard, when you're supposed to be psychic.

"So I will start by pointing out that I have made a precognitive impression that I have already sealed in this envelope, but let's save them for the grand finale... it's always a good rule of thumb to build up anticipation for the 'big surprise ending.' So if you can please hold onto this envelope? Thanks, we'll get to that in a bit, but for now you will need to get out a ring watch and key. If your key is on a key chain with other keys, please just remove one key, and I will also need you to remove your ring as well. Finally, take your watch band and clasp it so that it forms a closed loop."

(Go get your items and follow these instructions as you read)

"Alright, I am going to turn my back, so I cannot see what is happening. Place the watch on the table in front of you, while simultaneously picking up the ring in one and the key in the other, and place both of them so that they form a line either to the left or to the right side of the watch. It will be your decision as to which side of the watch to put the other two items, and in what order to put the other two items in. Okay?

"The point here is that I won't know the order of the three objects in front of you right now. However, I am going to try to tune into each one, psychically. First, let's concentrate on your ring. I am sensing that there could be an item to its right, but I might also be

27

wrong. So, I'll tell you what; if there is an object to its right, please quietly switch those two objects with one another. If there is no object to the right of the ring, however, just leave it where it is. Now let me focus on your key. I am sensing that there might be an object to its *left* this time. But I may be wrong. So if there is an object to the left of your key, please quietly switch those two. If not, just leave the key where it is. Finally, we will put focus towards your watch. So if there is an object to the right of your watch switch the two of them for each other. Otherwise, if I am wrong, leave the watch where it is. Okay. I sense that you are most likely, at this point, wondering when does the psychic part start... Was I right? Then it got started just then."

"Pick up the item on the left and now focus on it... Wait... I see something... it's flat. Are you looking at your key? All right! So far, we are on the same wavelength! Now you choose one! Do you want to choose the remaining item on the right or left? The right, you say? Pick it up... Concentrate... I see lots of moving parts, are you holding onto your watch? Thank you very much! All right, now, there is a prediction that you've been holding this entire time within the sealed envelope. It's now time for my 'big surprise ending.' Open it up and read it!"

It reads: *The item that will remain will be your RING. This object represents your past present and future. Knowledge and inspiration can be found just by personally connecting with the mystical value that is stored within this ring. Meditate on this from time to time and fortune will come as a result!*

BACKGROUND

A similar effect was created by me many years ago and had been published in a few underground manuscripts under the title *Nu Sense*. My friend, Lee Asher, who sells his own line of magic merchandise, still sells my original *Nu Sense* e-book. For more detailed information about the effect and its history, please do check out *Nu Sense* at Lee Asher's website. The short answer is that the lineage of this clever ruse goes back to a brilliant man named Bob Hummer. I added some presentational twists, unique revelations and developed a few clever ways of getting into it, which made it worthy of re-evaluation, but otherwise the original premise is by the late, Bob Hummer's clever mathematical formula.

BREAKDOWN

The above method of this effect is self-working. So long as you follow the instructions exactly as described, it will work every time. There are a few important things to know, however. So let's break it down:

The envelope (or business card) prediction is given to someone to hold before everything begins. The prediction is always the SAME. After you turn your back or have someone cover your eyes, the spectator must begin by placing the key and the ring to either side of the watch. The key and ring can be in whichever order to each other so long as BOTH items are placed either to the left or right of the watch. Note that in the description, the spectator is instructed to clasp the watch first. This is done in order to make it seem natural to justify picking up the other two items once the watch is placed down, giving the illusion of free choice. Since the two smaller items can be juxtaposed and the spectator can decide whether to put them on the left or right of the watch, there is little feeling of being forced to make one's choice.

The RING is ALWAYS the FIRST to be switched with the item on its RIGHT, *but only if there is an item to its right.* Next, the KEY is always the one to be switched for the item on its LEFT, and again, *only if there is an item to its left.* Finally the same procedure follows with the WATCH and whether there is an item on its *right.* This formula always follows the SAME pattern, but should feel, in performance, as if you have just decided in that moment for your volunteer to make those moves. Rehearse making it feel random and off-the-cuff.

So long as steps 1 and 2 are followed correctly, the order of the three items from left to right, will be that the KEY will always be on the left, the RING will always be in the middle and the WATCH will always be on the right. They will also be in alphabetical order from left to right, in order to help you remember the object placement.

Since you know the placement of each object, you simply first draw attention to the object on their left, thus revealing the KEY, which will ALWAYS be on their LEFT. Next, you will offer a two-way psychological gambit, by asking the spectator to choose one of the two remaining items. *"This time you choose one of them. Do you wish to choose the remaining item on the left or right?"* This is a tricky line.

Because if the spectator chooses the item on the RIGHT, you will simply reveal it to be the WATCH, and then call attention to the last object that REMAINS, which, of course is the RING. But if the spectator chooses as next object, the one on the LEFT, which would be the RING, you will be prepared to say: *"So you have just chosen the item that you want REMAINING. Don't tell me what it is. Just hold your LEFT hand over it, and now concentrate on the last item, the one to the right of the one you chose to remain... I'm sensing lots of moving parts... is that item your watch? Beautiful! But, remember, the item you chose to REMAIN was your RING... Open up my prediction..."* As you can see, either way, you always end up with their RING as the one that remains, thus allowing you to deliver your "big surprise ending" while leaving your spectator with your business card and a special message on it that invokes the memory of them having met a mindreader!

The Ring Watch & Key effect is impromptu, and will create a genuine feeling of mind reading. Of course, it will take some practice to present it convincingly. One of the best ways to practice this is to read it right off these instructions while talking to a friend on the phone. You can even email your prediction to them so long as you have them promise you that they won't open your email, until you tell them that it's okay to. You also don't need to end with a prediction at all. Just tell them where each object is. Remember to use your powers for good and not for evil.

NO THREAT ROULETTE

Here is an idea that can just as easily be done using a deck of playing cards, or by just using six business cards, and a simple writing utensil. It can actually be done over the telephone, as most all of the effects that are being presented in this first section, perhaps with the exception of *Do I Know You?* But even that demonstration can be practiced (if not in front of a live group, then) over Skype or face-to-face teleconferencing.

No Threat Roulette also has an element of danger, but it's only symbolic danger, so there's nothing real to fear. If you have a deck of cards handy, this works exceptionally well, when using an Ace of Spades and five other red spot cards (Two of Hearts, Seven of Diamonds, etc). The rest of the deck can be set aside, as only those six cards are needed. If there are no playing cards handy, six identical business cards would work as well by simply drawing a picture of a bullet on one of them with a pen or marker. Turn the other business cards so that they are all facing in the same direction, and you will be ready to begin.

For ease of handling, I will deliver the presentation as if playing cards are being used, although it will be clear how playing cards are not even necessary to use, once mastered. Because your back is turned throughout, it is very important that the instructions that you give are clear.

"Since the Ace of Spades, in old gambling circles, has been called "the Bullet," we will use this card for that very purpose. The other 5 red spots cards will be used in a different way. Hold them in a fan so that they are all facing towards you as if you were playing a game of poker. Now let's imagine that the fan you are holding is a 'chamber to a pistol' and you will now load the 'bullet,' the Ace of Spades, into that chamber. Go ahead and now place the Ace of Spades somewhere into your fan, but take note of its position. From left to right in your fan, count how many cards your "bullet" card is. Remember that number. In fact, we'll call it your "lucky number," as you will need it for later. You see, we are about to play something similar to Russian roulette. Not to worry, though. The only actual bullet we'll be using is the Ace of Spades."

"Square up all your cards and turn the packet face down. The only thing you know right now is how many cards down from the top of that packet the Ace of Spades "bullet card" is, as that also coincides with your Lucky Number, right?"

"Normally, at this point in the presentation, I will give the spectator (you, in this case) a chance to 'spin the barrel' by having you call out a number between one and six. But since you are only reading this, I'll assume you chose the number "four." Spread over four cards from the top of the packet and then cut the cards after the fourth card and move those top four cards as a block to the bottom of the packet. Now, just to ensure that they are really mixed up, do it again. Cut the top four cards to the bottom of the packet. Finally, cut the same amount of cards that correspond to your LUCKY NUMBER which you determined a moment ago and place them on the bottom of your packet. Please don't look at the position of any of your cards, because if everything went as planned, I have successfully gotten you to lose track of the exact position of the bullet card. Am I right?

Well then, let's play a game!"

"Without looking at the identity of any of the cards, hold the top three up to your forehead... Click. Click. Click. Look at them. None of them are the Ace of Spades, right? So far, you remain alive. This time, take the bottom two cards of the packet and, without looking at them, hold them up to your forehead... Click... Click. Look at them. Empty chambers... Both of them... Except of course the only chamber that wasn't fired... which means you are spared another day, my friend! No day is worth risking your life over, unless it's for your personal amusement. So, I predict that tomorrow, for you, will be a great day for skydiving."

If the above instructions were followed properly, you should have been left with the Ace of Spades, thus ending a *life or death* effect successfully and with no casualties. Because I wanted you to experience the effect as to what it does, I didn't exactly present the effect, as I would have had I done it live for a real audience. But the only thing I did differently (besides not actually give you a choice of calling out a number between one and six) was make the revelation of the Ace of Spades at the end happen faster. Normally, I draw it out card by card, sometimes allowing them to make the choice themselves as to whether they would like the top or bottom card. I also have a cool way of ending it after it gets down to two cards left. But for right now, allow me to show you through the entire methodology as to how all of this is done.

BACKGROUND

The first place this effect was published was in a limited-release manuscript of which I printed only 250 copies, called *Nu Secrets and Realities* (2006). The second place it showed up was in an even smaller limited-release manuscript called *Four Told,* which came out in 2007. The two gentlemen who helped me take this effect to the level that it is now are my good friends and co-conspirators, Dr. Raj Madhok and Joel Givens. Raj first brought the idea to my attention, after another mutual colleague of ours, Steve Banachek, had published his idea of using a "Bullet Catch" theme. He later adopted the similar premise in a later version called "Telephone Russian Roulette", that can be found in his book *Psychological Subtleties 3 (pg 142)*, is also worth looking into. The original formula for this effect came from the mind of a man named Eddie Joseph, who first published it in a periodical called *Swami* in August of 1973 (Volume 2, Issue 23).

FIVE OPTIONS

Once you have gotten your spectator to remember his "lucky number," a little math begins, based on the first number that you will ask him to choose between one and six. This will be best seen as an easy series of outcomes to memorize. There are only four that you need to remember, since he really can't choose the numbers 'one' or 'six.'

You say: "Square up all your cards and turn the packet face down. The only thing you know right now is how many cards down from the top of that packet your Ace of Spades 'bullet card' is, since that also coincides with your Lucky Number, right? But now, we're going to give the barrel a spin. In fact, why don't you start by giving me a number from one and six?"

The following are your only FIVE options:

1 or 6: Since your spectator has no analogue for what's happening, he should just follow your explicit instructions. You will need to be smooth. If your spectator says either one or six, say, *"Alright, now spin again, and call out a different number. Ones and sixes will unfortunately make it way too easy to follow."*

2: If the number two is called out, this is actually the ideal situation. Simply have your spectator move two cards from the top to the bottom and proceed to the "Lucky Number Phase."

3: If the spectator chooses the number three, have him cut the top three cards to the bottom. But now you must have the next numbers chosen add up to the number *eight* (Don't worry about why, it's just part of what needs to happen). Ask the volunteer to name another number between one and six. Hopefully, the number five will be chosen, because if so, again, you are home free (3+5=8). If he says 3 and then 4, then have him cut the next four to the bottom and then say *"How about we put just one more card from the top to the bottom just for good luck."* (3+4+1=8). If the spectator chooses three and then says two, you can say *"Now cut two cards from the top to the bottom. And since you chose the number three initially, let's cut another three cards from the top to the bottom."* (3+2+3=8) Proceed to the "Lucky Number Phase."

4: Should your volunteer choose the number four, this is also ideal. This is the same scenario as in the opening description, when you first saw it (hopefully) work. If your volunteer chooses the number four, he is asked to cut four cards from the top to the bottom of the packet, but then he is asked to do it again, in order to *"more thoroughly mix up the cards."* (4+4=8). Proceed then to the "Lucky Number Phase."

5: Finally, should your spectator choose the number 5, have her cut the top five cards under the one remaining sixth card, and then remark, *"Oh great, one card gets displaced. Well that didn't really do such a great job of mixing them up- I'll tell you what, let's cut the cards in half and complete the cut. That'll get us started nice and proper."* (5+3=8) Proceed to the "Lucky Number Phase."

THE LUCKY NUMBER PHASE

"Let's do one more thing that I don't even want to know about. Don't tell me your lucky number, but just cut that many cards to the bottom. Remember not to look at the position of any of your cards, because if everything went as planned, I have successfully gotten you to lose track of the exact position of the bullet card. Am I right? Well then, let's play a game!"

Part of the real life-lessons of learning to be a good mentalist is in learning how to give clear and precise instructions to your audience and spectators. So much mentalism, like this, is method based, that offering clear and precise instructions are crucial to being a successful performer in this field.

If your instructions are clear and confident, once the cards are cut at your spectator's secretly chosen Lucky Number, you will have no problem in knowing that the Ace of Spades will now be exactly FOUR CARDS from the top of the six-card packet. Remember, the spectator's lucky number also corresponds with the initial position of the "bullet card," making it integral to the success of this formula. (So within the cyclical stack of the six cards: 8+Lucky Number=4 / also 2+Lucky Number=4)

FIRST FOUR BLANKS

In this phase, all of the cards except the bullet card and one other will be eliminated. Unbeknownst to your volunteer, you already know where the Ace of Spades is (four cards from the top) before the process even begins. It is now a simple matter of keeping track of where the bullet is within each remaining group of cards.

Start by having your volunteer hold the top card up to their head without looking at it. Since your back is turned, you can't see it either. *"Click,"* you say, as you ask him to verify that the top card wasn't the Ace. Have him hold up the next card... *"Click."* Have him reveal that it, too, is not the Ace. Have him place the two revealed spot cards face up but over to the side in a pile.

The Ace is now the second card down from the top. Say, "It's a bit nerve racking, even for something that's just done with cards, right? I mean, put yourself in my shoes, your life depends on me... and that can get a little intense. So this time, I'll let you make tbe choice. Would you like to try the card at the top or the card at the bottom of your packet?" Whichever he chooses for himself, continue, by having him hold it to his head, and after a short pause, say, "Click." Then have him try the other opposite option just for kicks ... "Click."

YES/LEFT RIGHT/NO

"Now there are only two cards left. Don't look at either of them. Just put the top card in your right hand, so that you are now holding one card in each hand. I really want us BOTH to use our intuition now. We already know that one of them is the bullet, and the other one will bring us to safety. So for this grand finale, we will act as a team. I am going to count to three, and when I do, we will direct our energy to which one keeps us alive and which one is fatal. I want you to just shout out either YES or NO, all right? Ready? One, two three..."

As they are calling out their choice of *Yes or No*, you must determine whether you should call out *Right or Left* at the SAME TIME. Since you know that the bullet card is the card left in their RIGHT HAND, if they shout out *"Yes!"* you need to shout, *"LEFT!"* and if they shout *"No!"* you must shout, *"RIGHT"* at the exact same time. The idea is that they will end up feeling as if they played a part in saving themselves, since it appears to be their choice to determine a possible threat or safe zone.

"That was interesting! I said, LEFT just as you said YES, so if your left hand is a 'yes' that tells us that this must be the safe card, turn over the card in your left hand, did we find the final safe card? This must mean that the last remaining card in your right hand is the BULLET. "

Alternatively:

"That was interesting! I said RIGHT, just as you said NO, so if NO is being said of your RIGHT hand, that tells us that we should NOT go with the card IS IN YOUR RIGHT hand. This must also mean the final safe card is in your LEFT hand—is that correct? And is the last remaining card in your RIGHT hand the BULLET? I believe my work here is done, my friends." And so we live to fight another day.

CHAPTER **4**

REAL MIND POWER

PRESIDENTIAL MEMORY

A s you can see, mentalism is cunning, clever, and deceptive. Although, the discipline of mentalism does pull its more illusory nature from its resources in the magic world, it actually gets most of its knowledge from other mystery art forms, as well as other outside resources that show similarities and potentials for an amazement factor. So mathematical anomalies and formulas are used frequently, word and language phenomena, hypnosis and suggestion techniques, martial arts skills, arcane mysticism practices are employed and of course, unusual knowledge in physics and other sciences are also explored. Demonstrations of the mind can apply to any number of those things, and this has a lot to do with how mentalism continues to thrive creatively as an art form into our current times.

Mentalism is about showing people the extraordinary powers of our minds under all costs, and doing it in an incredible way. A demonstration in how people can develop super memory would fall right into line with the art of mentalism. The following demonstration will also show you how mentalism makes no distinction between amazing demonstrations that are deceptively astonishing and true mental/physical feats that also contain an amazement factor. This is why so many people have a hard time trying to figure out if mentalism is real... *it's because some of it is.*

There are a lot of other things to appreciate here. For instance, trying to track down some of the methods that one comes across can be sometimes difficult. We are people of the "mystery arts." We are bound together by secrets and honor behind those secrets, so the work that we lay down is sometimes only mouth-to-ear. Many of the most tried and true mentalism techniques go so far back that they have no known creator. The one that you are about to learn is one of those effects. My good friend, (and master mindreader) Ross Johnson, originally showed this to me, and his friend Bob Klein showed it to him, but the actual author is unknown. It's fairly modern as it most likely dates back to no further than the days of President Tyler. I also made some adjustments to the system in order to update it to more current times, and I offer it to you here for (perhaps) the first time in print.

"What I am about to do, is cause you to suddenly be able to remember 30 random things, that you wouldn't think you would be able to remember, in 15 minutes! And not only will you be able to remember this list, but you will also be able to remember it tomorrow and even next week... whether you like it or not! Feel free to clock yourself with a stop watch if you are reading this starting NOW."

"Are you ready for the list? I'll give you the first ten things I want you to remember:

Pen

Swan

Mustache

Sailboat

Hook

Golf Club

Cliff

Hourglass

Lake Monster

Bat & Ball

"Now at first, you might look at a list like that, and think of it as dauntingly unexciting to try and remember those ten items. But I am going to show you how it will be easy, and completely effective! Because what you are actually looking at is what is called a "visual memory peg system." This system is wonderful, especially if you ever wanted to remember a list of ten items, for say, getting groceries, or making a to-do list. I'll show you how to use it later, but for now, remember the list as follows:

Visually, the number:

One looks like a Pen.

Two looks like Swan.

Three (turned sideways) looks like a Mustache.

Four looks (sort of) like a Sailboat.

Five looks (sort of) like a Hook.

Six looks like (a very childish drawing of) a Golf Club.

Seven looks like the side of a Cliff.

Eight looks like an Hourglass.

Nine looks sort of like a Lake Monster poking its head out of the water.

Ten looks like a Bat & Ball.

Read the above list one more time, then put the book down and try to remember it for yourself. You will find that you can remember these first ten items with ease.

"Now the next ten things I will give you will be a little harder to remember, but I will show you how in a moment. They are:

Washing Machine

Atom Bomb

Chef

Medicine

Money

Another Atom Bomb

Car Jack

Moving Van

Harry Potter's Son

Necktie

"Upon first glance, this list, especially combined with the last list, may seem silly and nonsensical. But since the last list can also be used as what is known as a 'memory peg-system,' we can use our wild imagination to help us remember the lists we make, while making it fun and amusing at the same time. You will do this by creating an interesting and memorable picture in your mind that includes the numbered memory peg within each image that you visualize. This appears much harder to learn than it is to just do. So let me just give you an example of how it works.

ONE is a PEN, right? But we also want one to be a WASHING MACHINE. Well, imagine that you just put a shirt in the washing machine and that shirt accidentally had a pen in it... Your laundry is entirely ruined. So, ONE is now a PEN found having exploded in a WASHING MACHINE. You just "pegged" the image of a WASHING MACHINE into your memory as the number ONE!

TWO is a SWAN, remember? So to add an ATOM BOMB to this image, let's imagine that you just turned on the news, only to see a story of how recent military drills are now involving a special "robot swan drone" that is actually equipped with an ATOM BOMB. So, TWO is a now a SWAN drone with an ATOM BOMB hidden inside!

THREE is a MUSTACHE, albeit a sideways one. But since we want it to also be a CHEF, let's make it memorable by imagining changing the TV channels, only to see a cooking show, with a CHEF who not only is wearing a handlebar mustache of his own, but is also pulling from his oven a "baked MUSTACHE" dish. I predict it will be hard for you to forget that THREE is an unappetizing, hairy, MUSTACHE casserole prepared by a crazy CHEF.

FOUR is a SAILBOAT, so let's imagine a SAILBOAT full of orange plastic MEDICINE BOTTLES, and referring to the medicinal warning labels, the sail of the sailboat also has prominently displayed on it a skull and crossbones along with the word MEDICINE underneath it. So FOUR is a SAILBOAT, with a skull and crossbones on it, full of MEDICINE.

FIVE is a HOOK, so imagine being on a boat and lowering a hook (that looks like the number five) on a line down into the water only to pull it up to find wads of cash MONEY hooked onto it! You have now successfully connected FIVE and HOOK with MONEY.

SIX is a (deformed/abstracted) GOLF CLUB. But we also want it to represent ANOTHER ATOM BOMB. So let's this time just imagine a GOLF CLUB swinging, but unfortunately, it hits one of those nasty trick golf balls, that contain a tiny ATOM BOMB hidden inside so that it detonates on impact... Voila. SIX is now a GOLF CLUB striking an ATOM BOMB hidden in a joke shop golf ball.

SEVEN is the side of a CLIFF. So let's attach a CAR JACK to this image, by imagining the cliff in a state of disrepair, in which it oddly needs the help of a CAR JACK to keep it from falling over. Now the number SEVEN is visualized as a CLIFF in need of a CAR JACK in order to help hold it in place.

EIGHT is an HOURGLASS. So imagine a MOVING VAN with a large BUREAU strapped on top of it. On the side of the MOVING VAN, there is a large graphic of an HOURGLASS with a slogan that reads, 'It's Time to Move!' EIGHT can now be visually associated with an HOURGLASS painted on the side of a MOVING VAN.

NINE is a LAKE MONSTER. But you also want it to represent the more complex image of HARRY POTTER'S SON. Simply, imagine reading a review of the latest HARRY POTTER book, in which HARRY POTTER'S SON gets eaten by a giant LAKE MONSTER. Now NINE is instantly associated with the made-up story of a LAKE MONSTER eating HARRY POTTER'S SON.

As we can easily recall, TEN is a BAT & BALL. So let us now imagine a special game of BASEBALL, wherein the teams were made up of men all wearing NECKTIES. And by the end of the game, it was also a TIE. Now TEN can be associated with a BASEBALL game in which the players are all wearing NECKTIES.

At this point, put the book down and now see if you can remember the SECOND LIST OF TEN ITEMS. I don't think you will find it hard in the least.

So that's twenty more or less random things that you can remember so far, right? Now here's the awesome part. The last ten items I will give you will be a list of the FIRST TEN PRESIDENTS of the United States of America. We will do so using a mnemonic based on homophones, words that sound alike.

For instance, the idea that the word WASHING MACHINE could remind you that George WASHINGTON was the FIRST president of the United States.

Just as ATOM BOMB could remind you of the SECOND president of the USA, John ADAMS.

Or that a word as simple as CHEF could make you think of the THIRD U.S. president, Thomas JEFFERSON (or CHEF-ERSON).

MEDICINE can very easily remind you of FOURTH United States president, James MADISON.

MONEY associates easily with FIFTH American president, James MONROE.

ANOTHER ATOM BOMB just as easily reminds us of SIXTH president, John Quincy ADAMS.

The word CAR JACK mnemonically translates to the SEVENTH U.S. president, Andrew JACKSON.

MOVING VAN (with BUREAU strapped on top) nicely reminds us that the EIGHTH American president was Martin VAN BUREN.

HARRY POTTER'S SON, or 'HARRY'S SON,' can sound much like the NINTH president of the United States, William Henry HARRISON.

And finally, NECKTIE is easily associated with the TENTH president of the USA, John TYLER.

So how fast has that been? Did you try to time yourself?

You just learned TWENTY random items that will help you

develop your memory, as well as the first TEN presidents of the United States of America, in 15 minutes or less!

There you have it. A clever memory presentation that I'm certain caught you by surprise, which in fact, you could show to other people within about 15 minutes time with just a little bit of practice.

Furthermore, it's possible to apply the very same rules used in this system towards making a grocery list or to-do list, by simply associating the numbered memory pegs (Pen, Swan, Mustache, etc) to the visual image of the grocery store item, or actions on a to do list. The important thing is to let your imagination try to think of the wildest, most outrageous image that it can using the memory peg images combined with whatever you need to associate them with.

Let us say, for instance, that I need to get to the BANK, go to the POST OFFICE, stop by the GYM, swing by the CLEANERS, and then pick up MILK, EGGS, LETTUCE, BREAD and CHEESE from the GROCERY STORE. Well that's FIVE THINGS that I need to do and FIVE things that I need to remember getting from the grocery store. Technically, you could use the same numerical one through five pegs for both lists, but since there are only ten things to remember here, I will offer an example that just uses all ten numerical memory pegs. Let's spend some time with our imagination and see what we can now free-associate...

1) The BANK now has a box that recycles old non-working PENS. You can now take all your old pens and deposit them at your local BANK. It's the latest thing.

2) The POST OFFICE is offering a new SWAN delivery service in which live SWANS will deliver your packages!

3) It's "MUSTACHE DAY" at the GYM. So you may have to take that into consideration.

4) The CLEANERS now has cleaning service for the sails of SAILBOATS with a good introductory offer.

5) The GROCERY STORE is having a sale on edible HOOKS. These are HOOKS that you can use to hang your hats and coats on, but whenever you want, you can eat them.

6) Hitting a carton of MILK with a GOLF CLUB would not be

good at all.

7) At the local CLIFF, every Saturday morning, you can throw EGGS off it as far as you can.

8) There is a new LETTUCE that grows from seedling to full grown and ready for consumption as fast as it takes for an HOURGLASS to time an egg!

9) These days you can feed loaves of BREAD to the local LAKE MONSTERS, just like you can feed ducks, but with LAKE MONSTERS, you can feed them the loaves of BREAD whole.

10) A big CHEESE manufacturer has just recently bought the entire sport of BASEBALL from America. Now everything BASEBALL will be made of CHEESE.

With just a little imagination, you can remember a fairly lengthy list of some pretty complex things. Try it!

PART TWO

ILLUSION OR DELUSION?

In this section, prepare to be spun around in different ways. I will try to lead you through the following strange stories, while doing my best to show you how I have come to ultimately think the way I do and live the way I live. I will do this while telling you about my life, some fun facts, and some pretty incredible experiences, a few of which I have had first hand, and others that involve some of my friends who I am eager to introduce to you. You will also come to understand how I don't really see myself as too much different from anyone else.

I do try hard to not be dismissive of even some pretty outrageous-seeming points of view. However, at the same time I also try to be mindful of potential threats and hazards that can potentially be caused by wrongful misinformation. Thus my overall stance will always be more curious than completely firm about any of the subjects I will be discussing. Perhaps, at the end of my life, I will be able to look back and see that my experience, knowledge, and interests have conditioned me to live as more open-minded and thus, more confident, mentally healthy, spirited, and free-thinking? Or maybe my belief that I am the master of my mind and destiny is just a mental delusion of grandeur?

Maybe I was just lucky that the manner, in which I chose my experiences and learned from them, was what gave me direction and a way to express myself. Perhaps you will just be entertained by my stories. In any case, you are about to be introduced to the real me, as best as I can explain myself. You are about to learn my most secret thoughts along with my experiences and peculiar past while watching me reason with myself as to just who I am, and why I think it is important to live an explorative and creative life, that is open to the possibility that reality and consciousness touch and can come together.

The thoughts and experiences that I am about to introduce to you, all come from true origins. If some of the following ideas that you are about to reason through with me begin to feel like we are stepping off the cliff of logic only to find ourselves swimming through time and dimensions both hard to believe or far-out, all you need to do is take a moment and remember that I am doing my best to make it make sense even for me. Soon, you will be reading just how it is that I ended up becoming *The Man Who Knows*, not by trying to understand my illusions, but perhaps more by trying to reconcile some potential delusions. Let us now move forward.

CHAPTER 5

DOES IT EVER GET REAL?

I t's plain to see, by reading through Part One, that there is an entire art form and philosophy dedicated to creating theatrical representations and models that look and feel like the experience of mindreading and mental phenomenon. These, however, are (under scrutiny) seen more along the lines of being psychological illusions that demonstrate and replicate the act of mindreading as opposed to actually using it.

If one were an anthropologist or archaeologist, from a post-apocalyptic future, who stumbled across this strange finding that an *entire field of practice* during the civilization of man went to "fake mind reading," I can see a list of questions arising quite immediately. Three of the most obvious of such questions being:

1) What would learning demonstrations like those have to do with their genuine ability to read someone's mind (if that is what they actually did)?

2) Are these all just techniques and principles on how to create mind illusions and nothing more? What purpose would that serve? All that, just for novelty and entertainment?

3) If mentalism is supposed to represent real superhuman potentials in any valid way, then just what do we mean by that?

There is a theory that the origin of mentalism may have branched out from the late nineteenth century spiritualism and medium movement. During these spectacular presentations, a séance medium would sometimes attempt to contact the dead, manifest ectoplasm, and cause furniture to exhibit strange behaviors to complete a mysteriously entertaining evening for the paying public. Mentalism techniques were sometimes used during these evenings as a "theatrical aid" to set in motion the expectation of other possible synchronicities or forecasts of the future that may naturally manifest as the evening progressed. Grand pronouncements of mental feats have been recorded as entertainment as early as 16th century, Europe. I am quite certain that the overall idea of manifesting the inexplicable goes back as far as man was able to realize his own experience.

Therefore, my guess is that part of the reason why mentalism has been so much of a mystery is because at one time witnessing it also meant that one was experiencing a presentation that was likely to include genuinely mysterious stuff. This is actually not just my own conjecture, but also that of many who are historians of these hidden arts. Someone who actually had a strong belief that his or her powers were real, in most instances back then, would perform it as such.

There were indeed also many frauds that the great magician, Harry Houdini, made a name for himself by exposing. Nevertheless, an entire evening of doing the same thing from start to finish would become dull to watch for anyone. So, it isn't hard for one to imagine that at one time, such theatrical techniques were used in this subtle manner to both ignite the imagination as well as offer another facet of mystery for entertaining its audiences.

On the other hand, it shouldn't be too hard to imagine that although the day and age would bring about all kinds of scam artists and con men, that there may have also existed those people who had a genuine scientific or mystical interest in trying to realize or master a real understanding of our minds, its potential for true manifestations, links between soul and science, and uncovering arcane knowledge that may reveal secrets for the future. This would include everyone from philosophical mystics like Francis Bacon to forerunners of the hypnosis movement, like Franz Mesmer.

I believe that there is a difference between these two sets of people, however I also have a personal theory that as we came to the end of the 20th century, the media turned more towards calling attention to the scam artists than those whose interests were sincere. After Harry Houdini became known for using the media to generate attention by spotting and then exposing spiritual mediums that used fraudulent theatrics to speak to the dead, the media became hyper-aware of how effective such controversy was as a public interest story, and meanwhile, most all magician societies followed Houdini in this direction which was to eliminate the practice of such spiritual theatrics that claimed to be genuine. Magicians obviously felt this to be a more prestigious stance to take so that society would still accept the performance of magic in its culture.

PSYCHIC Q&A

Sometimes theatrical techniques are still used today as a creative addition to a séance or spiritualist medium's presentation, but in present days, when provided as entertainment, there is usually a disclaimer. It has also been frequently used as a way to change the pace, or add an entertaining diversion to a stage hypnosis show. But one of its purest uses would be applied to what is commonly called *Psychic Q&A*. During the Q&A portion of a psychic show, the entire audience is offered to ask the person acting as the medium, any question that they may desire and an uncanny display is shown of remarkably being able to deliver answers! It is during this section that much of the time, the performer knows nothing except how to maintain an audience's interest, and yet, if approached with openness, sincerity, charm, and charisma, more details can be answered and uncovered about the question being asked than even the performer is capable of explaining.

Much of the time, the "automatic impressions" that the audience witnesses, may be of things that will occur in the future, making it conveniently harder to know for sure if they will happen since one is still in the present. Other answers may come in the form of advice or guidance, so unless you are the person asking the question, it is harder to judge the significance of it. However, sometimes, very specific pieces of information become suddenly known that cannot be explained. Ironically, the astonishment and disbelief on the participant's faces at these moments are indeed also "mind read" by the rest of the audience that the spectator is having a truly genuine experience. So in these instances, everyone ends up participating in some genuine mindreading. I live for those moments.

Just off the top of my head, during recent performances, I have correctly guessed that a man's son's name was "Jayden", the age of a 14 yr old who wasn't in the room, that a guy's favorite sport was snowboarding, birthdates, breed of pet dogs, number of cats owned, musical tastes, favorite foods, color and make of a new white Jeep Cherokee, names of significant people, and that someone was planning on going for vacation in Thailand. These moments are real moments, in which I am challenged by spectators who are literally asking me questions like, "Can you tell me the name of my son?" or "Where do you think I will be going to this summer?"

What I try hard not to do is predict disasters, or negative things occurring. Often, people are insecure about a health-related matter. In such cases, I can offer guidance and inspiration, but I am not a medical doctor so I am open about admitting this. I am also of the mind that trying to resonate with happy feelings is one of the keys to a happy life.

Some believe that many of those who have legitimately predicted disasters were able to do so either because it might affect them or a loved one somehow, like a "jungle sense." But, in truth, the few times which I have managed to avoid danger by circumstance, it had never been from any feeling that anything bad would happen to me if I made a decision otherwise. It did always feel more like I was being protected somehow. Also, I have heard of more than one instance in which a nightmarish prediction was made without having any personal connection to the event.

A good example would be a story that came to me via a police chief from a New Jersey precinct who spoke with me after I gave a performance for the National Association for Chiefs of Police a few years ago. He talked about knowing a psychic woman who predicted a school shooting just days before it happened and told me that she was visibly shaken by the vision. Since nothing had happened yet, all he could do was reassure her that nothing of the sort was happening, and she was going to be all right.

It turned out that the shooting she predicted was in an entirely different state, to which she had no personal connection. He said that the horrific visions that she described were quite accurate to what ended up happening in this other location. There wasn't anything he could do about it at the time, however. It wasn't until after it happened that he was able to put all the pieces together regarding what she had told him.

CHAPTER **6**

THE PLACEBO IN ME

Of course, any theatrical and novelty presentations (card tricks and such), that might lead up to more inspired moments, help set the stage and add texture to the truly amazing organic connections that can be made if the "man of mystery" brought it to the audience's attention, or if those who were experiencing the magic would just take a moment to see something real unfold. The psychological mystery-arts can be (and have been) employed as entertaining interludes that support psychic and hypnosis stage or parlor presentations. Most of these are executed by using methodical processes that theatrically replicate it. The range of mentalism ideas, however, has exploded over the past 100 years, and more so lately than ever.

Nowadays, the vast majority of "stage mentalists" you will see would be more appropriately labeled "mind illusionists" who will use an entire repertoire of mentalism demonstrations and may hardly ever truly connect with his/her audience in any manner which really taps into a genuine place or spirit. They can sometimes be quite entertaining and usually come from a magician's upbringing. My personal preference, however, is that I'd rather see, experience or share something real...

I am more in tune with the original philosophy of trying to make the act of reading minds as truly baffling as it can be (for all parties) while maintaining good psychological drama and theatricality. I also like to include a good repertoire of audience participation demonstrations that will help me to stay in control of everyone's expectations. The theatrics are used to spark off a potentially trance-induced "placebo-like nerve" within the minds of those who are engaged, and thus cause the audience to become psychologically "carried away," but also potentially more susceptible to:

1) Memory of Something Forgotten

2) Motivational Empowerment

3) New-Found Hope

4) Personal Insight

5) Psychic Inspiration / Spontaneous Psychic Awareness

6) Recognizing Synchronicity

7) Spontaneous Inner Healing

I am quite proud, frankly, of being able to affect people in such a positively odd assortment of ways. What makes me believe that the seven items above are things my audience can become susceptible to? Firstly, the above are a list of things that have been commonly reported to me over the years by people just after experiencing my recent one-man show, *Invisible Connections*, which played for multiple-weeks in both Washington DC, and Las Vegas in 2010 and 2011. Many fans have written to me of how just seeing my show has "changed them." I realized early on that my performances have, like a medicine man's rituals, at times, created a reaction in people that motivated actual change and inspiration. Somehow I was affecting people in a way that sometimes gave them magical, even life-changing gifts and insights. As grateful as I am to have this affect on people, I have always felt it best to accept these comments as blessings. It is amusing to contrast and correlate the power of the placebo effect to the overall concept of mentalism effects. Both essentially embody the forms of two different kinds of "ritual theatrics." Yet both will create unexplainably positive changes in people, even when there's really nothing but a ritual representation for its existence in reality.

THE FAMILY HEALER

An interesting example of how the power of the mind can be seen to manifest in surprisingly powerful ways right in front of you, can be done simply by updating one's knowledge of exactly what the placebo effect is and can do. Oddly, when the placebo is "in effect," the only thing that is relevant to the healing process is the suggestion that it should begin healing in combination with the ritual that stimulates the healing process. Otherwise, in many cases, no other form of medication need be used. I never cease to be amazed by the power of what loving energy can do to the healing process. A good example for this would be seen in my own daughter. She very well might be one of my greatest skeptics. As long as she's lived, she has had to put up with her father, and the illusions he creates for fun and amusement.

Now, at the thoughtful age of seven, she has begun to dissect my little tricks, and started to debunk me in front of her friends. One thing that she is still convinced by, however, is my ability to heal wounds. She has witnessed herself as wounds that she gets will appear to heal faster if I "tend to them" with my magical gifts. Even as recently as the morning of my writing this, my daughter banged her shin while running through our house and cried out. I asked her if she would like me to try to help, and so she came to me and pointed to where it hurt. I casually caressed the area for about 10 seconds and talked to her about plans for the day, before letting her go. She walked away without even remembering why she had come to me, but then a moment later touched her shin, and looked at me with a smile, and said, "Hey! You..." I just winked at her.

Alain Nu, The Man Who Knows™

CHAPTER 7

PLACEBOS AND CONSCIOUSNESS

THE ASHER PARADOX

To be clear, I am not a university-educated doctor. I am really only a man with a brand. I am *The Man Who Knows*. My "crystal ball," through which all of my work is currently being done, is a beat-up outdated laptop. I have a PhD from the School of Hard Internet. It's not the same thing, learning about the world online, as opposed to learning from a real college professor, but I believe through perseverance, one eventually learns how to spot the difference between subjective from empirical evidence or peer review studies. It's always best to do research yourself and access qualified friends who can give you their expert knowledge as well. I always like to say, if you're going to be wrong, it's better to back yourself up with lots of people-support.

All of that said, I have always been intrigued by the notion of finding the places in life "where inspiration meets reality." So what you are about to embark on is my personal journey, as I take you into my contemplations, regarding this miraculous thing known as the *placebo effect...*

Notable London physician, Richard Asher, was known for saying back in the 1960's:

"If you can believe fervently in the treatment, even though controlled studies show that it is quite useless, then your results are much better, your patients are much better, and your income is much better, too."

This became known among physicians as the "Asher Paradox." Asher then goes on to say that this paradox is probably also what accounts for the remarkable success of the some "less-gifted but more credulous" members of the medical profession, as well as how some of the more-thorough but less-charming physicians may get worse results based on less attention put towards the importance of good social skills.

Asher even went a little further to add, "If you admit to yourself that the treatment you are giving is frankly inactive, you will inspire little confidence in your patients, unless you happen to be a remarkably gifted actor, and the results of your treatment will be negligible." This was quoted as late as 1989 (*Follies and Fallacies in Medicine*, Petr Skrabanek and James McCormick). So it wasn't until ongoing research within the field of hypnosis and other alternative treatments kept reporting back as having such positive results for therapy patients, did the placebo effect regain interest in the late 1990's.

ENTER THE ACUPUNCTURIST

Recently, in 2013, Associate Professor at the Harvard School of Medicine, placebo researcher and acupuncturist, Ted Kaptchuk, conducted a very interesting research experiment. The study played out in this manner, and his findings made its way into several news stories:

1) Subjects who participated were people who complained of severe arm pain. These people included those with carpal tunnel syndrome, tendinitis (such as tennis elbow), and individuals with other wrist and elbow pain. A total of 270 people participated in this experiment.

2) As part of the study, half of the subjects were given pain relief pills, while the other half were given acupuncture treatments.

3) Side effects occurring in the study were seen fairly equally in BOTH groups. The pills made some of the subjects sluggish to the point that they found it nearly impossible to get up out of bed. Some acupuncture subjects saw severe swelling and reddening of the arms. Some patients reported a severe increase in pain.

4) The majority of the subjects on both sides, however, did feel true relief, with more people who were treated by the

56

acupuncture feeling better than those who took the pain relief pills. These were seen as exceptional findings, since no one had ever made a thorough study, much less proven acupuncture's higher success rate over anti-pain medication in the past.

5) In the end, the only thing that was proven was that the placebo effect has an uncanny ability to trigger a correcting process within one's physical makeup, which can make us better or worse, depending on our approach and mental perception

6) The "anti-pain" pills that were prescribed to half of the subjects were made of compressed cornstarch. The "acupuncture needles" were retractable "shams" which never even pierced the skin. So the study was not aimed at comparing and contrasting two different treatments at all. It ultimately compared and contrasted two bogus treatments!

7) Therefore, there was a definite placebo effect found in both treatments that showed an affect of causing significantly improved pain relief in both instances of fake acupuncture as well as cornstarch pills. In both treatments, there was a larger degree of positive over negative effects reported by both groups. Although the fake acupuncture was found to be more effective than the corn starch pills, this could be attributed to the amount of "caring attention" that is felt from being attended to by an acupuncturist, despite whether or not needles actually penetrate the skin.

8) Most fascinating to Professor Kaptchuk, was that another aspect of the experiment was to warn patients to look out for symptoms of drowsiness, swelling, irritable rash, or increased pain. As predicted, those people who did not get a placebo effect that helped to make them feel better, actually ended up feeling the exact negative symptoms mentioned, and many of them were felt as exaggeratedly severe. A few who took the pills claimed that they were finding it impossible to get out of bed in the morning, others who received the fake acupuncture complained of redness and swelling. Those who felt increased pain felt it rise to unbearable levels. This phenomenon is called a "nocebo effect." Nocebo is Latin for

"I shall harm." Placebo is Latin for "I shall please."

Ted Kaptchuk, who received grants from the National Center for Complementary and Alternative Medicine and the Osher Research Center, Harvard Medical School, has made numerous studies in the field of placebo research. Although he is technically an assistant professor and not a tenured professor at HMS, I have found his experiments to be very interesting and would one day enjoy meeting him. Obviously, there is still more research to be done. Between his studies, combined with others in the past, it appears the placebo is most effective with headaches, mental re-patterning, muscular skeletal pain, back pain, and digestive and urinary problems.

Kaptchuk's approach to the placebo effect is a little more complex than just administering sugar pills and saline injections. It is ultimately the entire presentation. It is the ritual of doing something to jump-start the self-healing process. The entire experience of patient to physician is the complete treatment. "The placebo effect is the effect of everything surrounding the fake pill, or the real pill," says the Harvard associate professor. "It's the compassion, trust, and care. It's the ritual and symbols. It's the doctor-patient interaction."

THE OPEN PLACEBO EXPERIMENT

By the end of 2010, Ted Kaptchuk completed a study that would ultimately challenge Sir Richard Asher's assessment of his own paradox, over twenty years later. Colleagues of his at Beth Israel Deaconess Medical Center in Boston as well as the Harvard Medical School supported the study. There was a slight ethical problem that he had with the entire study in that the deceptive nature of the treatment just didn't seem to align properly with modern western medicine traditions. His goal was to see if he could just be completely honest and tell people what he was doing with them up front, eliminating the need to be deceptive all together. His findings were extraordinary. Here is what was said to have played out:

1) Two groups of eighty subjects were formed from participants who all suffered from irritable bowl syndrome (IBS). The control group was not to receive any treatment at all. The test group, however, was prescribed a specific dosage of placebos to take at certain times of the day.

2) The test subjects, who were prescribed the placebos, were told up front, this time, that the pills were "like sugar pills," *but that placebos have been known to successfully improve their condition.* Nothing more than the information delivered roughly in the manner above was stated. The experiment even went as far as to print the word "placebo" directly on the bottle, and to tell the subject clearly that they didn't even have to believe in the placebo effect in order to for it to work. All they needed to do was to remember to take the pills. This process was monitored for three weeks.

3) By the end of the experiment, nearly twice as many patients, who were treated with the fake pill, reported symptom relief when compared to the control group (the result was 59% versus 35%). In other parts of the same study, the participants who took the placebo showed an improvement that actually doubled the degree of perceived improvement, roughly equivalent to the effects of the most powerful IBS medications.

4) "I didn't think it would work," said Anthony Lembo, HMS associate professor of medicine at BIDMC and also an expert on IBS. "I felt awkward asking patients to literally take a placebo. But to my surprise, it seemed to work for many of them."

So over twenty years later, after Richard Asher's assertion (which if you honestly admit to yourself and your subject that the treatment you are giving is inactive, that you will inspire little confidence in them), a new understanding may soon surface. It may actually be quite possible to change such rules towards eliminating the dilemma of deception on the part of the physician. If replications made by different researchers prove that this is the case, we may have to add an addendum that states:

Placebos can be observed as effective at curing some physical conditions, even when the subject is told honestly that it is a placebo, so long as subjects continue to carry out the ritual process.

If exploration of this idea continues to advance towards effective treatment, it may one day be a game-changer for the odds of the *ritual experience.* That would certainly change the entire architecture of the rationalistic approach.

LIFE & MIND IN THE UNIVERSE

The whole thing still doesn't completely add up. I must admit, I am only scratching the surface here, and there is much that one can learn and know about the healing properties of the placebo effect. The very notion that even the remotest positive suggestion invoked can heal someone, however, is appealing to everyone, especially after they hit middle age. How can one understand this more, if at all?

Professor George Wald was an American scientist (1906 – 1997) who studied zoology and taught at Harvard University. In 1967, he won a share of the Nobel Prize for Physiology and Medicine with scientists Haldan Keffer Hartline and Ragnar Granit. At the Quantum Biology Symposium in 1984, his talk, *Life and Mind in the Universe,* examined very thoughtfully the subject of evolution and consciousness, and it was there that he made a somewhat scientifically staggering pronouncement. He said:

"It has occurred to me lately, I must confess, with some shock (at first) to my scientific sensibilities that both questions, meaning the origin of consciousness in humans and of life from nonliving matter, might be brought into some degree of congruence. This is with the assumption that Mind rather than emerging as a late outgrowth in the evolution of life, has existed always as the 'matrix.' The source and condition of physical reality; the stuff of which physical reality is composed is mind stuff. It is Mind that has composed a physical universe that breeds life, and so eventually evolves creatures that know and create science, art and technology-making animals. In them, the universe begins to know itself."

In his quote above, Wald references British astronomer and astrophysicist, Sir Arthur Eddington, who in 1928 said:

"The stuff of the world is mindstuff ... The mindstuff is not spread in space and time... Recognizing that the physical world is entirely abstract and without 'actuality' apart from its linkage to consciousness, we restore consciousness to the fundamental position."

DID GOD DO THIS?

Both Wald and Eddington's quotes bring up a few interesting observations that create some scientific controversy. The above statements have, in many ways, sprung forth a recent popular argument, especially among Christians, that this could, in many ways, prove that there may actually be a God, in particular with the Evolution vs. Creation debate. You may have already heard it stated somewhere or by someone using the following three notions:

1) Starting with DNA, one must understand that there is a "code" that is stored within every DNA molecule. That DNA code can be studied, as if it were an "owner's manual," ultimately allowing you to understand the entire organism it represents. One must also understand that DNA is a molecule that is self-replicating. Each molecule is able to make an identical copy quickly and efficiently. DNA is even seen to detect and correct replication errors. Protein enzymes that constantly travel up and down the molecule are seen to monitor its condition and will make moment-to-moment corrections and repairs. These enzymes literally have the ability to make "editorial corrections" to the DNA as it sees as needed. These are compelling facts just by themselves. In my opinion, you don't even need to believe in a God to see how curiously interesting this is.

2) According to the laws of "information sciences" (the scientific study of where information originates, is transferred, etc.), information has never been seen in any scientific study to originate by itself in matter. In other words, it has never been observed to spontaneously come about. Any time the copying of information is traced back to its original source, there is always an intelligent mind behind creating that piece of information. Since there does appear to be some sort of creative information stored within each DNA, this may indicate that DNA comes from *something intelligent.* Suddenly, the idea of forty thousand years of natural selection seems more preposterous than the idea that Wald reveals in his strangely more direct assessment.

3) Mathematics, like DNA, also has built-into its own system, many divine formulas, that can be ultimately perceived as an extraordinarily complex code. Pi, phi, fractal geometry, the Fibonacci sequence (which was referenced as the *Golden Mean,* in *Gödel Escher Bach an Eternal Golden Braid,* by Douglas Hofstadter). What came first, the universe or math? Max Tegmark's Mathematical Universe Hypothesis (MUH) is a

Theory of Everything model that essentially submits that our external physical reality is a mathematical structure. Is math God, or is math a clue to God's existence? Taking into account the many wonders of the world that we still have yet to understand, we can also see that *numbers and math* embed within it an endless stream of mysteriously perfect codes, each one through which we may use as tools for contemplation, as well as to continue to build the world around us. There is no human creator of math to whom anyone can trace back. Math is beyond ancient. Math is perhaps the strangest and most beautifully perfect of all phenomena. Is math an intelligence that is beyond human? Encoded language has never been seen to be born from matter; it can only be born from an intelligent mind, as the rule states.

I don't think you need to be Christian or religious in any way, however, to feel just how profound the above observations are. Certainly, it offers a good reason as to why some of the leading scholars in the field of evolution and consciousness have mid-career suddenly changed directions in their consideration of perceiving what it all means. Could it have really just been a series of random collisions and accidents after the Big Bang that created consciousness, as the old evolution theory states? Or could consciousness have been here all along?

THE PLACEBO RITUAL

Up until the 1990's, the placebo effect was mainly used to test newly introduced pharmaceuticals in order to scientifically prove to the FDA that a new drug is able to out-perform the placebo. The placebo effect was therefore used as a "stable medium." All the while, however, the placebo effect continued to prove itself to be a surprisingly strong contender against the drugs against which it was measured. Just think how powerful it must be, in that you can admit, completely honestly, to someone that you are using a placebo on him or her, and even explain to them that they don't need to believe in it. Yet, somehow, with the innocently "normal" appearance in which it disguises itself, the placebo has an alarming success rate that continues to surprise us at how effective it is as a mysteriously self-working healing agent.

Superficially amazing about the placebo effect is the fact that it has the appearance of a "magic spell." A magical wave and puff of smoke from a wand, a few incantations recited, and you're healed. Seeing it this way helps to contribute to the perception of absurdity that is still felt today with regards to self-healing and alternative healer practitioners. There is much to learn in order to fully understand even where the placebo effect stands today in the medical world. More controversial, is the notion that a further medical understanding may be found in other cultures' curing techniques that are still considered by many as bogus for-profit-only "faith healing" scams.

But from what I can gather regarding the phenomena of the placebo, it can boil down to:

1) Placebos can be invoked by ritual: The ritual of getting better.

2) The mere suggestion that it works will activate the process.

3) Stronger, weaker and alternative *rituals* may be used to adjust the process.

4) Stronger, weaker and alternative *suggestions* may be used to adjust the process.

5) Kindness, caring and empathy are useful characteristics to come across as having.

6) Confident, unpretentious, and professional attitude is also useful to communicate.

7) It is important to monitor a subject's improvements and fluctuations indiscriminately of what happens.

8) It is important to take thorough, detailed notes of all processes, conditions and observations.

THE REAL PLACEBO BREAKDOWN

As mentioned, the primary function of the placebo was to create a measuring stick to help know whether or not to increase the strength of a drug's effects that were balanced against it. Nowadays, there has become more of an emphasis on experiments to see if there is a way to focus solely on increasing the success-rate of the placebo effect itself.

In 2013, Kaptchuk and several of his colleagues from Harvard affiliated hospitals created the Program in Placebo Studies and Therapeutic Encounter (PiPS), which is headquartered now at the Beth Israel Deaconess Medical Center. To this date, it is currently the only multidisciplinary institute dedicated solely to placebo study, but hopefully it will inspire the work of other researchers to help continue the efforts to confirm all of these very interesting findings.

It is plain to see that the 21st century in science has begun to put serious research and exploration into the mysterious effects of placebo-related healing. From the seriousness of how it's being taken, this is an obvious example of some of the far-out research that is currently being studied in scientific laboratories. When it comes to the possibility of one day causing change to occur in the direction of circumstance using the power of thought alone, we are closer than most of us even know.

The breakthrough understanding here is that a placebo effect that is directly connected to consciousness will undoubtedly set in motion an endless series of other fantastic ideas. Its confirmed existence so easily leads to the confirmation that people's thoughts may also interact with one another outside the five basic senses, and indeed also seeing genuine aspects of the future, magnify healing energies in others, communicate ethically with all life forms... It becomes endless.

To begin with, it has been posited already by several serious scientists (and slowly gaining momentum as scientific fact) that what our minds believe to be true has the ability to alter the biology of our physical bodies on a molecular level for good and bad. So the idea here, on a basic level, is that if we become sick, if we feel pain, if we have a headache or stomach problems, we are able to use our mind to consciously think ourselves back to being well again. Likewise, if we are perfectly healthy, but negativity pervades our subconscious thinking, we may make ourselves sick. It should go without saying that people get sick for all kinds of reasons that stretch far beyond one's negative thinking. However, negative thinking may also lend itself to encourage illness as well as *negative consequences*.

By the way, the notion here is not that "One day in the future we may achieve this ability." In fact, apparently, we already have this ability, and it has long been tested. Over several generations of society programming, people have been conditioned to believe that we must see a doctor or take this or that medicine in order to feel better. The basic reality of our mind and body, however, is what we believe and motivate ourselves towards, we can make happen. If you want it, you can have it. It's basically about how easily you are able to believe it enough to make it a reality.

The practice of using placebos in medicine has been used since the 18th century, when John Haygarth, a distinguished British physician, became curious of a popular medical treatment of that time called, "Perkins tractors," which consisted of two metal rods with pointed tips that were used to pass over and poke at patients while suggesting improvements of whatever ailment was being complained about. He decided to test the Perkins tractors against a "dummy remedy" and found that there was no difference between the two. More curiously than debunking the Perkins tractors, it was noticed that both remedies, though considered "quackery," succeeded regardless, with improvements of the test subjects on both sides. Haygarth became the first to discover, "to a degree that has never been suspected, what powerful influences upon diseases, is produced by mere imagination."

Although the placebo effect has been used in the study of medicine for over a hundred years, it has never been taken very seriously as a medicine. I believe the reason why it is so dismissed by doctors, is because philosophically the concept of the placebo, as one gets deeper and deeper into its workings becomes very similar to that of faith healing. This notion must make most doctors' heads spin with justifications as to why it is a ridiculous notion; why it must not be the case. Most western doctors at this time in history have a negative knee-jerk reaction to hearing about mystical cures, much less wanting to be associated with them.

Because of this, constant and continual replication of placebo testing seems to be required throughout history. I think it is mainly because of the way we are taught at schools about science. The placebo effect is one of those true things that happen in reality that breaks the rules in such a way that scientists, because of their training, must continually see it to believe it. It's like cavemen who first discovered fire becoming simply transfixed by its existence. The placebo effect inconveniently, however, takes organization, people, time and funding to replicate as a serious study.

In 1999, a study discovered that 50% of severely depressed patients taking their prescription medication improve whereas 32% percent did taking a placebo. This came from The United States Department of Health and Human Services. However, physicians seem to trust the placebo effect more as a gauge for measuring the efficacy of newly introduced pharmaceuticals. They don't appear to be as interested in trying to simply improve the efficacy of the placebo treatment itself. If it was discovered that the placebo effect could be increased by using hypnotherapy, reiki, acupressure, qi gong or any other technique that offers an alternative, non-invasive, drug-free treatment and that shows a better-than-average success rate against most other treatments, the economy of the medical industry would feel a sense of panic. I personally don't believe that we'll one day not need hospitals and doctors. Rather, I believe that if we learned to heal ourselves of the less-significant health related issues, we can have doctors and hospitals focus more on helping and supporting those with more severe issues that would take the natural healing process too long to recover. Hospitals and doctors will always be needed, but we need to realize just how much it is possible to trigger healing within ourselves.

I used to take my animals to a local vet in Silver Spring, MD, who was a Korean man that called himself Dr. Kim. This was many years ago and yet his heavy Korean accent is still crystal clear in my memory when once he said to me, "Some medicine is a kind of poison. Use just a little bit, and it can be okay. Use too much; maybe not so good." Some medicine is a kind of poison. I saw what he was saying as if the intrusion of certain medicines into the body does something to change the pattern or disrupts the energy of the body/temple and triggers the body to correct itself. If a self-correcting element has a direct connection to consciousness, while the medicine does its job to make its adjustments, the energy of the body's own response to the taking of the medicine will also act simultaneously as it doesn't turn off just because a different medication is administered. Thus, if self-correcting energies are triggered by consciousness, then all medicines must work congruently alongside the body's own anticipation of healing. If the ritual of medicine is applied without the medicine, it's very possible that the mind automatically triggers turning the wheels of the body's immune system to focus on the area in question without the need of any actual active ingredient.

A surgeon, if asked if there is any placebo effect that can be done in place of surgery, would probably find it somewhat laughable. However, in the *New England Journal of Medicine*, July 11, 2002, a study was conducted at the Baylor School of Medicine, which tested knee-surgery against a placebo. The participants were all patients who complained of severe and debilitating knee pain. The patients were divided into three groups. The first two groups were given two different types of standard surgery that people who have severe arthritic knees normally receive, so that Group 1 had damaged cartilage that was shaved from their knee. Group 2 had their knee joints "flushed out." This involves removing all of the material believed to be causing inflammation. Group 3 were treated with a full dose of "fake surgery." The patients were simply sedated, and then tricked into believing that they had the knee surgery when all that really happened was that incisions were made, followed by a bit of salt water splashed on the knee as they would do normally anyway. They then sewed up the incisions like all the other patients. All three groups went through the same rehab process, and at the end of it all, the results shocked everyone. It was seen that the placebo group had shown physical improvements just as much as the other two groups who had gone through real surgery.

That same year, in 2002, Irving Kirsch, professor of psychology at University of Connecticut, published an article entitled "The Emperor's New Drugs" in the American Psychological Association's *Prevention & Treatment*. After filing for a Freedom of Information Act (FOIA), he was able to request information on the clinical trials of the top antidepressants. Through his study, he found that 80% of the effect of the antidepressants measure during their own clinical trials could be attributed to the placebo effect. His testimony stands:

"The difference between the response of the drugs and the response of the placebo was less than two points on average on this clinical scale that goes from fifty to sixty points. That's a very small difference, that difference is clinically meaningless."

As recently as July 23, 2014, the findings of a study funded by the National Health and Medical Research Council of Australia, were released in *The Lancet*, that showed how when it came to lower back pain, paracetamol, known more commonly as acetaminophen (or Tylenol) in the USA, shows no better results than a placebo pill. Dr. Christopher Williams, from the George Institute for Global Health at the University of Sydney in Australia, randomly assigned 1652 individuals, whose average age was 45, who complained of acute back pain, from 235 primary care centers in the Sydney area. Half of them were put on a treatment regimen of taking Paracetamol three times a day for four weeks. Three times a day, incidentally, is just under the maximum dosage required for paracetamol. The other half was given a placebo. As it turned out, the average time it took for the patients to feel recovered, took about 17 days for the Paracetamol group, but took only 16 days for the placebo group. As a result, Dr Christopher was forced to state, "Simple analgesics like paracetamol might not be of primary importance in the management of acute low-back pain."

Placebo treatments have been studied and practiced all over the world as both a science as well as a pseudo-science. Many scientists and physicians will avoid looking at the possibilities because they don't see it as real science. It is literally as simple as a strong suggestion made within a ritual, and this somehow manages to stimulate real biological and physiological responses within the body. Through visualization alone, you can notice changes in your heart rate, blood pressure, chemical activity in the brain, arthritis and even the overall immune system. There are people who have suggested that placebos have cured arthritis, depression, fatigue, anxiety, and even Parkinson's disease.

After volumes of tests and studies, (over the last hundred years):

1) There is ample proof of the existence of a placebo effect.

2) For the purpose of reaching stable health, placebos are used as a measuring stick to gauge a new drug's effectiveness.

3) It's hard to tell how much the placebo effect may also play a role in the healing process of the newly introduced medications themselves.

4) As the placebo effect appears triggered by the mind and ritual, the notion of higher levels of consciousness is also brought up.

5) If the placebo effect is linked to DNA and healing through consciousness (as already believed by many), perhaps there are things that western physicians can learn from tribal spiritual faith healers, after all.

6) If everyone began to open their minds and hearts and realize how we are not figuratively, but *truly connected* to one another, in very subtle ways, we may be able to realize new uses for our collective mind/spirit.

Just so that you are tracking along with where I am about to take you, back in the old days, we use to look at the placebo effect as a "something that comes from nothing." Others might look at it from the standpoint that eventually, people just "naturally get better." However, it must be understood that getting better faster and more effectively "than normal" can be observed when telling the patients to just take pills that contained no active ingredients. That is the real interesting thing about the placebo effect. So it seems that our mind has a lot more to do with our healing process than we may even know.

In fact, if we were to go there, it would lead us to wonder if it is possible that a "higher consciousness" that we may all have access to, may be linked to a subtle energy field that connects all living creatures and non-living entities through time and space. These are deep ideas that are shared by certain Chinese qi gong practitioners, Japanese reiki practitioners, and others who are familiar with Eastern traditional medicine as well as indigenous tribal shamanic and aboriginal traditional practices found all over Africa, Asia, South America, and nearly every island all over the world.

That our actions combined with belief can cause a powerful healing Agent to activate, gives reason to believe that such an Agent is born out of a suggestion. This suggestion creates belief, and somehow, whatever is *believed* will move in that direction. It appears that it can be any mind that creates the *suggestion to take action,* at which time the body readies itself to accept said Agent, which is represented by the ritual of performing *any mentally acceptable action* to activate the cure. Could it be that so long as the ritual is mentally acceptable by the mind, it somehow activates a more focused healing process?

Alain Nu, The Man Who Knows™

CHAPTER **8**

THE MAHARISHI EFFECT

The idea of our collective thoughts and intentions successfully exercising subtle control through such an energy field is quite old. However, as late as the 1955, Maharishi Mahesh Yogi began a movement called Transcendental Meditation (TM) that would combine the exploration of the inner mind with the collective mind. The movement was successful at sparking hope, uniting the efforts of scientists, philosophers, celebrities, philanthropists, and began research institutions as well as a new institution of thinking worldwide.

On August 1, 1993, *The New York Times* came out with this story:

THE silence was earsplitting. Less than 100 yards away, cars and buses honked on a busy avenue in a Washington neighborhood known for indiscriminate gunplay. But with eyes closed and minds "floating," nearly 60 men, women and children concentrated on not concentrating. Legs crossed, they lined up in rows on a foam pad in a dimly lighted college gymnasium. Trying to wipe their minds free of any thoughts, they focused on a silent mantra that only they could hear. More than 4,000 practitioners of transcendental meditation, including more than 12 Long Islanders, went to Washington on a six-week mission to slash the crime rate in neighborhoods like the one in Washington. 'We came to do this experiment, and the experiment is to show that if individuals do this technique, they can positively influence their world,' said Raymond Probs, 39, of Northport, who started meditating in Washington on June 7. Mr. Probs, chairman of the Long Island Capital of the Age of Enlightenment in Northport, said meditation could reduce violence by creating 'a powerful influence on the larger level of consciousness.'

The World Peace Group (which is run by TM practitioners who support the philosophies and teachings of the Maharishi) proudly makes the claim that over the past 40 years, Transcendental Meditation has been observed in over 600 research studies at over 200 universities and in 27 different countries. Surely meditation and

71

self-awareness can help one to become more in control of oneself, one's own relaxation and emotional control, but what about meditation's ability to remotely circulate positive energy unwittingly into others? How could they have figured out that could happen? Could that even be true? If it is, it flies in the face of most rational ways of thinking.

TM has amassed an impressive collection of hundreds of big celebrity practitioners, such as Jennifer Anniston, Russell Brand, Ellen DeGeneres, Clint Eastwood, Madonna, Paul McCartney, Jerry Seinfeld, Stevie Wonder, Oprah Winfrey, and famous cult film director David Lynch not long ago started his own foundation whose mission is to bring the practice of TM into American inner-city public schools and places to give options for children and teens who are in need of alternative methods of reducing stress. This has been controversial, as some skeptics and protesters feel that TM has deep roots in the Hindu religion and that since the practice of religion has been outlawed in U.S. public schools, that it would not be appropriate. The celebrity connection, however, makes it feel very appealing, however. I, myself, do not practice TM, but it is easy for me to see how strong its gravitational pull has become and how it can be positively effective for any individual.

Another odd practice within the TM community is their practice of a strange "levitation" exercise in which, while sitting in lotus position, the practitioner can move their spirit to such a state of ecstatic enlightenment that their body is jettisoned off the ground. Of course, it then comes back down. In fact, there doesn't seem to be any scientific proof that it actually levitates. On camera, it looks more like a strange "hopping" takes place, albeit while sitting in a crossed-legged lotus position. It rather looks both silly and fun, but try sitting in a crossed-legged position and then try hopping as high and as far *as they can* and you will quickly find that you cannot. Not even close. First, you must be enlightened...

The "hopping levitation" of Transcendental Meditation has also given detractors much to laugh about. It would be these "outside of normal" claims that would split people's opinions of just which way to turn. Nevertheless, when the Washington, DC, study on TM's affect on crime reduction was released, it did indeed show a significant drop in crime, and during a time when Washington, DC, was wearing the crown for being the "#1 Murder Capital of World."

TM promotes world peace and has since released study after study in different cities all over the world that have shown successful results worldwide of what the Maharishi believed could be a "consciousness field effect" that a certain percentage of people practicing TM could have over a population, which would affect everyone to the point of bringing the overall stress level, and thus the crime level, down to significantly show a change. And as it turns out, the TM hopping phenomena that seems so laughable to skeptics apparently produces a brainwave that can be visually seen on EEGs as being more harmonically coherent than any other brainwave state that can be achieved. For this reason, it is the only type of meditation that is used in studies at The National Institute of Health in Bethesda, MD.

Nevertheless, my friend, Steven Lawrence Heston, Professor of Finance and Economics at The University of Maryland, College Park, said to me regarding the work of the Maharishi, the whole thing felt to him like "a mixture of carny scam, gullible, wishful, spiritual thinking, and religious zealotry." That TM can cure any illness, reduce crime, and bring about world peace seems ridiculous to Steve. Says Professor Heston, "There is no conceivable mechanism- there is the totally arbitrary square root of 1%. There is one low-quality study with the preposterous conclusion 'The statistical probability that this result could reflect chance variation in crime levels was less than 2 in 1 billion.' (If you) look at the graph, the fluctuation could clearly produce an occasional dip."

This is the kind of reaction that is fairly typical among those who take a skeptical stance against these fantastic notions that may be more about luring your consciousness by selling utopian dreams. It seems that some people, plain and simple, don't agree with the validity of the information that is available online regarding the positive effects of TM and population. I must say, it comes across as highly improbable, and just as Steve indicates, potentially corrupt, particularly if one considers oneself to be a skeptic and therefore does not know the full story. But the full story is also quite worth making clear, as it too presents its own case plainly and comprehensively, as fantastic as that may sound.

A FRIEND OF MAHARISHI SPEAKS

I decided to call my friend for some clarification. He is an unpretentious, thoughtful, and passionate man, a longtime instructor of Transcendental Meditation and old friend of the Maharishi, named "Williams." The following is mostly from a single phone call in which Williams detailed the entire history of his time with the Maharishi Mahesh Yogi. It was indeed enlightening:

"Maharishi's early research came out in 1974 when they had 16 cities in the US where there was 1% of the population that had merely learned the basic technique, but not the advanced TM Sidhis program, and that was a very interesting study which showed a definite potential positive affect on the population as it was noticed in all 16 cities. That was seen to happen from the very basic ideas that the Maharishi emerged from India with back in around the mid 1950's.

"His basic premise was that there were so many attempts to achieve peace in the world, and all of the attempts have been through governments, peace treaties... essentially, one country going in and trying to make another country think like they do, or adopt their style of government. Or even through lawyers to settle and create peace legislatively, or through pro-peace organizations. This is a different approach. This is not 'positive thinking peace.' This is not meditating on peace. When TM is taking place, no one is sitting there thinking, 'Peace, peace, peace. All world peace...' It's not on their brain at all. It's not the focus. It's not what this kind of meditation is.

"There are all kinds of meditation. That's showing up in the research too. Different meditations activate different areas of the brain and have different functions. (Physicist) Orme Johnson talks about this on his website. Maharishi taught that trying to meditate on positivity or being positive to create peace was what had been done up until then, but 'the basis of world peace is individual peace.' In other words, you have to be at peace in yourself, because the world wars, the world strength of intentions are due to nothing but the accumulation of individual stress and conflict that then breaks out in the collective consciousness as global and international conflict." Williams explained.

"If you don't have a method that brings the individual peace then you have nothing. That would be like trying to spray-paint a forest green instead of watering the roots of each individual tree in that forest"

Williams continued regarding the Maharishi, "He projected in the early 1960's that the effects of individuals practicing his basic technique should take only 1% of the world population. Only 1% would be needed to begin this practice in order to create permanent world peace because it is so powerful and neutralizing.

"He had a systematic breakdown of what are the effects of TM for an individual in terms of full mental potential. What are the effects of TM over health, and how does that affect social behavior. Social behavior, he said, is about giving, but in order to give you have to 'have.'

"If you only have $5 in your pocket, every time you spend a dollar it's a big pinch. But if you have millions of dollars in the bank and a check book in the pocket, then there is no pinch felt from spending, and that is the same with energy, love and intelligence. If you have a limited amount to spend and you feel tired and stressed and exhausted, then it's a struggle to do anything, but if we are overflowing with any of that from a boundless source, then it just flows and giving becomes effortless and spontaneous. You no longer even have to tell people that they should be giving. It no longer has to be a prescribed behavior. It just overflows from an abundant and lively inner source. He said that this energy would overflow in a way that will start affecting an individual family, or a neighborhood, or a city or a state, or a country or the entire world. That was when he originally theorized that only one percent would be enough to neutralize the collective stress because of the power of that inner peace and bliss, and positive energy and love that naturally radiated from 1% of the people."

Of course, this still causes one to wonder how he became excited about the concept of only 1%. Well, it turns out that 1% is quite a prescient number. Williams continued,

"In 1974, one of Maharishi's practitioners noticed that there were 16 cities where TM meditation was reportedly practiced by 1% of the population. So given the Maharishi's prediction regarding 1% of the population, they asked themselves, 'Where can we measure this that it might have an effect?'

"That was when someone proposed the idea of studying the crime rate. Criminal behavior pretty much occurs completely out of stress, so if we reduce the stress, we should see the crime rate go down. So they paired up 'sister cities,' which had similar demographics for each of the 16 cities that had 1% of the population meditating.

"They were selective in making sure to pick sister-cities with similar socioeconomic demographics, population density, etc. After pairing them up over a period of time, they were able to see that over the time of their study that the trends of the 16 cities that didn't have any TM meditation program compared to the ones that did had all gone up in crime rate, whereas the 16 cities that did show a significant TM population did go down on an average of up to 16% and for some significantly more."

As the research first started to come in which showed that the 1% concept he had seemed to be working, this was during the time that Williams was practicing with the Maharishi. He remembers vividly being at those meetings with him. "He was so excited as the researchers started coming in, bringing him the data and crunching the numbers for him." Williams remembers the Maharishi even challenging the data, asking lots of questions of what this and that was. It wasn't until his people showed him that it seemed to be a reflection across the board that this was happening, that the Maharishi decided to embark on a world tour to promote what he saw as a new idea."

Williams continued on, and told me how Maharishi's theories began in 1972, recalling:

"That was the time that Maharishi had originally developed his theory of 1% for every billion people. When he said that he sat down and he identified the 3600 cities in the world that would cover the population, which at the time was 3.6 billion people. This guy was incredibly precise.

"By 1976, he decided to come up with ways to deepen the experience. He would say things like 'Let's see if we can intensify it. Maybe we can somehow up the amperage of how powerful we can bring our minds to. What would stimulate even greater brain wave coherence and all of the effects in these people so they can all end up with a far more powerful effect?' That was when he decided to incorporate the Yoga Sutras of the Patanjali, the classic definitive text on yoga.

"Patanjali is where all of yoga comes from, and yet, for those who are familiar with this text, it really only had a total of two sentences that applied itself to the yoga asanas, the postures that most people are familiar with. The rest was about Samadhi, consciousness, permanent Samadhi, Sidhis, super-normal powers, all the deep mental stuff-- the Asanas were only there to support the flexibility which they say will allow them to 'maintain the experience.'"

YOGIC FLYING

The year 1976 was when Williams was involved in the courses with Maharishi, and that was when he began to make everyone read the Yoga Sutras. He remembers reading through those texts and feeling the heavy weight of not being able to completely understand what he was reading. But when those who had trouble with the Sutras would bring them to Maharshi, he would tell them to just keep reading them and meditate on them afterwards. He would say "Just read it out loud in your groups and then go do your meditation. Just keep reading it, and it will eventually filter and make sense." Eventually, the more everyone did as the Maharishi advised, the more they became less troubled with *trying to understand* the sutras, and the more they started to ask the questions that would actually begin their true learning. "Maharishi was an unbelievable teacher. He basically taught people to think for themselves," says Williams, "and then he would tie it back to the experience of meditation."

"The third chapter of the sutras was of the 'Sidhis' the 'Special Abilities.' As they all reached that chapter, the Maharishi was intent on encouraging us all to try it. He was excited and eager to test these qualities of what it would take to have such special abilities that would be written in such an ancient text." Williams remembers the Maharishi telling him if these special powers could be achieved, how incredible it would be. "It was during this time that people started having these unusual experiences that were hard to explain.

"They started to notice that the "Flying Sutra," The sutra on 'Levitation and Movement through Space and Air,' was producing very powerful effects, and spontaneously people started to have what they were defining as the early stages of that sutra (which was the 'lotus-position hopping' that was mentioned earlier). The hopping phenomena started happening spontaneously among us. Internally it was just the experience of great bubbling bliss. That was when the

Maharishi started to say things like, 'Let's bring in Orme Johnson, and let's have a real close look at all of this with regards to what the brain waves are saying,'" recalls Williams.

"When they reviewed the brain wave functions during the practice of all the different sidhis as well as TM, what they discovered was that, it was actually during the Yogic Flying Technique, that was when the periods of brain wave coherence was the greatest. It was the most intense and most prolonged."

Williams remembered that in those days, it actually made many of his practitioners concerned that, if this was leaked to the public, people were sure to think that they were all just some ridiculous and crazy cult. He remembers many of them making suggestions to the Maharishi not to let this out to the public. But instead, the Maharishi insisted. He said, "We should show everyone, so long as we can prove it works, it's like Superman, right?" Before anyone realized it, there were TM Superman posters.

Williams laughs, "Maharishi was very simple and instant about this, and he didn't seem to care at all that it was bad PR, more than the fact that it was interesting knowledge. The fact is, it did hurt us, PR-wise. He knew it would, but he cared more for those who knew what it was, and those who would pay attention to it and experience it. His feeling was that he didn't need the whole world to believe him. He only needed 1%. He just needed some serious people to help produce the effect that would take care of the whole population."

THE SQUARE ROOT OF 1%

I would like to say that my friend, Williams, did not want his identity disclosed because he felt that he did not want to interfere with factual mistakes that he might make with regards to the entire history of the Maharishi. He encouraged me to send this interpretation to the David Lynch Institute for fact-checking, and I was told that it was being sent to David Orme Johnson, who has been with the Maharishi at least as long as my own source. So far, there has been no word back from them, so I am assuming that the information that I am offering here is at least fairly on par with history. My goal in all of this was to get to the bottom of two TM claims:

1) To find out more details as to how they can take their Yogic Flying techniques so seriously. (Since most people can't help but see it as ridiculousness.)

2) To find out to what degree they felt they could claim that TM could reduce a city population's crime level.

Williams recalled the Maharishi sitting down and discussing the Sidhis with his scientist friends "Maharishi would be sitting with physicists, looking at the brainwave research. One of them would say to him, 'Maharishi, this looks like super gravity,' or 'Maharishi, this looks like laser light.' The brain waves in normal waking states of consciousness are kind of like normal light waves that come from a normal light source. Whereas in TM, and even more so in the Sidhis and the Yogic Flying Technique, the brainwaves become coherent and orderly, and whereas they might be seen as jagged or spiky, the waves become more even and smooth. They also became synchronous. In other words, the wave formations from different parts of the brain became synchronous or harmonized with each other.

"Physicists would often sit with Maharishi and get into deep conversations with him. At one point, they were talking about the subject of *temperature*. The idea was that if you lower a temperature to absolute zero, you are also making the most coherent wave formation as everything else slows down to essentially zero movement. So as you lower the temperature of something, you are also raising the coherence of it, which is why food doesn't spoil as fast when put in a freezer. Maharishi made the analogy, saying, 'That is what is happening in the brain. You are lowering it to the temperature of absolute zero. You are lowering the activity of the brain to nil, to that vacuum state of pure consciousness, where consciousness is in its simplest form of awareness.' Deep silence, no object of consciousness, you are not conscious of anything. It's just consciousness being conscious of consciousness. It's the only experience where the perceiver, the object of perception, and the process of perceiving are all seen as the same thing—this is ultimately the experience of Samadhi, pure consciousness. In fact, that is actually what yoga is: that is what unity means in the word Yoga. It is the unity of perceiver, perception and perceiving.

"Then Maharishi asked the question, 'How can you take a regular light source and turn it into a laser light? How does that happen?' And they said back, 'Well, there has to be a trigger-effect, there needs to be a certain number or percentage of wave which you deliberately induce in order for it to become coherent and synchronous.' This causes the other light waves to begin shifting automatically, and once you reach a certain threshold, you reach what is called a 'phase transition.' There was a process that they explained to him which would cause all other light to shift automatically into laser light. So Maharishi asked them to tell him the number that this was, and after they made their calculations, it was the square root of one percent."

Their studies then took them from city to city to see if they could record consistencies that used a proportion in conjunction with the square root of one percent of the Maharishi's specially trained "Yogic Flyers" to affect a local population. It turns out that the way they came up with this square root of one percent number was that it was an analogy of a formula that was told to him regarding normal light to laser focus. Furthermore, it seems that his purpose was to use such a study to test out the effectiveness of what his Yogic Flyers, who already exhibited an impressively coherent brain wave function, could do when it came to their pin-point accuracy of bringing down the crime rate through meditation techniques of the Sidhis. If all things went as planned, theoretically it would generate a field of bliss that acts contagiously on the outlying environment. What they noticed, was that it, too, seemed to be working!

"They continued to try this out, each time trying to ensure that they had a minimum of a square root of 1% of a city's population of Yogic Flyers to be flown to a city to stay for a couple of months to see if the crime rate would go down. And for about the next year and half, each time they would go into a city with a high stress/crime rate, the effect would be similar. First the crime rate would increase slightly, and then the crime rate would drop about 18% to 25%. Oddly, what they also noticed during this time was that each time they would leave one place to go to another, the crime rate of the city that they were leaving would then go back up.

"After they felt that they had tried this enough times to prove that an effect was happening, the Maharishi got real excited and said, 'Now, let's see how well we can do in Lebanon.' As crazy as it sounds, the Maharishi sent over the correct number of his people that corresponded to this 'square root of 1%' equation to war-torn Lebanon. And within the time that they were there, the city that they went to became quiet. This was a significant moment, because it seemed clear to everyone who was witnessing it by this point that something was happening. A real consciousness 'field effect' was taking place. There was never any fanfare about their arrival into the cities that they went to. They would just rent a warehouse or a facility to do their Yogic Flying, and made no big deal of it. All of their meditations were done in private. The exercise was not to execute this in public, but rather in private, just within the vicinity of a crime zone, in order to see what would happen just by their presence while in the act of sending out this strong brainwave brought on by the elation that is felt during the act of Yogic Flying.

"So this was not about a suggestion or a placebo effect, this was about a new kind of 'cause and effect physics' which happens through meditation and consciousness. It was around this time that it became important to them to find a way to document this scientifically. Orme Johnson, who is a physicist, was one of the Maharishi's scientists, and the professor of psychology at the Maharishi University of Management, in Fairfield, Iowa. He was instrumental during this time at running thorough experiments for the Maharishi.

"Not long after they left Lebanon, they also tried it in several other crime zones, but there started to be a concern around the fact that they were noticing that the although each time they would show up in one place and watch as the vicinity would quiet down, it would be no sooner than they would be leaving before, the area would often spike back up, sometimes even higher than before. This really disturbed the Maharishi. He realized at that point, establishing a group temporarily would only mean that when they left, the turbulence would erupt again potentially worse than ever, and that was certainly not his goal.

"The Maharishi became interested then in experimenting on it more in the United States, as experiments done here in the U.S. tended to be more organized. So by 1983, as there was close to 4.9 billion people in the world, the TM community was also trying to up their own numbers to match the Maharishi's 1% rule. It was then, that the Maharishi decided that they had done enough studies on cities and the effects on smaller countries. He wanted then to really try to match the world's population by bringing in a minimum of 7000 people to Fairfield, Iowa to meditate in order to see if they might show an affect on global world peace. Within one month, a building was erected to house 7000 people in Fairfield, Iowa, specifically for the Yogic Flying.

"Once they were able to bring 7000 TM practitioners to come to Fairfield and train with the Maharishi's Yogic Flyers, they carried out their research and looked closely at the global statistics. They looked at everything from statistics of civil unrest to the worldwide crime-rate, reviewed statistics of countries bombing each other, and what they discovered was that, oddly, it seemed as if the 'Maharishi Effect' was working. All the indexes that they were reviewing were all turning up to appear significantly related!

"It was then that the Maharishi decided that he wanted to try and set up a permanent group of about 7000 to 8000 in one location in the world to meditate in order to monitor the energy of world peace. Of course the world population has grown significantly over the decades, so the number of yogic flyers will end up always needing to change. Maharishi emphasized that a smooth transition was important because he was concerned that, similar to laser waves, the 'phase transition' of changing the brainwave to smooth and coherent often went through a temporary chaotic phase wherein, as was mentioned earlier, the system would become more chaotic just before it becomes smooth and coherent. As this seemed always to be an unwanted byproduct of the effect, Maharishi was always concerned and emphasized that the goal in mind should have an intention of smoothness for each 'phase transition' for all wave functions as they take affect."

THE WASHINGTON, DC, EXPERIMENT

Sometime just before August of 1993, Washington, DC, was crowned the "Murder Capital of the World." As far as any of us who were living here were concerned, at the time, we were willing to try anything to end the violence. Hearing that the "Transcendental Meditators" were coming to town was not entirely surprising to anyone. By then, the TM community had been experimenting on different cities for nearly 20 years, even though at the time, I don't know how much even that was talked about, since even *The New York Times* story didn't mention their many years of prior experience with experiments conducted on other city populations. Nevertheless, I personally remember the excitement coming in from those who were curious of the results. It even seemed to work on Washington, DC.

The DC experiment began on June 7 and lasted until July 30th, 1993. By the time they had come to DC, they decided to make it an "announced study." Before their arrival, the researchers had publicly announced that they were predicting a 20% drop in crime by the end of their study. So as opposed to secretly coming in, they staged it as a two month-long "demonstration for world peace." This would be one of their most carefully controlled experiments. The study began with a "coherence group" of about 800 and accumulated about 4000 over the trial period. Before their arrival, violent crime was steadily increasing during the first 5 months of that year. Within a week of their beginning their study, violent crimes called "HRA crimes" (homicides, rapes and aggravated assaults, measured by the FBI Uniform Crime Statistics) began to decrease and continued to drop until the end of the experiment. Mentioned on the World Peace Group's website regarding this study:

"This prediction had been ridiculed by the Chief of Police who asserted that the only thing that would decrease crime that much would be 20 inches of snow." In the end, the maximum decrease was 23.3%. This significant reduction occurred when the size of the group was at its largest in the final week of the project and during a blistering heat wave.

"The statistical probability that this result could reflect chance variation in crime levels was less than 2 in 1 billion (p < .000000002). When the project disbanded HRA crime began to rise again. The research is extremely reliable by the usual standards of social science. As a result we know that the effects of the coherence group can not be attributed to other possible causes, including temperature, precipitation, weekends, and police and community anticrime activities."

Maharishi Mahesh Yogi continued to work steadily on the effects of TM and the Sidhis on population and was able seed many parts of the world with his amazing ideas that somehow merge together the seemingly disparate concepts of both physics and mysticism. He died in February 2008 at 91 years of age. Williams is convinced that

Maharishi was a man who not only lived a long life, but also was able to do so while working at least 20 hours out of the day. Some have said that in the last couple of years of his life, he was hardly sleeping at all. He was a brilliant, caring and advanced spirit whose research continues to inspire many top thinkers in the world to this day. Furthermore, I would personally like to add, he is perhaps the single most powerful advocate of the notion of a "consciousness field effect" between the twentieth and early twenty first century.

So it's plain to see that there is a lot to be controversial about with the subject of the Maharishi Effect (consciousness field effect). Might it one day become common knowledge taught in schools, that the coherent brain waves created by focused meditation can bring down stress inside oneself to the point that it begins to show signs of bringing down the stress levels of also those that live around you? What if it did have something to do with an overall percentage of a collectively formed consciousness that would affect the entire field in a spiritually medicinal way? The tendency here is to *wish that it were true.*

One of the ideals underpinning the David Lynch Foundation is to offer a most basic and simple process of the stress-relieving aspects of TM as "basic knowledge," to be taught as an alternative curriculum to inner-city schools, schools for troubled teens, juvenile detention centers, etc. Might the knowledge of how to use an effective meditation technique help to bring more awareness to the stress-relieving benefits of youngsters who haven't been taught such skills?

The Maharishi had made a sound point. As you nourish one tree with plenty of good water, sunlight, and healthy nutrients in the soil, those nutrients, water and sunlight, will automatically also work on nourishing the other trees nearby. It is this automatic nature of "conscious nourishment" that is created simply through meditation, which brings coherence of our thought-patterns that actually makes it so effortlessly powerful.

Aside from the work of TM and those inspired by the Maharishi's thinking, our collective thoughts do appear to exhibit some interesting possibilities which only begin with a consciousness field effect. We may one day be using our minds collectively, as a single unifying force. And although it may at first seem idealistic, there are many who believe that it's just that we haven't gotten to the point of exploring it enough.

It is awesome to imagine that one day we might learn how to change the course of the worst storms to navigate them into areas where they would do less damage, or even change the course of a giant asteroid that appears destined to collide with our planet by focusing our collective minds. Our collective minds may one day be used to heal one another in more practical ways, so we can reserve our doctors and hospitals for the more complicated matters. The placebo effect, the consciousness field effect, and the self-regulating, self-repairing nature of the DNA cells within us are still not fully understood, but as we continue to understand this new terrain of space, there is a good chance that it will lead us to a new milestone in our evolution that may sanctify a new classification of man. Could that be at all on our horizon? Or is this just science fiction-talk...?

Alain Nu, The Man Who Knows™

CHAPTER 9

WHAT I THINK

With all of this now being brought up about placebo and the potential effects of field consciousness, you might begin to start making a few odd connections. For instance, might the symbolic performance or illusory representations of mysteries also enhance an aspect of the placebo within consciousness that can affect a multitude of people? "Master demonstrations" are well known for taking place during religious festivals where people will find themselves ecstatically being "slain in the spirit." Other annual events, as well as sacred rituals in other third world and tribal cultures exhibit similar trance-like phenomena. They are generally displayed as a special skill that the grandmaster, medicine man, priest, or shaman embodies during the gathering.

Regardless of the talents that he or she exhibits, the master is always seen as the most preeminent. However, he or she is not the master because of his or her skills, necessarily. Usually, it is simply that he or she is seen as being somehow connected to the divine. Therefore, although the skill also becomes symbolic of divine powers, the master is already revered for his or her knowledge and connection to a more sacred world. The skill artfully and ceremoniously calls the attention of the people to gather and is a representation of the infinite within his or her own self-mastery. It is the moment that is created; as all elements come together that draw the *reality of the infinite* into each of us. It is this moment that the great mysteries are revealed within. The experience ultimately plants a seed into our memory, and as the mind contemplates the seed, an inspiration is born. As it forms connections, the inspiration becomes solid, and as it continues to grow, it can be felt growing as each continuing connection forms at a steadier pace. Could either or both of those two oddly connected, yet seemingly disparate concepts (that is to say, illusion and placebo), have been brought together at any point in history, by mysticism?

In the world of hermetic mysticism, one of the most powerful wisdoms was found inscribed as the first words to be read on Hermes Trismegistus' most sacred and revered *Emerald Tablets* which, translated, states:

"That which is Below corresponds to that which is Above, and that which is Above, corresponds to that which is Below, to accomplish the miracles of the One Thing."

Most people know this phrase by its shortened version, "As above, so below." The significance of this phrase is that it is believed to hold the secret key to unlock all the mysteries in our universe. That wisdom, which Hermes, "The Thrice Great," embedded within this statement, gives us the hidden formula of the universe in that:

All things that happen on one level of reality, happens on every level of reality.

DUALITIES

Mentalism is an artistry born of consciousness that reflects the image of cosmic phenomena, similar to a reflection in a mirror or a pool of water that reflects the space around it. The image is not the same as the reality, and yet, it casts such a realistic representation that an understanding may also be learned from the reflection. In the case of these 'performance-reflections,' the difference is that it is harder for one to picture it as manifest of a present reality, but rather, more that of a possible reality.

There is another way of seeing mentalism, generally seen through the eyes of *skeptics* or people who relate to modern skeptical culture that, on the severe side, might be read more like the following:

Mentalism is a realistic and clever way of making it appear as if one can read minds, see the future, or exhibit other uncanny abilities that many people, even today, are tricked into believing is really happening, but is actually a hoax. The most commonly known purpose for its existence is for unsavory persons to sham the unsuspecting and gullible into believing that something real is happening in order to make profit, control friendships and alliances with those who are willing to 'drink the Kool-Aid' and revere them as gurus.

Of course, we must always try and distinguish the difference between a distrustful person and an art form. Being aware of people's intentions is a natural part of adult human interaction. There is always a chance of meeting someone who has underlying intentions that may be manipulating. In my opinion, however, the "reality or sham" comparison is distracting

The duality of mentalism is not between whether it's a reality or a sham. Mentalism is a "mystery art," thereby the duality is between *reality and illusion*. The slight difference in perception here, I believe, is a difference worth understanding. An illusion is, like a mirror reflection, simply something that has a striking likeness to what it is representing. As in all of the arts, whether it is a painting, a film, a story, or a performance of a Civil War reenactment, the appreciation of such presentations may offer a kind of wisdom or teaching about that very thing, without actually being the thing it is representing. The beautiful duality of reality and illusion is that in the similar manner as night and day, male and female, or yin and yang, they are both polar opposites and one and the same. Many of the greatest artists (just like the great mysteries) have inspired our greatest wisdom and achievements. So when I have seen performances by tribal shaman and ceremonial magicians, I have a different appreciation. I wonder what such people have to offer of themselves. Surely, they are gifted in many ways that allow us to learn from them as reflections of our own powers and us.

Part of appreciating the mysterious enigma persona is in the "not knowing" of what aspect of reality is being engaged. A mysterious practitioner desires those to be affected by the experience he or she is casting in such a way that meaning is felt and accepted for what it does to their spirit emotionally and purposefully. As the performer does this, the emotion created from the reaction ultimately manifests into a *direction* of sorts. Those manifested directions result in patterns of behavior that may entertain, provoke curiosity, or even transform one's reality. This is where experimentation with genuinely connecting to others can become very real for both such performers as well as their audience.

If there is a genuine way to read someone's mind, exhibit clairvoyant powers, predict the future, or energetically heal and affect yourself and others, the only way that could be possible, would be by using our minds somehow to cause an aspect of itself or our body to sense, or somehow mentally interpret a hidden language found in a cosmic form of conduction or a frequency or vibration. Every so often, for reasons that no one has yet been able to pinpoint, we find ourselves accidentally or suddenly receiving thoughts that somehow connect to unknowable information, other people's thoughts, or receiving projections of the future. Could those moments really be only a "coincidence," or might there be something more? You have most likely heard many times of how someone who is near the end of their life, suddenly rallies back even when they are at their worst, only to live for sometimes months to years later. Might there be an aspect of consciousness which modern science has forgotten about and still refuses to reconsider? Perhaps, is it an aspect that we haven't yet considered which may one day become tangible in ways we could have only dreamed of in the past?

It is better to think of any of our ideas that come to us as genuine possibilities than as complete impossibilities. To say something is impossible is not only the wrong frame of mind mentally, but it completely destroys the excitement of making it come true. As long as you believe an idea you came up with is impossible, you will never let yourself attempt it. Should you, however, consider what possibilities may be gathered in order to fulfill your ideas, paths will be forged, and within time, opportunities will manifest.

I have always been interested in things that science has a hard time explaining. At first, I was very skeptical of people who made claims that seemed too extraordinary. As I delved deeper and deeper, however, I began to take note of experiences I, myself have had, which by now has become too many instances in my own life in which something happens that defies explanation of any kind. I used to shrug off those experiences, usually making up outlandish reasons as to how things like that would have rationally happened to me. Later, however, as I started to replace my own cynicism with a more investigative approach, I realized that there was a lot that I could not personally explain from simplistic rational reasoning. I started to take note and accept everyday strangeness as more of an exciting blessing each time something inexplicable or particularly noteworthy would happen to me. Ever since I have started to do this, I feel I have started to see and understand the universe in a completely different way.

Sometimes they are little things. Just a few days ago, as I was writing the "As Above, So Below," paragraph, which I was already planning to write for some time, I noticed that there is now a new film advertised on television called *As Above, So Below*. My writing that section had nothing to do with having seen the TV commercial prior, however, or even knowing that such a film would be coming out. I might also go so far as to predict that the movie won't be nearly as good or as popular as the original text, but of course, we are talking about comparing Hollywood to Hermes.

Most people will have experiences like this from time to time, but usually an experience like that gets filed as "just a coincidence," and especially if there is no personal connection to the experience besides the random occurrence that it was. There may be something deeper about such random occurrences if one is vigilantly aware, rather than dismissing these moments entirely and not giving them a second thought. It can be a fun mental exercise to try and find the hidden meanings in things.

Sometimes they are larger things. Once, while in the middle of a two-week experiment, with a scientist and researcher friend of mine named Eugene Kovalenko, in Los Alamos, NM, a strange thing happened. His standing challenge, though, is perhaps one of the most difficult challenges set to any psychic, and to this day, still has not been successfully achieved even by well-known psychics, Peruvian shaman, nor myself. Eugene is oddly convinced that one day he will find someone who will be able to successfully cause one of two pendulums he has hanging in front of his 24/7 surveillance cameras, to inexplicably move. Both metallic disc pendulums hang from the lid inside of a large glass jar. This prevents wind or air-conditioning to affect their swinging. The idea here is to choose which of the two discs to move and then choose the time in which to try to connect with it and cause it to move by itself, while not affecting the other pendulum of the other disc. All this must be done within a reasonable amount of concentration time, but you could choose which ever time you wanted to record.

One disc is silver and the other one is painted red. They hang under surveillance cameras that run continuously. To not affect one pendulum, while affecting the one right next to it is the challenge. The challenge set for me was to give me two solid weeks to try to move the red disc pendulum, and to simply record the times that I focused on them and send them to him. He would then check the surveillance of the pendulums during the times noted to see if there was any significant change. I was near the end of my two weeks of trying unsuccessfully to swing the red pendulum, when I took a drive up to Princeton and was met with some inspiration.

It was a little over a week after the Fourth of July in 2010. I had gone up to visit with two friends of mine who I had just met, Bob John and Brenda Dunne, and some of their team at the International Consciousness Research Laboratory in Princeton, NJ. Robert Jahn is a retired (emeritus) Dean of Engineering at Princeton University. He founded the famous PEAR (Princeton Engineering Anomalies Research) Laboratory along with Brenda Dunne who has co-authored all of his most recent books and participated in the majority of the onsite experiments regarding the mind-over-matter phenomenon. I had just gotten back from visiting them and finding out about a couple of interesting new devices that I had just gotten from them. I felt as if I had a possible answer as to how I might move the pendulum in Texas based on my experience I just had in Princeton.

It was while there, that I was able to try out a few new "games," which Psyleron, their then newly-sprung sister company had been developing. From a thought I had about how to become successful with the game I was introduced to, I decided to go home and try the idea out on my soon-to-be-ending pendulum experiment with Kovalenko. I woke up very excited, the next morning just before 5am and walked into my studio that sits detached but behind my house, so I could get some privacy. I sat in the middle of the floor and began to concentrate. As I meditated on raising the level to a swell of emotion within me while forming a musical pitch within my mind. Suddenly, I started to shake. I could hear a sound like a vibration that sounded like a large truck was passing by my home, or perhaps it was a helicopter passing overhead. The room began to shake even more violently. A couple of rocks that I had balanced on top of one another suddenly fell over. I was now fully awake, but the room was still shaking. What the heck was going on? It was dark in my studio because I had left the lights off. The whole reason for my waking up so early to try my experiment was to try to meditate during a completely quiet time of the day. But now there were moving lights flashing in my window... What in the world was happening now? Was I being raided?

When my senses came back to me seconds later, I realized that the searchlight in my window was my wife looking for me with a flashlight. She noticed that the lights in my studio were off, but also knew that I wasn't in the house after calling for me several times. The shaking had awoken her as well. We were trying to figure out if it was a low-flying helicopter or a large construction truck, but as we turned on the television and found the news, we realized it was an actual earth tremor (in Maryland!) that registered 3.4 on the Richter scale. This oddly took place at the exact same time that I decided to spend time on this "new idea" that I was experimenting with on this seemingly impossible remote psychokinesis study of Eugene Kovalenko's. I will talk more about the method I was using to attempt to swing the pendulum, in Section III of this book on my personal experiments with mind over matter and *Psyleron*.

In the end, this was one of those hard-to-document circumstances, as the tremor seemed to be triggered from somewhere in the northern region of Montgomery County and I live in a more centralized region, closer to Washington, DC. For a person who has lived in Maryland for most of my life now, I have felt about a good half-dozen small tremors while living in this area just in my adult life. A few of them, I have felt while driving, as I can feel my entire car vibrate uncontrollably. Usually, I am not focusing my attention on it, or anything like it at the time. And it's usually after the fact that I start asking myself if it was an earth tremor. However, this particular moment of the early morning, at the quiet hour of nearly exactly 5am, and while in the process of trying to do what I was trying to do, it was hard not to find it oddly significant. The fact that I would be meditating on trying to make something move that was hundreds of miles away, only to suddenly feel the earth beneath me shaking violently and find out that it was a 3.4 earth tremor that had occurred, (which are not frequently felt in Maryland at all) made me slightly concerned whether I might have somehow contributed to this random geological event.

Even with my wife as a witness from being there, Bob Jahn's and Brenda Dunne's testimonials that I had just visited with Psyleron and interacted with their psi-games, and Eugene Kovalenko knowing that this positively took place during the two-week time span of our experiment, it is an experience of which I can only write about in memoirs, like I am doing right now. At the time it happened, I also blogged about it, but that only resulted in a *skeptical blog* response which wrote about how ridiculous it would be if I was trying to claim responsibility over the local earthquake. To be clear, I only asked the provocative question, *"Could* that have been me?" because I am such the publicity scoundrel...

Has anything strange like this ever happened to you that you cannot explain? Maybe even an odd story that has been in your family history? Maybe you always found it too hard to imagine because it felt too far-out, or too otherworldly? Could it be, that somewhere embedded within that experience might be a hidden clue, a secret message or untapped knowledge that may reveal itself as somehow significant in the future?

It was indeed the world of secrets and possibilities such as these that has set fire to my imagination ever since I was old enough to read.

AN ASIAN OUTCAST BECOMES A KNIGHTS TEMPLAR

My father would be what I would call a semi-agnostic Catholic. This means that if you ask him what religion he practices, he'll tell you that he's Catholic. My mother, who came originally from a Chinese traditionalist upbringing surrounded by Buddhism, was baptized to be Catholic after marrying my father. So if you ask her what religion she practices... She'll tell you that she's Catholic. Now these days they do attend church... on occasion and especially now that they are in their eighties. But when we finally settled down in the outer DC suburbs of Bethesda, MD, (when I was eight years old) and I told them that I would really rather not go to church, their reaction was to say, "Well, ok then." I don't think they were necessarily happy about this decision of mine, and perhaps even felt slight disappointment at my complete indifference, but they were too busy to fight with me about it. My sister was born a year later when I was about to turn nine, and she lived her whole life with them never going to church either. Wait a minute... we were made to go to church on Easter and Christmas. Let me be clear at this point by saying that I never thought of myself as a sinner. I much more innocently preferred to see it as being *spiritually invincible*.

My parents who were both Library Science majors and who met each other in 1962 in Laramie, Wyoming (which is an odd place for two Asians to be in the 1960's, I know) saw themselves as new-comers to this country. I think their overall policy was to try to survive with a nuclear family in the US in a way that would be in the least stressed way as they could make it. I used to jokingly call them "fake-Catholics." But what they really were was a newly formed but hardworking middle-class Asian American family trying to make a home in the DC metropolitan. As librarians, my father and mother both found decent jobs, and worked for The Library of Congress and The National Library of Medicine, respectively.

Throughout my early life, I was taught to remember that both my mother and father were minorities who came from different cultures. Therefore, the most important thing for me to know was that *all people* must have tolerance and respect for other people's different beliefs and cultures, *but especially us because we were minorities.* It seemed simple enough, especially in America.

Different systems of thought should try to tolerate and/or co-exist with one another. That was just before I learned about racism and bullying. My school years were sadly not ones that I would recall as being the greatest times of my life. I learned, between my third through eighth grades exactly what it was like to be bullied and discriminated against. Those were a difficult six years of my life. I was the new kid on the block, the new kid in school, and one of only two Asians in my grade. The other girl was Filipino, and she didn't seem to like me at all.

In my ninth year (1974), my sister was born, and a process of bringing all of my relatives from Vietnam to the US after the war was well underway. Somewhere in my ninth year, eleven of my Vietnamese relatives, who I had never met before, moved into our home in Bethesda and slept on army cots and sofa beds all over our house. It was an entirely different culture than what I was used to, but these were my father's brothers and their families. This became a new culture for me to try to understand, based on the fact that I was being raised by my surroundings as an American. .

I became conflicted. Why does everyone at school treat me like I am so different than them? Why do my own relatives see me as so different from them? Who was I? What did I believe in? My father put it succinctly by saying, "It's just the differences between cultures." What does a nine year old do with that information? Maybe it was that I felt I needed to learn as much as I could about *other things that other people wouldn't know about?* Maybe that would help compensate for my inability to easily understand the people around me, who I felt guilty of not being able to understand? So began perhaps my most motivated reasons for why I fell more and more into my own private world of personal mysticism and desire to learn magical secrets. Like most all people, it was my underlying hope amidst it all to establish some sense of personal control and integrity.

I was taught the meaning of what it is to be *tolerant*. I had to now become tolerant of new customs, new foods, and privacy restrictions- all while living in my own home. We all lived together for about a year. During that time, my parents even tried encouraging me to tolerate bullies at school because there were just too many other things going on and so long as I wasn't coming home with any major injuries or broken bones, what real harm could be done, anyway? I do feel that this is relevant as to why I am prone to becoming sensitized when I am feeling bullied or when I feel that bullying is taking place.

During those six years I realized that *being tolerant of bullying is not the answer*. If one were to look within oneself, I think it becomes easy to see how difficult it is to be tolerant or open with anyone who finds it fun or amusing to insult and condescend on other individuals or groups of people in a hateful way, based on differences in appearance, belief and lifestyle. As things transitioned for me through middle school and high school, I ended up experiencing prejudice in so many different ways, that I am all too sensitized to how unified groups will construct special language patterns among other ways and means to diminish, disgrace, and isolate those who are targeted (and usually someone who is not as strong-minded).

In fact, it was during middle school and high school that I was to become aware of just how segregating the public school system can be. Two of my best friends (who were brothers) joined the Masonic fraternity of DeMolay, as their father was a Mason. I ended up becoming a member myself sometime in my thirteenth year. Suddenly, I realized that I was indoctrinated into one of the largest and most powerful secret societies in the world. One that was accepting of any other culture of person to become a member, and one whose own history is so rich in ancient magical traditions and secret formulas that it boggled the mind. It was exactly what I was looking for, actually.

The initiation ceremonies were filled with meaning and symbolism. The robes were pretty awesome too. As a young man interested in magic, I was able to also have some very interesting discussions with older and wiser men who filled my head with a whole new meaning to magic along with thoughts of deeper secrets that could be attained with perseverance and making the right connections. Also, being a part of the group, gave me a sense of community that I had never felt before. I would make it through my high school years, knowing I had the support of my new brethren that now networked the entire DC metropolitan (not to mention, the world over). In later years, I became the Master Councilor (considered the highest ranking youth member within a DeMolay chapter) of both Samuel Gompers and Potomac Chevy Chase DeMolay chapters.

Jacques DeMolay, who the Masonic fraternity was named after, was the twenty-third (and last) Grand Master of the Knights Templar, leading the original society from 1292 to 1314. In 1307, after Pope Clement dissolved the order, DeMolay and many of his men were captured and subsequently burned to death by France's King Philip IV in the fourteenth century after DeMolay retracted all of his previous confessions that were made to the King. The French Templars were wealthy and powerful during the days of the Crusades. The King, who was deeply in debt to them, decided to instead use his power and greed against them by having as many of them as possible, be arrested, imprisoned, tortured and killed. The remaining Templars are believed by many to have fled to Portugal, Scotland, and it is even believed that some remaining Templars founded the country of Switzerland.

This was the type of history that I got to experience in ritual form, within the walls of the Masonic temples that we inhabited. Most importantly, to me however, I no longer had to be disappointed by any lack of approval given to me from my peers at school. The fraternity of DeMolays gave me others, both older and younger to reflect off of, and was also paired up with the Masonic sorority known as Jobs Daughters. My first "steady girlfriend" was, in fact, a Jobs Daughter. It is still amusing to me to know that much of my adolescent years were actually spent within such sacred walls.

Through the perspective given to me by the experience of being an active DeMolay member, I was able to see history from another perspective. This, I believe, helped to open my eyes to the relativity of truth. I started to become hyper-aware of how nothing was necessarily happening the way I might have originally perceived it was. This is not necessarily because of any sacred Masonic knowledge, mind you, but just from where I felt I was personally coming from. Having never been raised by going to any church regularly, my first practice in worship was literally *Masonic* by experience, meaning and symbolism.

It is through one of the DeMolay initiations that the story of Jacques DeMolay is recounted. Seemingly, reality can be shaped by whomever it is that has the authority to write history. This seemed to work, at least, for King Philip IV, who brutally murdered DeMolay along with many of the most significant Knights Templars on that same day. It seems that from long before that, but certainly from then on, information exchange has been in constant confusion with the issue of the spreading of untruths and lies to misguide the masses, just as the Templars were accused of doing to the King. Thus, it is difficult to fully trust a philosophical ideal whose intention is shown to suppress or squash-out other ideas or research by using whatever forces are necessary to create suppression and leave untrue negative impressions. The truest place of power, I learned, was between those who one would call either family or brethren. So although there seems to be much which one should be skeptical about, I learned that power and inner-strength could form by establishing bonded relationships.

I was able to join DeMolay as my family had claimed to be Catholic. It is my understanding that if you claim that you do not believe in God, you will not be permitted to join a Masonic fraternity. Most of my friends were more in it for the fraternal social circle it created, so even if they weren't completely on board, they at least "played along" in a serious manner with all the ceremonies. Of course, however, as one reaches a certain age, there does come a time when one's faith is challenged. I was no different...

ON SKEPTICS

Before we move on from here, I would like to talk about a group of people who form an association of whom I am friendly with, but who do not share many of my personal perspectives. This is a smart, fun-loving, science-based group of people who exist as a part of modern day culture, who have labeled themselves "skeptics." Isaac Asimov, Richard Dawkins, Harry Houdini, *Mythbusters* hosts Jamie Hyneman & Adam Savage, Penn & Teller, Bertrand Russell, and Carl Sagan are all famous, diverse, and intelligent people in history who claim or claimed) to have a skeptical rationalist philosophy, and also that *The Skeptics,* as a group, claim as their own. Let it be known that I have a great respect for all of the aforementioned people. I love all my friends who are skeptics, and much modern day skepticism is approached quite thoughtfully. Many of my skeptical friends are some of the smartest and nicest people I know.

Oddly, however, there are a few self-appointed skeptics who will be the first people to begin foaming at the mouths like a Pavlov experiment as soon as any such words as *alternative, consciousness, cosmic, energy, holistic, or vibration* is heard by them. I am not sure if these are the same people who disregarded such things as superstitious from years long past, if they are just closed minded people who enjoy being critical just for that sake alone, or if they are advocates who work for businesses who launch disinformation campaigns against ideas that may ruin them. These couldn't possibly be true skeptics, however. Not like the friends I have made. So just who are these "cloaked individuals"? Are they skeptics? Or are they brainwashed individuals who support the profiting of such big-business agendas or our poorly considered health care system? Conspiracy theories abound.

Many skeptics will be among the most fascinating and brilliant people you'll meet. They are passionate, articulate, confounding and creative. Critical thinking education shows the importance of understanding the scientific method, as well as all the observational flaws that many perceptions can be mistaken for. But Critical Thinking also tries to bridge the worlds of science with art, philosophy, history and religion through a rationalistic viewpoint. Many of these people have become "experts with an agenda" who get you rattled enough to think and form your own opinion. Artists like Penn & Teller and James Randi. Scientists like Richard Dawkins. Authors like Issac Assimov.

In the mid 90's, I became friends with then Professor of Sociology at the University of Michigan, Marcello Truzzi. Although he wasn't necessarily famous like the others, he was one of the founders of the Committee for Scientific Claims of the Paranormal, otherwise known as CSICOP. He was also one of the founding members of the Society for Scientific Exploration, which I will talk more about later. In my opinion, Marcello brought so much class to both organizations. Paul Kurtz, who was a fellow co-founder of CSICOP, dubbed Truzzi as "The skeptic's skeptic." Since his death, a little more than ten years ago, Marcello has been very much missed by me as well as by many others from both sides of the paranormal/skeptic fence. Marcello Truzzi was also the very first man known for saying the often-heard quote:

"Extraordinary claims require extraordinary proof."

The skeptical movement has these days become more widely known as the *critical thinking movement*. These are mostly people who want to get to the bottom of paranormal and mystical claims, which they lovingly call "woo," by showing people how if you cast light into the shadow, what you generally find is that there was nothing really there all along. My personal belief is that if you are going to try to find out something mysterious, it's always good to run it by a skeptic, as they will be the first to let you know if they detect a scam. As such, the vast majority of skeptics do not believe in a God or necessarily even living a spiritual way of life. But that is still the area, where I, as well as mystics, psychics and skeptics, enjoy observing and keeping an eye on the most. The things in which there seems to be no easy answer, even though you might have run it through all of the available filters.

One of the most controversial fellows within the skeptical community, James Randi, founder of the James Randi Educational Foundation (JREF) and The Amazing Meeting (TAM) is someone who I have long considered a very close personal friend of mine. He is best known for his *One Million Dollar Paranormal Challenge* to anyone who believes that their paranormal powers are keen enough to withstand the JREF criterion for the scientific approval of such powers existing. So far, many have taken the challenge, some have come close, but there have been no winners that have ever fully satisfied the JREF team. Some will argue that the JREF testing requirements are unfair, or that they have been given all the proof they need but that no amount of proof will ever meet their demands. Most fairly, it does prove that the questions herein brought to our attention are not easy questions to answer. Another close colleague of mine, Steve Banachek, has recently been ceremoniously handed the overseeing of the *One Million Dollar Paranormal Challenge*. In fact, I have known both Randi (since the 80's) and Steve (since the 90's), and the relationship that we have with one another effortlessly moves past the realm of personal philosophy. In fact, it feels to me as if somewhere between their strong beliefs, yours and my own, there is an agreement of sorts. We are all seekers of truth.

CHAPTER **10**

IMPRESSIONABLE EXPERIENCES

SHIP TO TAIWAN

My grandfather on my mother's side was Lieutenant General Hsiang Chih Yeh, who was the chief of Taiwan's CIA (Chinese Intelligence Bureau of the National Republic of China) to General Chiang Kai Shek during the Communist Party takeover of Nan King and Shanghai (February, 1949). My mother was at that time, the second oldest of six children. When it was time to move his entire family over to Taiwan from the mainland, my grandfather arranged seven tickets to be given to my grandmother and all of their children to board the steamer ship called, the *Taiping*. My grandmother noticed that there were only seven tickets. But there were eight total people in their family. My grandfather explained to her that it was urgent that she go to Taiwan with their children on the next ship out. Mao Tse Tung's Red Army had just invaded Nan King where they were living and they would not be able to hold them back. The news of the communist victory over Nan King had spread quickly and 2 million Chinese were now trying to flee the region. They would have to get to Shanghai and take the next steamer boat across the Taiwan Strait to freedom. There were huge passenger vessels taking people to Taiwan as an escape plan. But he would be staying on the mainland to take care of some business with the general. He would meet up with them in a few days.

The plan was already set in motion. The tickets were already bought. But my grandmother had a funny feeling at that very moment, that this was not the right thing to do. She begged my grandfather to not put them on the ship. But that's silly. Everyone was trying to get off the mainland, and it was urgent to him for the lives of all of their children that they get on one of the first ships to leave.

Assertive as my grandfather was to get his wife and family to flee the country, my grandmother refused, telling him that she had an "intuition" that told her that the family should not separate. She said, "If you're not coming with us, we're not going!" She was insistent and started to cry uncontrollably. He was forced to concede. He told her that she and all their kids would then have to stay with him on the mainland until he was finished with his current assignment. It was easy enough to find a happy family to purchase the seven tickets from him, as the ship was completely full to capacity with Chinese Nationalists wanting desperately to leave.

Ultimately my grandmother got what she wanted; yet only shortly after the ship (which they were supposed to be on) left the port, it sank. Apparently, it was in the act of leaving port secretly and didn't want to call attention to the large ship leaving port after dark, so most of the lights were turned off on the ship. As poor timing had it, another smaller vessel that, as a result, could not see the larger Taiping steamer ship directly in front of it in the darkness, accidentally collided with it. There were just too many unprepared people on board and it was too dark and crowded to organize a last-minute escape plan that would rescue them all from a sinking ship. The death count was over 1500.

Since I have lived all of my life in America and my grandmother, who lived in Taiwan, died when I was nine years old, it made it impossible for me to establish any real personal connection as her grandson. So my understanding of my grandmother throughout my life was really one based on this mysterious woman from another time and place, but whom I am nonetheless a part of. My mother regularly prays to her mother to give protection over us and even prays to her whenever she flies on an airplane. One thing is for certain. Had my grandmother accepted those seven tickets unthinkingly, and boarded the Taiping that day with her children, *you* would now be reading a completely different book.

THE SHOW MUST GO ON

In my late teens, I ran away with the circus. Well, not exactly, but close. My first "on the road" experience was when I was only a nineteen year old college drop-out, becoming hired as the stage/road manager for a magic illusion show back in 1984, called the Denny & Lee show. Denny Haney or "Denny Lee" was most respected within the industry for his rendition of the famous "Metamorphosis" Houdini box escape, but performed everything from producing and vanishing cards to floating a lady in the air. His company was out of Baltimore, but he was always busy playing club dates, corporate events and universities across the country. It was from my time working with Denny which gave me my initial ideas of how to market myself as a "mind power show" to these same industries later in my career.

The Denny & Lee Show, when I first started up with him, only consisted of himself, his assistant Minh, and me. He and Minh (aka "Lee") were the stars of the show, and I was essentially the guy who made everything happen around them. I pushed the equipment in, I set it up, I ran their sound and lights, and when driving with them in Denny's 1980 Chevy cargo van, I sat in the back, just behind Minh, on a beanbag chair surrounded by crates and boxes. Seat belts were for sissies. Because it was a beanbag chair, what would generally happen is I would crawl into the back of the van, and since Denny would always insist on driving his van, and I would just fall asleep in the back, and when we arrived to wherever the venue was, I would wake up and start unloading.

Generally, it would be a two to five hour drive, so it became a habit of mine to fall asleep in the back. The majority of his work consisted of stage shows for what were called "club dates," as in clubs like the Masons, Shriners, Knights of Columbus, fire halls, golf clubs, and then also resort clubs like the Poconos and Catskills that scheduled regular entertainment, usually consisting of a variety act opener and a comic or singer to close the show. Denny & Lee was a hot live east coast act back then, and he would later earn the respect of entertainment professionals worldwide. I remember needing to hand sheet music to the musicians in the live orchestras that would need to play them on and off the stage as well as add accompanying music to their illusion acts.

Usually, the routine was always like this: I would drive up to Baltimore from DC, hop in the van with him and we would then both go and pick up Minh and head to the gig. I would jump in the back when Minh would get in and then usually that's when I would fall asleep until we got to where we needed to be. One day, back around February of 1988, we were scheduled to perform that evening at a Masonic Temple in Reading, PA. On this day, however, I told Denny that I would just drive myself and meet him there in Reading. Back then, the reason I gave him was that I just wanted to be by myself and listen to music. I remember this not making any sense to him at all. It wasn't worth it for me to do this. Especially given how much I was being paid. Normally he would buy us food on the way, and I would be also missing out on that.

My reply was to assure him that I will be there in plenty of time for set up, that I will probably beat him there, and that I just felt like driving, for this one time, by myself. I remember feeling a little odd about it myself, but I also remember feeling a sense of relief to not have to drive with them once Denny gave in to my request. I got onto the highway, turned up the radio and started off to Reading, PA.

As an illusion show, one tries to get everywhere as early as you can in order to set up your show, so by the time I had arrived, I got there before everyone including the client or any of the guests. It is truly amazing what an illusionist of Denny's caliber will go through in order to entertain an audience. All variety artists, for that mater, will put in more personal work, time and energy to execute a perfect performance than any other type of performer I can think of. Surely musicians will sometimes do the same. But as far as getting to the venue as early as possible and making sure all the smallest details are covered, not to mention all the practice and rehearsal that takes place up until that point, variety artists work about as hard as they come. Specifically, I am talking about the magicians, the jugglers, the acrobats, animal trainers and clowns. Often they are the earliest to arrive and just as often they are the last to pack up and leave. I've even seen tiny aerialist girls carrying their own steel-hanging rig from their car in the parking lot to the stage (of course, I offered to help).

In this case, I was the first to arrive. I thought they wouldn't be too far behind, and yet it was taking longer than I estimated it would. Thoughts went through my mind of how he and Minh probably went to a sit-down place to eat and was taking a longer time to spite me for having driven up myself. Most people, these days, would wonder why I didn't just call him. Well, it was the 1980's, and cell phones were not yet invented, so waiting was all I could do. It's crazy to think that this is how we all lived back then. And that day, I waited a long time.

The client showed up and I was able to introduce myself and check out the space to know how to ready it once Denny and Minh arrived. The time was getting later and later, and everything was in place except for the act. Usually the show gets preset before people walk in to have dinner, but this time, people had arrived all dressed up and were already seated. Still no sign of Denny. The client was starting to get concerned, but during these types of events, there is so much that is happening all at once, that all he could do was check in with me every so often to see if Denny had arrived yet. Now people were just starting to nibble on their first course.

I remember walking outside and waiting for his van to pull up. It was a cold snowy and blustery day, and though I had tried to put it out of my head, his getting into a serious accident did occur to me. I tried to stay positive. Suddenly, an old beat up station wagon pulled up to the Masonic Temple, and strapped on top of it were the same black cases, that I knew Denny packed his show in. Denny and Minh had arrived! But where was the van?

As it turned out, on their way to the get to the event, a man in a large pick up truck apparently came out of nowhere and T-boned Denny's van, striking it at nearly full speed. He had tried to apply his brakes, but had hit ice, slamming into the back of Denny's van at *exactly the same spot where I would have been sleeping*, had I decided to drive with them on that day. His Chevy van was totaled. But incredibly, he and Minh were shaken but unharmed. So as the old axiom states, "The show must go on." A witness who saw the accident take place, just happened to be driving an old beat up station wagon, so after all the important information was exchanged, Denny offered to pay him to drive he and Minh to the event, which miraculously, he was able to oblige for him.

Though it might not be the first thing that I would think about when it comes to all the things I had learned from being a real classic magician's apprentice, perhaps one of the most amazing things about having worked with Denny, was seeing just how successfully things could be accomplished even under the most excruciatingly impossible working conditions. That night, immediately after dinner and a few announcements, the Denny & Lee Show, went out on stage, did their thing, and received a standing ovation, which was back then, something they rarely missed getting.

Had I decided to drive with them on that one day, I would have been at least crippled from the incident, and there would have been no show at all. My mother would believe that it was my grandmother looking out for me.

LUCKY PSYCHIC FORESIGHT

My friend, Loyd Auerbach, teaches at two different universities. He is a professor of Publishing and Media at John F. Kennedy University, in the San Francisco Bay area near where he lives. But at Atlantic University, in Virginia Beach, VA, Loyd teaches online classes as a *Professor of Parapsychology*. This is an accredited university, which was originally founded by perhaps one of the most fascinating and prolific "prognosticators" of all time, the "American Prophet" Edgar Cayce. Still run today by The Association for Research and Enlightenment, this is where Professor of Parapsychology, Loyd Auerbach, still teaches a class called "Principles in Parapsychology." Loyd also teaches non-academic courses on parapsychology at HCH Institute in California.

His parapsychology classes can be seen as an overview of extrasensory perception, psychokinesis, and survival of bodily death. Much of it involves the history of parapsychology, quite a bit about what the research findings are (the kinds of experiments that have been done), as well as some exercises the students can try themselves to see if they can be a little more psychic. Loyd is also the author of several books, as well as articles on parapsychological subject matters including remote viewing, mind over matter, and just trying to get down to the truth of some very complicated mysterious matters. With such credentials, it is not surprising that he gets calls all the time from Hollywood screenwriters and film directors, people whose homes need investigation of a paranormal claim, as well as other authors and scientists who are constantly sharing the latest discovery or scientific curiosity.

One week after the fateful September 11, 2001 tragedy, Loyd spoke to a pilot who was supposed to be the pilot on Flight 93, but who woke up that morning, with a feeling, not of dread, but that he "just shouldn't go to work that day." He had no reason to believe that anything bad was going to happen, but for some reason decided to call in sick. He also told Loyd that one other flight attendant did the same thing. Curiously, the reason why he called Loyd was because he was suffering from "survivor's guilt," having called in sick and sending someone else in his place. It is obvious that because he decided to go with *how he felt*, that this historically tragic experience was completely avoided by him. I suppose sometimes it's best to just be grateful of every lucky thing that happens in our lives.

NATURAL KNOWING

Producer and director of TV and film documentaries regarding the UFO phenomenon, James Fox, is known for his 2012 TV series, *Chasing UFOs*, as well as his documentaries *Out of the Blue* and *I Know What I Saw*, among others. He is a driven personality, and a fun guy to hang out with at a bar. While sitting with him and some other friends at Madam's Organ Blues Bar, in the Adams Morgan district of Washington DC, he recounted an interesting story (completely unrelated to UFO's, incidentally), from just a few years prior.

It begins in 2010, in San Francisco. He and an associate of his, "Tim," were in a meeting in his office, when a disagreement between them suddenly started to escalate. After it became clear that the two of them were clearly not going to settle the argument at that time, Tim stormed out of James' office.

Moments after, a strong image suddenly flashed into James' mind. In fact, it was the image that Tim had just scratched James' car with his key. He decided to, at that point, walk down and check. Sure enough, as he got closer to his car, he noticed that someone had put a deep key scratch into the side of his door that was about 8 inches long.

Immediately, James called Tim and said, "Why did you 'key' my car?" Tim denied that he had done anything to James' car. "What? I didn't key your car!" James felt that there was no other answer. "Look, I know that you just keyed my car. So why don't you just say you're sorry, and we'll move on?" Tim remained adamant. He refused to admit that he did it.

Over a year later, Tim finally admitted that he scratched James' car with his key.

Of course, you don't need to be a UFO chaser to have had something like this incident happen to you. Nor does it even have to be about something bad. Some may come to the conclusion that James, after such an escalating argument, might suspect that his associate would do something like that in a worst-case scenario, and upon seeing that it did indeed happen, it only magnified his reason to accuse Tim of being the culprit. As James put it, however, something inside him made him absolutely certain that Tim "keyed" his car, in fact, enough that he immediately ran down to confirm that indeed his car was vandalized. Could that have been only his imagination? If not, how could such a situation have occurred?

The following are suggestions (which I have used) that may help you to connect with otherwise unknowable things. I have used this technique in so many different ways, from finding lost items to making decisions.

1) Something which I've tried, that has a pretty good percentage-rate of receiving uncanny results is to receive impressions which surround certain emotions. Just take a moment to take a few deep breaths. Fill your lungs with air and simply imagine that your mind is a receiver of information.

2) Since it seems apparent that emotions are the easiest impressions to pick up on, I can first begin by meditating myself down to a "neutral" state of mind. During this time, I summarize all the things that I have felt throughout the day, and place them aside into a "safe, peaceful and relaxing" place, allowing myself to enter a state of neutrality. This is typical self-hypnosis procedure.

3) As I imagine my subconscious self, transferring these conscious feelings, issues, concerns, plans and responsibilities into my "safe place," I am simultaneously visualizing myself examining each emotion in a detached and thoughtful manner. I then tune into recognizing what I feel is the *most obvious* answer that comes to me in that moment.

4) The most *obvious message* is most likely your truest answer, so think about what you feel like it is truly saying. Contemplate its meaning. This is the information that you need to

understand the most, and on all levels.

Usually, you will see the message clearly and directly in front of you. This entire process should take no less than one to three breaths. You do not need to think for long as it should not even feel as if you had a choice. Of course, this does not include any psychopathic or deranged thoughts that lead to hurting anyone. Those don't count.

Try to stay with your first gut feeling response, not because you will be correct, but because you don't want to ever disregard it. A careful analysis of that feeling while in this state of mind may form an inspiration that will pull you from your dilemma. Be fully honest and compassionate as you bring to words your impressions. By breaking down the meaning of each significant word, you may find that they also contain a secret message that will add meaning to whatever question is being asked.

I believe that little messages can be found in everything around us and in the feelings that we experience. Everything that happens in our lives has meaning, and everything that we observe; we can choose to learn from. How you apply your learning along the way that is always the most important path. I think eventually everything comes together, even certain things that might initially feel as if it's really going badly. I find that it is most advantageous to change the direction of one's fortune by simply being patient and vigilantly prepared so that you are 100% ready for when the right opening manifests itself.

To remain balanced, we need to learn how to pull out our objective lens so we can be more objective about our emotions. This can be done with whatever matter is being focused on. If we can observe that something feels wrong or out of place, by zooming out and seeing the larger picture, sometimes it's even possible to see how changing something else altogether different can correct an issue, sometimes even more than the need to work directly on the issue itself. This would be similar to re-introducing wolves to Yellowstone National Park; it inadvertently saved and flourished the vegetation, wildlife and even the flow of the rivers that ran through that region. By observing one's situation by zooming out one's "mental lens" and trying to bring into focus all the different perspectives, sometimes it is even possible to see clearer the objectives, as well as the purpose, intentions and directions which can be taken from there.

Realizing and understanding how to work with your natural knowing can be fun, introspective, and insightful. No one should be any less than completely confident of their ability to make the best and most positively intuitive decisions by trusting their hunches, instincts, and sense of brilliant obviousness. It's amusing to keep track of and fun to try and get better at. A friend of mine claims to have a special instinct that she calls her "shopping instinct." If she decides to go shopping on a day that she has this instinct, she always manages to bring home a "perfect find." This is an example of how it can also work with positive-feeling hunches.

Another friend of mine, Bonnie, told me about how her daughter, Sarah, had recently gone to Europe, and mentioned that she was planning on going sky-diving while in Switzerland. Sarah didn't mention when she would be going skydiving, or even which country she would be in during her two-week trip. One morning, however, Bonnie had a dream that she was flying through the sky at an exhilarating speed. Coming out of the dream, she remembered distinctly, only the fact that she was flying, noticing the sound of the wind rushing past her ears, and feeling in a state of complete excitement and joy.

As she awoke with a jolt, she noted the time on her bedside clock. It was 6:00am. Then a feeling overcame her that this must be the day that Sarah was going to make her jump. Later that morning, Sarah called Bonnie to tell her that indeed she made her jump. When she noted the time of Sarah's jump, it was not only a prediction of the day it would happen, but the jump took place precisely at the same time that Bonnie had awoken from her dream.

Just the other day, while writing this, I was with my daughter, with a group of her Friday home-school friends, called Free Range Kids. The ages of these kids span from 3 to 11 year olds with usually one parent present per family. We were all hanging out in a nice little oasis in Rock Creek Park just outside the DC city limits. There are hiking trails and little beaches and cliffs, in that area. It's quite pleasant, really. As we arrived, there were three of the older boys who had waded across the creek and were climbing on a tree that had fallen mostly in the water. Realizing suddenly that I had not brought a change of clothes for my daughter, I told her that I would rather she not get her clothes wet. She was very disappointed at this and protested greatly.

I took one look at the three boys and then turned to her and said, "You know how I can sometimes tell the future? Well, I will tell you right now that within the next three hours, one of those three boys... I cannot tell for sure which one, but one of them, will fall into the water, will get soaking wet, and will probably get hurt doing so." She retorted, "How would you know that?" I calmly said back to her, "Because sometimes I can tell the future." From that point, I would privately glance at my watch to make sure I took note of when three hours later would be. In fact, it got to be past two hours when I started to feel as if this was one of those times when my prediction just didn't work. But just before the three-hour mark was to pass, both she and I heard a large splash. It was one of the three boys I originally pointed out. As he stumbled from the creek and onto our little beach, it looked as if he had slightly jammed his right thumb, as he was squeezing it tightly. I walked over to my daughter and showed her my watch. "Remember what I said about one of those three boys?" I asked her. It was exactly at the three-hour mark.

CARTOON DINOSAURS

When my daughter was as young as four years old, I had a funny experience that happened within a dream. It was early in the morning, around 5 am, and I was in one of those half awake, half asleep states in which I knew that I was dreaming of these funny brightly-colored cartoon-like dinosaurs, but sensible enough to wonder why I was dreaming of these peculiar images and I remember wondering why these things were in my head. As I lay there, slightly confused from the content of my dream, I started to wake up more and realized my daughter must have slid in bed next to me in the middle of the night, as she was now asleep with her head touching mine. Suddenly, while still asleep, I heard her whisper, "Dinosaurs."

Did my daughter just read my thoughts while talking in her sleep, or perhaps, could I have been tapping into my four year old daughter's dream? As much as I enjoy occasionally contemplating dinosaurs on my own, it seemed less likely that I was the one dreaming of dinosaurs, especially cartoon ones, so it seemed logical to assume that in that fleeting moment, I was the one who was seeing into my daughter's subconscious thoughts, and not the other way around. But either way it doesn't matter. I simply love the feeling at being amazed enough within a moment that it causes me to contemplate how little (and yet how much) we know about everything around us.

CHAPTER **11**

MANIFESTING WISHES

If I were to tell you my most special gift, it would certainly be the gift of being able to do what I had dreamed of doing all along. In fact, in many ways, I have far surpassed it. I have a cozy little home just outside of Washington, DC, in Kensington, MD. My office is just behind my home, and my desk faces a flowery garden with a small pond. I have a beautiful and talented wife who is the mother and home-school teacher of my bright and artistic seven-year-old girl. All my life, I have loved animals, and my little family today includes a Shepherd Collie, a Pomeranian and three cats (as well as frogs and fish in the pond).

I am not an exceptionally wealthy man, and as much as I appreciate any popularity that I have received, it is not that important to my ego, so long as I feel somewhat as if someone out there understands what I'm talking about. My life, however, is rich with my time spent with family and close friends. My peers hold me in high respect, and I have won distinguished awards for excellence in my work. I have been asked to travel to many countries and exotic locales just for people to experience my performances or hear me speak. I have been on television, radio and Internet programs to talk about different aspects of my work. I have headlined shows at prestigious casinos and cruise ships, and have been asked to attend important political functions and fundraisers, as well as several presidential inaugurations. Most importantly, I have been able to explore, throughout my life, all the things I have found the most interesting. As long as I can remember, I have had a fascination for things that are mysterious. Maybe it was because of the timing. I was born in 1965 in San Francisco, and spent the remainder of the psychedelic sixties there, absorbing all sorts of energy from that area during the most impressionable time of my life. Maybe it was because by the time I was seven, in 1972, the ever popular TV that decorated living rooms all across America was buzzing with weird sightings of UFO's, lake monsters, and people who claimed to possess extraordinary powers and who talked about developing such powers that could live up to scientific scrutiny. Or perhaps, this fascination for the fantastic is just what happens to everyone who is about that age and begins to develop interests in such things that defies their sense of logic and ignites their sense of wonder. Of course, within a few years, this is usually a phase which wears off as individuals continue to get older and begin to develop more "mature" social pursuits in sports, the opposite sex and academia. With me, however, it never left. I kept feeling that if I just tried to learn more, understand and contemplate deeper into these strange mysteries that I might just find something that I would grow into.

It is interesting how an early interest in magic, mastering ways to trick the senses and our perception can lead to deeper levels of understanding mentalism, and how that can then so easily transform into a love for hypnosis. From there, if one can open one's mind just a little more, it may lead to a hidden unknown source of power that reveals a truly cosmic or even extraterrestrial awareness. Don't worry. Considering such odd notions will not make you gullible or vulnerable unless you choose to be. What I will ask is that you simply keep in mind the question, 'What if?'

Consider that I am not anyone in particular, but just an average man who probably has strong ADHD traits. My mother and father are Asian college immigrants who moved to America seeking a better life in pretty much exactly the way that anyone can imagine. They both ended up with jobs working for US government libraries. We never lived excessively. So my choosing this odd direction in life was certainly a shock to both my father and mother who did everything to try to encourage me to finish school and find steady employment. Yet, here I am. I am now a homeowner in the vibrant DC metropolitan area, the president of my own LLC, and a father to an amazing daughter. I travel the world as an entertainer or a spokesman for leading businesses, I have authored my own books, starred in my own TV shows, and occasionally, I still play guitar.

TIMING, FLOW, & ASKING FOR MIRACLES

I am absolutely grateful for having been blessed, as it is as mysterious to me (and to my parents) that I could have possibly made the choices I have and gotten away with it. Nothing could have challenged this idea more than the devastating economic crash that recently put almost everyone in the non-celebrity rungs of the entertainment business into financial ruin. I started to feel it happening while I was in production for my series with TLC back in 2004/2005. This was one of the reasons why I was so appreciative of having gotten that opportunity. I believed, at the time that, if anything, it would help to keep me afloat while trying to weather an upcoming bad economy. What I didn't realize was just how long that bad economy would last. Concerning me even more than that, my wife became pregnant in 2006, and my daughter was born later that year in September.

I decided that this was a sign to stay home and spend more time with my family. I had become one of the busiest entertainers in the business back then just traveling and performing for universities and colleges. However, as business became slower and more cutthroat in competition, I decided that it might be better to hang back and try not to lose my composure. It was back then that I watched a fairly impressive savings account get smaller and smaller until there was hardly anything left in it by 2009. I wasn't going to let something like that bring me down, though. During that time, I secured myself with a personal manager, in Las Vegas, Clinton Ford Billups, Jr., who has stuck by me from that point on. Many years before he and I met, he was the manager and TV producer for the Amazing Kreskin. As an artist, who likes to work on my writings, research and more specific details of my performance and life, it has been nice to have Clinton, who has since been the man steering the direction of my odd, but organically chosen career. He is an experienced professional.

By 2010, Clinton convinced me to dip my feet into the world of authorship, and my first book was published. *Picture Your ESP* was a book which presented itself more as a "coffee table pictorial self-test book" to test one's intuitive ability over chance expectation. Within the first week of that book's printing, it became a "#1 Hot New Release" in its category on Amazon.com. For that, I must thank all my fans and family for helping to make that become a reality. I had never written a book for the "real public" like that before, and yet, now I am an author.

So what does any of this have to do with the manifestation of dreams?

Is there some marketing secret to my ability to have caused any of that to occur?

Yes. The first secret is to reach out to others while applying what makes you flow and allow those people to broaden your personal network. Mihaly Csikszentmihalyi describes that the optimal experience of "flow" happens when one's highest level of skill is matched with one's highest challenge.

The adverse to this, would be if one needed only to put in the least amount of one's skill towards something that required very little challenge for one. The only feeling that would result from a circumstance like that would be apathy. Things that require one to use the least amount of skill but have the highest amount of challenge would cause anxiety. In the same way, a spectrum of qualities can be observed by mixing and matching skill sets with challenge levels. Mixing a low challenge task with something that only took a moderate skill level to perform would cause boredom. Combining a high challenge task in which one only has a moderate skill level would produce arousal. Flow happens when both performance of challenge and skill are high.

To live life in a manner that gives you a solid mental foundation to build your dreams upon, one must find some kind of flow. Flow creates an optimum mindset. I would also highly recommend the works of Mihaly Csikszentmihalyi's, *Creativity, Flow* and *Finding Flow* for a complete understanding of this concept. Flow is what Csikszentmihalyi characterizes as the "psychology of the optimal experience." In many ways, an understanding of flow will begin to open the gates for you to manifest your dreams. There are, of course, other aspects to this that reveal itself by understanding Flow. For now, by experimenting with ways that you can reach your full potential of skill, while pulling off your greatest challenges, you will be practicing your ability to operate at "flow capacity." At the end of the day, take a moment to check and realize how trying that made you feel. You ought to feel pretty good.

By May 2013, I had made a few successful runs in Las Vegas, and was entertaining frequently for private events held at the International Spy Museum in Washington, DC, where I also became a regular public headliner. Just the year before, I was the official "man of mystery" who provided entertainment for President Obama's

Inaugural Ball put on by the American Legion, who holds the oldest and most prestigious private Presidential Ball. For that event, I was specifically there to entertain the recipients of the Congressional Medal of Honor and their families. Later, in the fall, I would work on educational fundraisers with Sir Richard Branson and Buzz Aldrin. I had made trips to the Netherlands, Hawaii, England, and Australia, but the truth was now that I was providing for a family, I was still just barely earning a decent living. With the balance of trying to survive through one of the worst American economic depressions, while on a traveling performing schedule and also trying to be a good father to my little girl, I was apparently taking a while to adjust my patterns to accommodate flow...

May of 2013, there we were, sitting in our dining room, holding hands across the table. My wife and I were having a discussion about school. Our daughter had a very successful kindergarten year at a Montessori school that was very close to our home, but with everything that we tried to scrape the remains of all our money together, it was just too expensive for us, living in Montgomery County, to make it work for another year. What should we do for the next year? The Montessori School was strongly suggesting that we should send her back the following year, and was even offering us a nice scholarship. Nico loved the Montessori School. We were just too tight on funds. The summer ahead looked bleak. What could we do? "I will personally home-school our girl before I put her in public school," my wife said to me. Could we home school? Is that feasible for our family and how we operate? A quick Internet search showed us that our county certainly did have many resources for homeschooling, as did the Internet. So it was settled. By the end of summer, we will register ourselves as home-schoolers and then, we the parents, would school our daughter.

I remember both my wife and I looking at a completely barren summer 2013 calendar. It felt like up until then we were surviving off of what seemed like a miraculously steady trickle of work, but that trickle had become an excruciatingly slow drip. I turned to my wife and said, "What we need right now, more than anything, is a miracle."

ASKING THE UNIVERSE

That evening, as I sat in quiet contemplation, I asked the universe,

"Our decision is that we will be trying to school our own child, so what happens now?" Within the next three days, my manager called me with contacts in Louisville, Chicago, and New York that allowed me to live the rest of my summer without financials worries. Within that same time, I received an odd Facebook instant message from an old friend of mine who I hadn't heard from in quite a while. This associate of mine had co-written and was producing a brand new show on one of the newest and latest model cruise ships scheduled to set sail in 2014.

The contract, which would be for nearly 5 months, would begin with me moving in and sailing right out of the dock it was being worked on in Germany, and would give me a headlining spot in a state-of-the-art show, work with a Broadway director, have special music scored for me by their own composer, and a special-effects introduction designed for me by an amazing team of animators. It was really quite a blessing. The thought, especially just after making the decision to home-school seemed perfect, especially if my family would be allowed on board to live with me on the ship. Of course, at this point, I did not know much about any of the contractual details; we just saw it as a delightful opportunity. The chances of me actually getting the contract, despite the fact that they were showing an interest, were still small, if not tiny. I had become, frankly, used to watching large potential opportunities evaporate into nothingness over the past seven years of bad economy.

What I needed was to get my energy up. I needed to use all the resources which I had immediately available to me. If there were a time in which I needed something like this to come my way, it would be now. But the obstacles ahead of me were quite real. There was little chance that a large cruise line was going to count on only me to take them up on becoming their headliner. There were probably a good three or four people that they might be looking at besides me, and that was just from who I suspected out of the states. I needed to make this opportunity manifest for *me* despite being compared against, perhaps other very likely candidates to get chosen, but how?

As I receive inquiries for appearances or performances, I pass them along to my manager. As an artist entertainer, one thing I have always found difficult was the negotiation process of talking to clients. I love to meet new people, I enjoy what I do and I believe fully that what I have to offer has value to the world, but if I spent my time concerned about whether I was going to get this contract or that contract, I would be spending all my time worrying and hardly any of it would be going to balance a livelihood of artistry, administration and associations, not to mention family, friends, and fun. This time, however, something else needed to happen. That evening, in quiet contemplation, again, I asked the universe to give me a sure sign that this would happen for me.

TO RECOGNIZE THE UNIVERSE ANSWERING

The next day, I received another instant message over Facebook. It came from a comic magician, who I knew from seeing on TV, but didn't know him personally. I also knew he had been working for the past several years at the Tropicana in Atlantic City. So I asked him how his show was going at the Trop, and he responded that he, in fact, moved (after a five year run at the Tropicana) to Kona and was just starting a new show there on the islands. He had been given, as a gift, a replica of an ancient Japanese story-telling device called a *Nankin Tamasudare*.

He had been told that I knew how to use one, and was asking me if I would give him lessons. Why would I want to give a guy who I didn't know lessons on how to use a device that I hadn't used in years? The Nankin Tamasudare is an ancient story-telling instrument, which looks very much like an over-sized bamboo sushi mat, but is linked together by an arrangement of cotton thread loops that makes it possible to change its shape and create a variety of complex symbolic images which support the ancient poems and puns that were told during the traditional Japanese festivals, known to go back to the Edo period. Oddly, at the time that he had contacted me, the Nankin Tamasudare was still considered very "underground" outside of Japan, was not easy to find on Youtube, and I was really one of only a small handful of people in the United States who knew about it and its functions. In hindsight, it would have been easier to say no to him. Instead, however, thinking about it quickly, I realized that I did know a friend in Los Angeles, who had a video copy of me using the tamasudare. It would literally be the only video of this in existence, and I didn't even own it myself.

So, within a time span of no less than a few minutes, between D.C., L.A. and Kona, there was an exchange of information. I messaged my friend in L.A., and asked him to send the video of me using the tamasudare to Kona. Because my friend in L.A. is one of those guys who seems to always be online, the whole exchange was done almost instantaneously. Then I told my new friend in Kona that he could go ahead and have my personal permission to use whatever he wanted from the work I had on the video. My feeling was that I was just happy someone was interested in actually using it, since I wasn't planning to. Well, my new friend in Kona was ecstatic. It was, exactly what he needed, and he got it by just taking some time out of his day and reaching out to me.

Immediately, he wrote back to me, saying that if there was anything that he could ever do for me in the future, that he would make sure to do whatever he could to accommodate. I remember suddenly, at that moment, putting it together, that this might be the moment I was asking for from the universe just the night before. After all, it was through Facebook Instant Messenger just the day before that the cruise ship offer had come in. Up until that point, the only client that I have had who ever contacted me through Facebook was Facebook (for an event in which I performed for both their national and international divisions, in 2012). Would this random message have any connection with my request to the universe the night before? It truly wasn't until the moment he told me that he would be willing to do a favor for me in return, that I suddenly thought about the above connections.

Quickly, I messaged him back and asked if there was a chance that he might have any connection to the cruise ship that I now felt I should try to pitch myself to. "I do!" was his reply. "And he owes me a really big favor!" Bingo. He was a best friend with the producer. The big lesson here would be that it is equally as important to ask and request from the universe your practical wishes, as it is to also be aware and listen to the universe, after you ask, for direction. The way it responds can sometimes be tricky. If I chose not to be curious, would I have gotten that gig anyway? It feels quite likely that I wouldn't have.

A few minutes later I received a message, telling me that he had just left a voice-mail on the producer's cell phone to call him back. The next day, he let me know that he spent an hour on the phone with the producer, and to prepare to pack my bags to spend a winter in the tropical Caribbean. Of course, by that time, I still had no personal word back from the ship. No contracts were being sent to me so I was still feeling uncertain. It did take a few more weeks of patience, but soon thereafter, a contract was being drawn up and verbal confirmations were being made.

MY MYSTERIOUS MANAGER

Now that I had that gotten over that hurdle, I had another one yet coming, and this was going to be tricky, because it involved getting my family onboard. I wasn't sure how to go about doing that in the least, so I first asked my manager if there was anything he could do about it, and he said that he would look into it. My manager, to me, is a strange creature. He understands aspects of the business that I do not, and with his main advice, which is basically, "Trust me," I have found that he manages to always exceed my expectations of how we come through on contracts. So leaving it to him, and having no other options, I decided that night to focus myself into my deepest contemplative thoughts and ask the universe, yet again, for a sign. This time, I remember it feeling more like a cry out to the universe of how far I have come with my family to arrive to this point, and what I needed the most was for my family to come with me on this contract. I remember feeling as if there was no other way to make this work out. Either they come with me, or I wouldn't be able to go.

Three days pass, and I get a call from my manager, Clinton Ford Billups, Jr. It turned out that when he asked the producer who his direct contact was for the cruise lines, he was told that it was the Assistant Director of Entertainment. And as it turned out, Clinton and the Assistant Director knew each other from way back, and Clinton had even attended the guy's wedding from many years ago. One wonders if I had not asked the universe for this favor, might reality have collapsed in a completely different direction? It doesn't seem likely, since rationally speaking, everyone was already who they were, and everything was already going in that direction anyway. Nonetheless, I got what I wanted out of it. My family was allowed to come with me, and my daughter was about to see different parts of the world, outside the U.S., for the first time in her life.

Although this is a recent story, I must say that it is not the only of its kind in my life. It is truly only one example. My life is full of these kinds of blessings, and I am never unappreciative. It may not stop me completely from feeling the pressures of everyday situations, but

I have learned that I don't have to "give up" in order to just "let go." At these times, I let myself just go with the design of the universe, to take me to where it will, and surprisingly, by just being a little patient, I end up being in a much better place than what I would have expected.

CHAPTER 12

SPOOKY

NOT AN ILLUSION?

Having worked as a roadie to a traveling illusion show for as many years as I did, allowed me to meet and mingle with enough magicians in my life to easily come to the conclusion that *most magicians don't believe in magic*. Some of them do, however. There is a group in Las Vegas, called *The Wonderground* and it is master-minded by my friend and shaman/magician, Jeff McBride, who does have a very deep spiritual belief in magic. Many of those who are taught by him, as well as others, who practice with his group and within his "magic circle" are fairly open-minded to both concepts of spirit and ritual. Regardless, this "spiritual revival" within the world of magic performance would represent perhaps less than 5% of everyone interested in magic. It appears that to the perception of the average person these days, magic is seen more as a way to prove how the mind can be fooled, and thus (in a roundabout way) disproves the origin of true mystery. On the extreme end, it also disregards any reason to explore in that direction without ridicule. Oddly, it seems that many of those who are the most interested in magic are also those who tend to be the least interested in spirituality, religion, or paranormal/parapsychological experiences.

Well, at least that would be the case for Denny Haney, Minh Duc and the rest of the Denny & Lee Show. Back when I was their stage manager, if I ever tried to talk about anything deep with Denny or Minh on the road, I would get tormented and teased by both of them. Of course, it wouldn't be fair to say that they are not spiritual people either. I think Denny just liked to keep the spirit in the van as lighthearted and jokey as possible. The majority of our time on the road was definitely spent making jokes and trying to crack each other up.

At one point, I had taken a year off from being with the show. Denny had hired two fellows, Ron and Richard, to replace me as his stagehand and roadie. So I was not present on the trip the night that they experienced what they did. But what they did experience on one evening, in an old hotel outside of Dallas, TX, was clearly no illusion and nor was it a laughing matter, at least while in the moment.

I already mentioned about how people in this industry are all quite skeptical of anything otherworldly or bizarre, but especially when it comes to inexplicable paranormal events. Personally knowing them, I can attest, as a friend of theirs, these are not the kind of people who ordinarily encounter weird inexplicable things happening to them, nor do they care or think about such things. On the contrary, they were used to traveling on a regular basis, and are quite free of any mental psychosis much less traveling anxieties. Joking and laughing would take precedence over all else. The four of them would always split two rooms, and Denny and Ron, being late-night TV watchers would share one room, while Minh and Richard, who preferred the "lights out" approach to sleeping, would split a room between themselves.

On this night somewhere outside of Dallas, TX, however, something weird happened. Ron had already fallen asleep in the other bed. Denny had just put out his last cigarette of the night, turned off the TV and lights, and laid down to rest. Suddenly, it felt as though something quite heavy, but invisible, started to press down on Denny's body and chest to the degree that he could barely breathe, much less speak or try to wake up Ron for help. Allegedly, he had just gotten into bed, and was barely even asleep when this happened. As described by him, when I met with him to recollect his memory of this episode, "I could barely breathe, and even though I was fighting to get it off me, it kept pushing down on me until I finally gave in. It wasn't until a few minutes after I gave in, did it finally let go of me. I couldn't check the time, but I'd swear it was on me for at least ten, maybe even twenty minutes. At the time, I thought that was it for me."

At around the same time, in the hotel room just next door to where Denny's experience took place, the lights were out in Minh's room and Richard was already fast asleep. Minh was still lying awake quietly trying to sleep. Strangely, she started to feel the blanket

126

(which was over her) begin to slowly be pulled off of her. Was she so close to the edge of the bed that the blanket was being dragged off one side of it due to gravity? Surely it wasn't Richard, who she trusted would never approach her in this manner... She grabbed the blanket before it was dragged off completely and jerked it hard to pull it back over her. Suddenly, she was thrown onto her back and felt something invisible pressing down on her. Similar to Denny's story, try as she might, she found herself unable to speak. Struck by the inexplicable nature of what took place she said, "That was one of the strangest things. The weirdest thing about it was finding out the next morning, when Denny told me that he felt the same thing. I couldn't believe it! That thing was on me for a long time, and I kept screaming as hard as I could, but he (Richard) just kept on snoring. I was just glad I was alive the next day."

Sleep paralysis has been well documented throughout history across practically every culture. Basically, it is a feeling of a sudden inability to move which happens usually while falling asleep but also while waking. This is usually associated with terrifying visions and nightmares linked to *muscle atonia* (muscle weakness) since the victims find themselves unable to react due to the paralysis. It is said that this feeling of terror, which is usually also accompanied with the feeling of an intruder invasion, is activated by the brain when one wakes up and finds that they are vulnerable to attack. Wikipedia goes into quite some depth on the subject of sleep paralysis, but basically states, *"This* (feeling of) *helplessness can intensify the effects of the threat response well above the level typical to normal dreams; this could explain why hallucinations during sleep paralysis are so vivid."* Wikipedia later explains the commonly experienced *incubus hallucination* in the following manner:

"The incubus hallucination is associated with the subject's belief that an intruder is attempting to suffocate them, usually by strangulation. It is believed that the incubus hallucination is a combination of the *threat vigilance activation system* (as well as) the muscle paralysis associated with sleep paralysis that removes voluntary control of breathing. Several features of REM breathing patterns exacerbate the feeling of suffocation. These include shallow rapid breathing and slight blockage of the airway, prevalent in sleep apnea patients. Attempts at breathing deeply fail, and give the individual a sense of resistance—which the threat-activated vigilance system interprets as someone sitting on their chest, suffocating them. The sensation of entrapment causes a feedback loop that involves the threat-activated vigilance system: fear of suffocation increases as a result of continued helplessness, which makes the individual struggle to end the episode. The intruder and incubus hallucinations highly correlate with one another."

The next morning, Denny immediately told Ron of what happened to him, and Minh likewise told her story to Richard. It wasn't until later, when the four of them all re-converged for breakfast, that they found themselves stunned by the likenesses of each of their respective stories. Said Richard "All I know is the next morning, Minh told me that she felt like somebody was sitting on her chest, like she felt this heavy weight and couldn't breathe. She said she kept trying to call my name over and over but that I wouldn't wake up. Later that morning, Denny came over to our room from next door and said, 'Man, I had the weirdest night last night, I felt like something was laying my chest for the longest time and I just couldn't get to sleep.'" Furthermore, after puzzling about it, they realized that Denny's' bed in his hotel room was positioned essentially head-to-head with Minh's bed!

Neither Denny nor Minh have had any weird episodes, night terrors or sleep paralysis since that time, and yet on that one night, in that hotel near Dallas, TX, in 1991, both had nearly identical phenomenological experiences. What makes this story interesting to me is that I know these people personally, not as people who go around telling tall tales of themselves (besides their being entertainers). Also noteworthy is that they both reported their all-too-similar stories to the person sleeping in the same room with them first thing the next morning, and then were able to, all four, find themselves amazed later when verifying that their paranormal experiences the night before were virtually identical!

So what could that have been? Unfortunately the name of the hotel has been forgotten, otherwise I would have wanted to know if there had ever been other reported encounters there before or ever since then. Denny has since retired from being on the road, as did the rest of them. Upon asking him or any of the others about the exact date or location of this strange happening, it appears it was also too far in the past, and they could not recall. Although I am sure that knowing the exact date or location of the hotel in Texas would help to broaden the picture that may give us more of a clue as to the spirit (if any) that may have manifested that evening, I find it noteworthy enough of a story, since it was experienced by four people who I knew. This experience has, for a long time, had an impact on *me*, since I remember vividly how animated they all were at recollecting the experience just after it occurred to them. They were all in shock, and try as they might, they could not explain how that could have happened.

In this year of 2014, as I try to relate the Wiki definition of sleep paralysis to the Denny and Minh experience, I can't help but feel new questions arise. Sleep paralysis seems to be overlooked often because it is generally not life threatening, at least at the stages that it's referred to as *sleep paralysis*. The thorough explanation of what neurologically happens in sleep paralysis, however, including the feeling of another presence, or an intruder, along with the terrifying feeling that accompanies it, seems to conclude quite offhandedly that there is a simple reason for what is happening, and that simple reason has to do with the brain and its paranoid associations with feeling paralyzed. After hearing Denny's and Minh's encounter, however, and recalling their true disbelief of what happened to them, I find myself more curious than ever about the phenomenon and whether it is purely neurological or if there's something more, like a strange dimensional layer that was somehow penetrated in that specific area at that specific time.

Indeed, the legendary reports of an *invisible intruding entity that presses down on the chests of its sleeping victims* spans both time and space, throughout history, and across countries, cultures, and creeds. In Finnish and Swedish folklore, this phenomena is known as a *mare*, (hence, the very word "nightmare") which is supposedly a locally residing "damned woman" whose spirit body will uncontrollably (while she sleeps) visit nearby villagers and sit on their rib cages while they are asleep, thus causing them to experience terrifying dreams. In China, it is known as *guǐ yā shēn*, which literally means "ghost pressing on body." In Vietnamese culture, it is known as *ma đè,* which means "held down by a ghost" or *bóng đè,* which means "held down by a shadow." In Turkey, sleep paralysis is referred to as *karabasan,* which means "the dark presser/assailer." In Swahili, the creature that sits on one's chest, making it difficult to breathe, is called a *jinamizi.* The Zimbabwean Shona culture used the word Madzikirira to refer to something "really pressing one down," but this mostly refers to the spiritual world in which a possibly evil spirit tries to use its victim for an evil purpose.

Many of us in Western culture are familiar with the words "incubus" of whose earliest mentions come from Mesopotamia on the *Sumerian King List*, ca, 2400 BC. An incubus is essentially a mythological demon who lies on top of his sleeping victims in an attempt to impose sexual intercourse. An incubus is said to attempt sexual relations with a woman for the purpose of fathering a child. In the *Historia Regum Britanniae* (c. 1136), which introduced *The Legend of King Arthur* to the non-Welsh-speaking world, Geoffrey of Monmouth was the earliest to mention how an incubus impregnated the mother of the legendary Merlin the wizard. Thus, the father of the Great Merlin was an *incubus*.

The word "succubus," incidentally, is the alleged demon-spirit in female-form who victimizes men in the same way. By legend, they are the same creature, which has the ability to extract the seed from men so that it could transform into an incubus and impregnate their female victims.

I don't believe that Denny or Minh knew this much about this legend at the time, though I'm sure they would be both quick to point out that in *no way* did Minh get pregnant by that experience. Nevertheless, it is interesting that this phenomenon actually occurred so precisely to both of them within such close range and roughly around the same time. To me, this indicates not something completely neurological, which would be a phenomena created by the brain within itself, but rather something that would be more akin to what people actually feel when the phenomenon happens to them: that there is some kind of an intruding energy that is imposing itself on them, either subconsciously, or physically, or both.

THEY CAUGHT ME

As I am writing this book, I am performing as *The Man Who Knows* as part of the premier installment on one of the newest luxury ocean liners on the seven seas. While diligently writing my thoughts backstage in my dressing room each day, one of the understudies to one of the actors, who is a theater technician that works with us, Will Hardyman, ended up telling me a story from his past, of paranormal proportions.

When Will was 6 years old, he remembers spending a lot of time at the Boise Little Theatre, in Boise, ID. His mother worked there as a set designer and was allowed at times to bring he and his little sister, Katie, to the theatre when working on an upcoming show. Will and Katie were pretty used to playing on the stage and in the theatre while their mother worked nearby. It was a magical place to be with their mom, at the Little Boise Theatre. It was even known for being haunted.

There were stories of strange and mysterious things that happened there from time to time throughout the local theatre community. Certain chairs in the house were known to creak and wobble on their own as if someone were sitting there. In the attic of the theater, techs would sometimes hear crying noises and moaning.

One evening, Will's mother was working on a set piece up on a ladder, while six year old Will and his then three year old sister were playing around the stage. Will remembers that he was playing with his Hot Wheels cars on the ramp leading to the stage, when, terrified, he heard his mother scream, "Nooooo! Katie, don't go there!" Will looked up, and right in front of him, watched as his sister, who was walking across the stage one moment, suddenly and completely disappeared, the next. The trap door on the stage was open, and Katie had just fallen in!

Everyone there simultaneously ran towards the trap door while a few ran downstairs to where she was. The drop was eighteen feet. Three-year-old Katie would easily be crippled, if not dead, after falling that far. But as Will and a few of the others ran to the trapdoor and looked down, in amazement, he saw his little sister standing at the bottom looking up at him with a big grin on her face! Will remembers that it was completely dark down there except for the small patch of light she was standing in. She had a small scratch on her chin, but otherwise, didn't look upset in the least. Meanwhile, his mother had quickly run down to where Katie was, and in shock, grabbed and shook her, and cried, "Are you okay?"

"I'm okay," said Katie, "They caught me." Cynthia gasped, "Who caught you?" There was no one there to catch her. Katie shrugged her shoulders. What would a three year old know, anyway?

THE COOL SPOT

My friend, Professor Loyd Auerbach, who I mentioned earlier (re: the 9-11 airline pilot who called in sick), refers to this story as "The weirdest thing in the world that I've ever experienced in any case." Of course, Loyd has experienced as well as researched a vast assortment of scientifically anomalous things from spirit table tipping to mysterious ectoplasm manifestations, but considering that this case had been measured, recorded and documented in so many different ways, made this particular investigation, quite a significant one for him.

In 1993, Auerbach was helping some friends of his shoot a TV pilot for Japanese Television, called *Haunted America*. On this particular show, which I did get a chance to see, they were introduced to a famous Japanese medium named Aiko Gibo. "Mrs. Gibo," as everyone on the set called her, was actually quite popular in Japan, with regular appearances on Japanese TV. She had worked on a few cases with police and even had a series of Japanese manga written about her life of when she was a young seer.

The TV crew and team all met at the home of the Kosicki's in Archer, FL. Linda and Bob Kosicki, who were civil war re-enactors, had apparently not lived in the house long before they started to experience strange ghostly apparitions of a faceless man checking his tie in the mirror, sleep paralysis combined with hallucinations of seeing a terrifying face, the sound of footsteps when no one else is there, and doors that are purposely shut that are later found open. The house, itself was built during the civil war. In fact, they had heard the house was haunted, and so as Civil War enthusiasts, they found themselves even more eager to live in a house where it might be possible to actually contact someone who had lived there during that time.

They offered for researchers with "ghost-hunting equipment" to come and take a look to see what they could find. Loyd, along with his team of top paranormal investigators that included James Bosworth, Barbara Gallagher, Russell McCarty and Robert Andrews were heading to central Florida, to meet some friends, a Japanese television crew, and the Japanese medium, Mrs. Gibo.

"One of the ghosts turned out to be a little girl, named Mary

Margaret who was one of the daughters that lived there, and of 'Cora,' whose ghost is believed to haunt the house searching in vain for Mary Margaret who had died, possibly of consumption, in the house. It turned out that she was buried in a cemetery not far from there," Loyd explained, "So there we were with a whole slew of equipment—this was back in the early 90's, so it wasn't as sophisticatedly small as the equipment used today... it was big. The Japanese had rented all sorts of stuff for us. So on the first night, Mrs. Gibo, at one point, starts talking to the ghost, and suddenly, all of the equipment goes off. Although the temperature gauge remained the same, we had four different kinds of EMF (electro-magnetic field) detectors, we had a geo-magnetic sensing station, which measures the earth's magnetic field, and at one point during the height of all this, it actually got skewed so much we had to recalibrate the thing. We had a Geiger counter that was going off like nuts, and we were also getting effects on thermal-vision video. This was all quite bizarre and it was all happening (during this one window of time). We were getting pulsing heat fogs underneath her hands (and on her thumb in particular, where she claimed the spirit was said to be tugging). Her hands were a bit hot, which could be a blood flow issue, but she said the ghost was holding her hands. What we could see looked like pulsating 'heat fogs' under her hand as well as (quite mysterious) heat fogs that went across the camera. Now the guy who was running the thermal vision had been trained by the company to use it for sinus issues in university hospitals, so the machine is normally used to look at sinus patterns. We ended up sending the tape to AGEMA, who is the company that makes these things, and when they looked at the footage, the only conclusion that they could make was that the camera might be picking up on pockets of argon gas that was floating around in the room that would reflect the thermal vision. But that's not possible when you have 15 people in the room and ceiling fans. So that was weird. We also got some very unusual stuff on audio, on one of the recorders (VTRs).

"On the second night, Mrs. Gibo was going to have a session with the ghost, in the same room with only one of the producers who was sitting with her. We had a video camera, a thermal vision camera, and we were all out in the dining room, watching the monitors. So she starts having a conversation with the ghost, and entices her 'in.' I happened to notice on the thermal vision, because this is the middle of July in central Florida, and the house had no air-conditioning. It was 97 degrees in the house. With thermal vision, you can tell by the walls how hot the room is, because the walls are a warm color. Suddenly I was noticing they were starting to get darker and darker and the temperature in that room actually somehow dropped to 75 degrees. It was significant. So I wouldn't call it a cold spot... but it was definitely a cool spot.

"We actually all ran in there—it had taken about 20 minutes to drop to that point. We all went in there and the room was definitely cooler, and then we noticed that the bedroom for the couple who lived there, which was right next door to the room Mrs. Gibo was in, (and they were both in there at the time trying to sleep), in that room, the temperature had gone up to 110 degrees. So there was actually a 'heat transfer' and we actually could see on both sides of the door that it was cool on one side, and hot on the other so the heat was actually transferring into the other room. To me, this was interesting, because psychics and the mediums generally say that ghosts need to absorb environmental energy in order to manifest. That was clearly not happening here, because the heat was being transferred out."

Although Loyd was not able to explain, with any scientific certainty, how any of that could have happened, he did tell me that Mrs. Gibo's explanation was that the little girl just wanted her to be more comfortable in the room, and since it was too hot for her, getting rid of the heat was her way of being kind to her while they were in spirit-connection with each other.

A SIGNAL FROM BEYOND

One of the most incredible stories I have ever heard, occurred about 8 years ago after my friend, Eloise, died. Originally, I knew her through her brother, Warren, who went to the University of Maryland in 1984. I met Warren, as he was the dorm-mate and a best friend of one my best friends, Kevin, from grade school, who also used to be a DeMolay brethren of mine. Warren and I became fast friends from the first time we met, partially because we found out that we shared the exact same birthday, down to the year. His family lived in Huntington, Long Island, and not long after that, I became close friends with all of them.

Warren's two younger siblings, Alex and Eloise, were twins, just two years younger than us. Warren's mother, Irvey, and I also became very close friends and I have regularly kept in touch with them all throughout my life. However, at age 42, Eloise, an amazing mother of two, succumbed to cancer. She had been sick for a while, and eventually, her time had come to pass on. Her life was way too short. To this day, I can remember my feelings of not wanting to believe it. Eloise was such an amazing, kind and beautiful person.

Within the first few days after she died, many members of her immediate family reported their lights flickering in a similar way. They would dim down and then get very bright. Both Alex and Warren reported this dim to extremely bright phenomenon happen on their computer monitors as well.

A week later, they were visiting Eloise's old home It was extremely emotional and sad for everyone. Alex, Warren, Kevin and Andrew were upstairs, while Irvey, and the kids along with a few others, were downstairs.

Upstairs in her home, Alex was distraught. Out loud, he said to her and for everyone else who was present to hear, "Elo, I just want you to send me a message, just to let me know that you're okay. I just want to know that you're in this other place and that you're okay." Within five minutes of Alex saying out loud that request, he received a mysterious phone call.

People have reportedly received "phone calls from the dead," throughout history, in fact, since the invention of the telephone. I have many times, even throughout my own life, heard stories from others of how their telephone rang at a mysterious time of the night that correlated to a recently deceased relative. Like most people, when I heard about stuff like that, I generally attribute it to random coincidence or superstition. When I was younger, it even sounded a bit corny to me. A "phone call from the dead" sounds about as ridiculous as "real magic." In Alex's case, however, it was much more than just that.

As now we all live in the twenty-first century, it was his cell phone. As opposed to a landline phone, all cell phones have built-in caller ID. This means we now all have the capability to see who is calling us before we answer. There's an old saying, "ghost in the machine," like the odd flickering of lights, getting from dim to very bright. I have always wondered how a spirit of any kind would be able to get into the machinery of something like a telephone to actually make a call to a person. Rationally speaking, this seems highly unlikely, even if at all conceivably possible.

Within five minutes after making his request for a sign from his deceased twin sister, Alex's phone rang. When Alex looked down to see who was calling, he noticed that peculiarly, it was his own cell phone number calling himself. Wait, that's impossible. You can't call yourself. So looking at it more closely, he noticed that it was actually off by three digits. It was in fact his exact cell phone number calling himself, with the exception of the area code. His area code in New York is 917. The area code that was calling him was from 914, Eloise's area code.

Alex told me that he might not have, at that point, made the connection that it was Eloise's area code of his seven digit cell phone number calling him. He was somehow trying to reason that maybe it was his own voicemail calling himself, but it didn't make any sense to him. So he just didn't pick up the phone. The caller didn't leave a voice message. So he decided to call the number back, realizing that regardless of the flukiness, it was after all, a different number calling him. What he ended up getting was *no answer*, but a random woman's voicemail who he didn't know, and who had no reason to call him that he could think of (he owns a music/sound mastering studio). He didn't leave a voicemail with her, because he didn't know her. He reasoned that she was probably trying to call her own voicemail by calling her own number but then didn't dial her own area code correctly. I personally don't know why he chose not to investigate further by trying to reach whomever this mysterious caller was, but this must just obviously be how New Yorkers think.

The next day, Alex was back at his home in Queens when he noticed that of his home phone number's "missed calls" list, there was that same number that had called his cell phone the day before. Quickly putting two and two together, Alex then realized that he had forwarded his home phone number to his cell phone number, and what that meant, was that the "wrong number" that was almost identical to his own cell phone number (that called him the day before) actually called his *home phone number* and was not even trying to call his cell phone to begin with! How likely is it that a number so close to being his own cell phone number, especially as a wrong number, would call his home phone number so closely after he made a request for a sign from Eloise? Why would that person want to get in touch with him at all? We may never know.

Alex confessed that he never tried to follow up with the mysterious caller, but then, nor had that caller ever tried again to get back in touch with him. Could this have just been a wrong number coincidence that happened to occur five minutes after Alex requested a sign to come from his recently deceased twin sister? To this day, Alex still wants so badly to believe that it must have somehow been Eloise that he has since never made contact with the owner of the mysteriously identical seven-digit phone number that came from Eloise's area code.

CHAPTER **13**

THE ELECTRONIC VOICE PHENOMENON

B efore I take you any further into this chapter, allow me to take a moment to say that throughout the course of reading the remainder of this book, on occasion, I will be making mention of certain products that can be purchased online and my personal experiences with them. In no way will I have mentioned any of the products in the following sections of this book for the purpose of trying to help sell such devices. I would more encourage only those who take a strong interest in such things to consider doing their own research. I may consider, one day, writing an entire book on nothing but strange new spirit/consciousness testing products that come out on the market, as there are currently enough out there to do so already. For the time being, however, I am only reporting my own personal experiences, as they truly have happened, recently and quite organically in my life. The main reason for introducing you to any of the items that you will be reading about are simply to document my personal experiences with them as my experiences did, remarkably, turn out quite interesting.

I also feel that these experiences are worth mentioning, as they introduce strange concepts that you might stumble across on your own, and thus should offer a few possible ideas regarding how you might want to try them out for yourself. Of course, not all of the following stories will take into account such technologies. Taking note, however, that there are now so many gadgets that purport to pick up on paranormal signals, this allows us to see the current level of interest shift in examining historical mysterious phenomena, as nowadays, it seems it can be experienced through shifts in the atmosphere combined with seemingly random events.

As a presenter who has, at one time, performed a lot at colleges and universities, I used to attend several college vendor conferences every year. One such conference was being held up in Boston at a Sheraton Hotel. My college agent at that time was representing me along with just about every ghost hunter you could see on cable, and then some. So back in March of 2010, while at a National Association of Campus Activities Conference as we were wrapping up after the last exhibit hall, I went to a bar in the hotel we were staying at, with ghost hunter Chris Fleming (From the TV show, *Psychic Kids*) and an African American comedian named Donnell. Despite the fact that it was a comedian, a ghost hunter and *The Man Who Knows* walking into a bar, what was about to happen, was no joke...

WHAT WOULD YOU ASK A SPIRIT?

I was actually quite curious, as I had never gotten a chance to sit across the table from a modern ghost hunter from TV before. So I asked him what I thought was the obvious question to ask. "What is it about all the electronic gadgets that you use to capture ghostly impressions? How do they work? And how would you know if it's an actual spirit?"

"I'll show you!" he replied back and quickly reached into his backpack, and pulled out what looked like a small black AM/FM radio with some portable iPod speakers. It turned out that the reason for this was because that was exactly what it was. Except that this radio was reprogrammed to sweep through each station, one at a time, allowing only short intervals of time to be spent on each station. He set it so that it would sweep backwards on the AM dial, allowing only about 1.5 seconds to be spent on each channel, and then turned the volume up. He explained that what would happen is that spirits will learn to use the radio in order to manifest their own voices that will respond to your interactions as the radio goes through these cycles.

I said jokingly, "There are spirits who are willing to speak with us here at the bar?" Chris looked at me completely seriously and said, "Spirits are everywhere. They connect themselves to other people. They can be found practically anywhere that anyone has ever been." I remember being impressed by how confidently he said this. "So is there anything that you would like to ask the spirits who are with us tonight?"

I looked at Donnell, and he looked back at me. "What do you ask a spirit, especially if it's a spirit you don't know, and whom you're not so sure what you might be getting into?"

"Ok, then I'll start." Chris said. "If there is a spirit who is out there and who would like to introduce yourself to us, can you please send us some kind of a signal..." The entire time, since he had turned the thing on, it was spending a little over a second on each station before continuing to hit them in sequence while going backwards on the AM band. Each time it went to the bottom of the dial, it would start again at the top. Occasionally it would hit a station in which you would get to hear a fraction of an announcer's voice, at differing levels of clarity, or just a fraction of music. So it seemed likely that some kind of noise would come from the radio in some form. But what came out within seconds of Chris Fleming asking for a "signal," sounded without a doubt, as if someone from the radio said, "Yes." The reason why I feel fairly confident in saying this did happen, is because I remember distinctly the look on Donnell's face as well as the confirmation coming from him that that was what he had heard as well.

Almost as if he were reading both of our minds after confirming that we all had heard a voice say "yes," Chris said aloud (to no one in particular), "We're not sure if what we just heard was just a coincidence or if that was really someone trying to contact us, so can you give us something a bit more to go on, like a countdown?" At first, I didn't know what Chris meant by saying that. The odds of any response at all that would sound to us like a confirmation seemed unlikely, at best. But within seconds of him saying this, we heard at least four distinctly different voices, come from the radio in sequence, but differing in clarity, calling out the numbers two, three, five and seven, possibly more.

The more time that passes since having that experience, the less I even want to believe my own story, because what had happened was *so unlikely*. The only reason why, in fact, I feel as confident as I do is because Donnell was there to act as a third party, who could confirm with me that he was hearing exactly what I was hearing. I remember us both being completely flabbergasted. Without missing a beat, Chris continued his interaction with the eerie voices by pointing to Donnell, and asked, "Can you tell us what his name is?"

I remember thinking to myself, "There is no way in hell that whatever random voices he's talking to is going to know the answer to a question like that." But no more than a few seconds later, a pretty crystal clear voice came through, and it sounded just as if a radio announcer was speaking and the channel was swept over to hearing him just as he said the word "Don." Now Donnell, who apparently has personal friends and relatives who call him Don, sat frozen for a second and then visibly shaken, got up out of his seat and walked back a few steps. That was basically his reaction. He was so disturbed that what came out of the radio was actually heard by all of us, that he didn't know what to do except move out from where he was sitting.

For Donnell, that was it. He was ready to call it a night. For me, I needed to know more. I shook Chris' hand and congratulated him for being able to deliver my first "on-demand paranormal experience." We talked for a bit about just what electronic voice phenomenon was.

As Chris and I continued to speak, the radio continued to sweep through the stations, but as I listened, I didn't noticeably hear anything significant that seemed as if any type of spirit was trying to speak to us while we weren't speaking to it. After a few moments of talking to him, however, I asked, "Just curious, but how many spirits are we speaking to at one time, anyway?" It occurred to me that it could be one or possibly more spirits present, especially if spirits attached themselves to other people like Chris said. The bar we were at was pretty crowded with people. "Why don't we ask them?" Chris suggested. "How many of you are there?" he asked. Again, within seconds of him asking, a voice came on and said what sounded like "Hey." Then another voice came on and sounded like it said "Hi" but in another voice and frequency. Then another voice said something like "Yup," then another said "Yeah." Chris looked up at me and said, "Did you hear that? There might be around four or five of them out there." I was pretty excited by the experience, as I have always been curious to know how one finds a ghost, how one can interact with it and exactly what any of that means. I had a feeling that, if anything, I got the experience of EVP's that I was asking for from TV's *Psychic Kids'*, Chris Fleming.

I'd like to reiterate, at this point, that I am merely giving you my experiences (which are 100% true) having come across these unusual electronic devices, and offer those experiences in the hopes that it may lend a perspective to other similar experiences. Outside of that reason alone, in no way am I endorsing the sales of any of the devices I mention in any way that can guarantee your own success with them.

Nonetheless, not only do these odd devices and machines fascinate me, but it is important for me to point out that even academic research scientists have constructed their own ways of studying fluctuations in certainty and uncertainty using their own random signal devices that will be discussed later (in Part III). I find that offering my readership a direction to go in for personal research is most easily done with many of these odd machines for those who are interested since many are accessible online. So although I am not writing about these to sell them, what I am giving you here, is an honest review of my own experience with them.

EVP'S PREDICT SNOW

The next morning, I was talking with Chris Moon, from Haunted Times Magazine/Radio, and who was also part of the crazy goon squad that comprised of who we all were, at the NACA conference in Boston. We were preparing ourselves in the exhibit hall to meet the entire college and university student programming board delegates and to deliver our info packets (complete with a memorable impression) to them. Having heard about my encounter with Chris Fleming the night before, Chris Moon was now eager to introduce me to his own machine.

Unlike Fleming's portable sweeping radio, that he called the SB7 (for Spirit Box 7), which seemed to collect random voices on each station as it continually cycled through them, Chris Moon's machine is what is known as a "*Franks Box*," created by a man named Frank Sumption. Frank Sumption is still alive today, and appears to be continuing to make his *Franks Boxes* (available on his website), but Chris Moon claims that there's something special about his particular Franks Box (a claim that is widely disputed among other *Franks Box* owners), in that it was one of the first ones that Frank Sumption ever built. Frank Sumption does number each box he makes and many of them appear to be slightly different in appearance, giving them all a "collectors aesthetic."

As I remember it, Chris Moon's was an actual wooden box, with a silver metal face, about the size of a small shoebox, with red and black knobs, a meter, sliding adjusters, and speaker holes drilled into its face. Truthfully, it looked like a prop out of a science fiction B-movie from the 1950's. Instead of trying to interpret second-long voices, however, his sounded like an ocean of static frequencies with all kinds of odd sounds and voices surfacing and dropping back.

Chris Moon has a belief that he has been paired up with a spirit friend, named Tyler, who has been following him around for some time. Tyler was an 18-year-old boy who had died in a motorcycle accident. The story about Chris' chance meeting with Tyler's mother is gripping, and well worth its own chapter (in a future book) just to look into that experience as being completely separate from this one. I am sure he will even tell you himself, should you ever encounter one of his ghost programs. But in this case, I was meeting Chris for the first time, so as far as I knew, he was introducing me to an imaginary friend.

He was positive that his machine could get results just as well as Fleming's did from the night before. So with only a few minutes before the exhibit hall opened up to the entire conference, Chris turned on his Franks Box and adjusted the settings to receive EVP feedback. I remember him calling out for Tyler just after he turned on the machine, as if requesting that his spirit be the one that surfaces over the others. Moon seemed pretty certain that Tyler's spirit would be the dominant spirit that communicates over his machine.

Feeling like I had done this before (since I had just been introduced to Chris Fleming's *Spirit Box* the previous night), I decided to take the initiative of now knowing what to say. "If there is anyone out there who would like to communicate with me, will you send me a sign?" Almost immediately I heard something that sounded like a "yes" surface, and Chris heard it too. Continuing, I said, "I think that is someone trying to say hello to me, can you give me a little more to go on, like a countdown?" Within only a few more seconds, I heard voices count "two... two... four..." almost as if it was being spoken by the electronic woman's "not in service" voice, but then it trailed off.

I must say, the weird thing is that although I felt quite aware that I was hearing what was being said, I also observed that Chris heard all of this as well, and we were confirming off of each other that what was being heard, was indeed being heard. So something was happening, and I really have no idea what, as this was now the second encounter I had within twenty-four hours and I was paying attention pretty closely, especially the second time around. It was the morning, around 11:00am, and I remember it feeling a bit odd that these unique spirit encounters can be had at any time of the day or night!

The next question I asked was said to be daring. Slightly concerned that I might be driving into a forecasted blizzard the next day on my way back home towards Washington, DC, from Boston, I asked, "Will I be making it home tomorrow?" I waited to hear a reply, but all that either of us could hear was white static. We waited a few more seconds, but since I was nervous that I heard no answer, I asked, "Will I hit snow?" Suddenly, three distinctly different voices bubbled up, which truly sounded as if it was saying, "Snow, snow, snow!" So there I am, not intoxicated mind you. Somehow, it is still the first thing in the morning, and yet I am hearing all this. To get clarity on what was just said, I pressed on, "Will I be hitting traffic?" We waited a few seconds, and then what sounded to me like a weatherman's voice said the word, "Delays..." before disappearing into the static. Each time we heard a voice, we would confirm off each other that what we heard sounded like what was heard. It was really quite fascinating.

I was quite curious to ask more questions. But the exhibit hall opened up, a swarm of college students came flooding through, and we were immediately thrown back into the "real world" of shaking hands and building face-to-face relationships. I was having the wildest time-sharing the booth with all these ghost hunters. But in the back of my mind, I wondered what all of that (which I heard the Franks Box say) actually meant. I would have to wait until the next day...

REAL GHOST PHOTOS

My agent represented the TLC Ghost Hunters, Ghost Hunters International, Psychic Kids' Chris Fleming, John Zaffis aka "the Godfather of Ghost Hunting" and Chris Moon, among others. We all had lunch that day immediately following our exhibit hall. Sitting at a table with 6 ghost hunters for lunch is an interesting experience.

What these individuals do for universities and college campuses is set up "ghost hunts," usually in the Halloween month of October, but during any part of the year it's possible. College students get to go with them to the "oldest," or "most haunted" areas on their campus where they attempt to capture ghost images on their own cell phone cameras, hear ghostly interactions take place and learn about these historic sites and why they are said to be haunted. Had I not heard for myself the EVP's that I did, I would have found little interest in any of this stuff. But now I was interested. Even if all of this was a total synchronistic coincidence, I was now enthusiastically interested that I could have even been made to feel like that at all.

During lunch, Chris Fleming took out his laptop and was showing the other ghost hunters about a dozen of his past year's "spirit images" caught in cell phone camera photos taken by himself, as well as students at some of the schools he went to. Many of them looked like typical Instagram shots of college kids dressed up in Halloween costumes, but then Fleming would point out a tiny white dot in the picture that looked like a speck of light just over the photographed person's shoulder. As he zoomed into the white dot, you could make out a person's face within it. It was weird, and frankly, it looked so good, I was pretty sure it couldn't be real. Jokingly, I said, "Chris, are you sure you're not touching that shit up with Photoshop?" It was interesting, because at that point, all the other ghost hunters who were sitting there rose to his defense. These photos were NOT fakes. This is their *work*. I was apparently being ignorantly dismissive of the stuff that they do. Well, I saw this as an obvious chance for me to pick up some great do-it-yourself ghost hunting factoids.

For best results in getting ghostly photographic apparitions and weird EVP recordings:

1) It's always good to have an ion counter. The basic idea is that when the ion count gets low, spirit manifestation is most probable. Apparently, spirits tend to somehow use up the ions in a room. Any unusual shift in the atmosphere, it is said, might indicate the presence of a "spirit entity," and this is a good initial signifying characteristic for the potential of recordable ghostly manifestations.

2) It's good to come equipped with a "cheap cell phone camera." Apparently, the cheaper, the better. Because the

best way to get good photographic results is to use a camera that doesn't have any automatic light filters, like infrared filters, which might limit the type of light that may be the source that can pick up the apparition.

3) When your ion counter detects a sudden decrease in ions, it is indicating the strong possibility that spirits are present. The idea is that this is the best time to just start snapping photos in every direction, and then later examine each photo to see if anything can be spotted. This is also a good time to simultaneously try to establish contact by listening for any significant EVP interactions and trying to maintain communication.

There are other devices that have been known to pick up on ghostly effects, including electromagnetic field detectors, pendulums, Ouija boards, and other similarly based techniques that involve noticing the fluctuations and interpreting the significance of virtually anything that emits a random signal. Finding unusual connections between yourself and something mysterious is now not only exciting and fun, you can also get to learn how to use cool techno-gadgets to compliment your techno-sorcery. Most of the time, the kids on campus would come along on these "ghost hunts" not because they considered themselves future paranormalists, but because it was provided as a free after-class function that the university Student Activities Departments, Office of Student Life or Campus Programming Boards paid for. These ghost hunts would offer the students something both spooky and social to do during the Halloween month of October. What some of the students would end up finding quite surprising, however, is just how possible it is for them to experience unusual fluctuations in the atmosphere as well as even capture ghostly apparitions on their own cell phone cameras.

Upon being told all of that, and being shown some strange "photographic anomalies," it still, to me, sounded like hearsay. My head was still spinning slightly from the EVP sessions that I experienced the previous night with Chris Fleming, as well as that morning with Chris Moon. I remember it being difficult to process everything that didn't make sense that seemed to have just happened to me, despite my own skeptical nature.

So immediately after lunch, I headed off to my room. On my way there, while walking up the staircase, I bumped into some close friends of mine, Jeff and Tessa Evason (known as *The Evasons*), an amazing mindreading duo who also perform for universities. They asked how the convention had been going for me, and I told them all about my prior encounters with Chris Fleming's crazy spirit radio receiver. As one would suspect, they listened skeptically to my story with that "Are you *sure* that really happened?" look on their faces. But suddenly Tessa turns to Jeff and says, "Remember when we were at that one school where after our show that girl took that picture of me? We were on one side of the stage talking to some other people, when I noticed a small commotion happening where she was standing with a bunch of her friends. Well, they came over and showed me the picture that she just took of me and just above my head, you could see a tiny white spot, that if you zoomed in real close, you could actually make out a face."

How random is that? I ran into two friends who actually told me that story *just after* seeing and learning about photographic ghost phenomena from professional ghost hunters? What the ghost hunters told me at lunch was true. This all-too-perfectly confirmed for me that what the ghost hunters told me at lunch was true. All the ghost hunters apparently do is instruct students on how to be observant for those kinds of photos, after they are taken. Hearing about Tessa's mysterious photo almost instantly alleviated much of my earlier skepticism of the photographs that I had just seen that Chris Fleming had. Ghost hunters have a real belief that what they are capturing on tape and on camera are real spirits. They are not like magicians who entertain you with their own self-created deceptions. Ghost hunters entertain with perception. And apparently, all it takes is a crappy cell phone camera, a sudden decrease in the ion count, and the ability to observe and interact open-mindedly with things in the room you are in, that aren't necessarily there.

DELAYS

The next morning, I woke up to sunny skies. Temperature was at about 45 degrees, almost moderate. I thought about what the EVP from Chris Moon's Franks Box had told me the day before, and I even prepared well in advance to get out as early as I could. I remember thinking to myself that if knowing the future meant that I could *change the future*, and then this would be my chance to prove the Franks Box wrong.

I started out in my Audi A4 Quatro (which is an all-wheel-drive sedan). The fact that I might hit snow was not too much of a worry for me. My car has handled nicely in pretty severe weather conditions. However, this was a beautiful day in Boston, so I remember leaving with the feeling that everything was actually going to be all right...

The drive through Massachusetts and most of Connecticut was quite pleasant and with hardly any traffic. But upon arriving somewhere near Bridgeport, I suddenly hit a heavy blizzard. It was a whiteout. The snow had not taken long to turn to slush and I'm supposing that it didn't take that long for the slush to turn to ice. There were deep tracks made by the vehicle in front of me that I had to try to drive in just so that I wouldn't have to drive into these deep icy slush mounds. Traffic was moving at about 35 miles an hour. Suddenly, I felt my tires run over something that caused them to slip into the side of the hard slush tracks and lose control. My car was starting to spin and there was nothing I could do about it.

I was now spinning in a clockwise circle, my Audi doing a 35mph "ballet" across the I-95 freeway traffic from the left and across three lanes to the right. Praying that I wouldn't hit a car with children in it; praying that a truck wouldn't hit me, suddenly the right side of my car hit the right hand curb, and my car bounced over the median sideways and onto the emergency lane of an off-ramp from a service area. Front tire completely destroyed, I was left sitting there by myself in my car, as snow quickly came down and blanketed my windshield, saying, "Delays..."

RANDOMLY GENERATED PLANE CRASH PREDICTION

Once I went through everything that needed to be done to tow my car to a nearby Audi dealership and rent a car to drive the rest of the way home, I found myself needing to tell someone what I just went through, but particularly someone who would believe me. So I called up a close friend of mine currently living in Boise, ID and who is also an American Zulu Sangoma (healer). His name is Jerome Finley. I told him of everything that I had just gone through over the last seventy-two hours that culminated into my car crash, and as I told him, he patiently listened to my every word. By the time I was finished, he said, "Well I must say, you have really intrigued me." But there is always a lot to talk about whenever he and I talk, so by the end of our conversation I was left wondering if he even bought my story as having really happened. To this day, I still have a hard time believing it myself.

Two weeks later, Jerome called me up and said, "Alain, remember how I told you how much you intrigued me, after you told me that crazy story of what happened to you in Boston? Well, you have turned me into a monster. In the past two weeks I've bought close to $2500 worth of ghost hunting equipment."

Over the next few weeks I would call him and check in with him and he would usually have at least one or two interesting stories to tell of his evening encounters with his "ghost boxes." He had structured a regimen so that every night at around 10:00pm, he would spend around 20 minutes listening and trying to interact with the voices he heard. He was collecting a good handful of pretty eerie stories that he would report back to me. On one occasion, he said aloud, "Is there anyone there?" Almost immediately, he heard a voice that sounded like a reply that answered, "Look right." Jerome was rather stunned and a little unnerved at the thought of even turning his head to look to the right. When he did, however, he didn't see anything at all except for his nightstand and a blank wall. Voices started coming through that sounded like a string of numbers. Confused, Jerome wrote four or five of the numbers down that he could gather. Later, when he went back to his nightstand, he noticed that there was a book that was sitting there that he paid no attention to earlier. When he looked at the string of numbers underneath its barcode, he discovered that it correlated to the same sequence of numbers that he wrote down earlier!

Of course, this came to me as a single eyewitness experience, so as much as I believe that Jerome would only tell me stories that are true, since I wasn't there, I can only write about this based on hearsay. I do want to include this story, because if Jerome heard a string of numbers come from his spirit box at all, and I remember on two occasions (and from two different machines) that I myself had heard a string of numbers, what does that mean? Remember, that this is a radio that is sweeping second by second through each channel. If this were as common as it seems, why would it even sound as if multiple numbers are being spoken at all if each channel

2

operates as a separate entity? Does it only *sound* as if numbers are coming up, or are we actually hearing numbers?

One of Jerome's machines is called the *Ovilus III*, manufactured by a company called Digital Dowsing, who specializes in building machines for the purpose of establishing ways of communicating with spirits, electronically. One of the modes of the Ovilus III is that it measures the area's electromagnetic field and this somehow gets filtered randomly through a basic dictionary software program that, once generated, will sound-out actual English words with a computer voice. This makes it so that one doesn't have to get frustrated trying to interpret second-long voices in mid-sentence. So you end up getting a string of electronically spoken, full and complete words taken randomly from an English dictionary program based on its reception of the local electromagnetic field. Now, mind you, I do not know the people of Digital Dowsing, nor do I own such a device (yet). However, I am a tad more curious now, after what I know to have happened.

One day, Jerome called me up and said, "I'm just going to put it out there, but I think there might be a plane crashing pretty soon. Of course, I hope it doesn't happen, but my *Ovilus* box has been repeating certain words that have been making me feel like it might happen. For two days now I have gotten repeating words, like 'fire, airplane, screaming, crash, sadness,' stuff like that. So just put that in the back of your head, ok?" The next day, Polish president Kaszinsky died in a plane crash near Warsaw. The strange thing is that, at that time, Jerome was living in Salt Lake City and the plane crash he had predicted happened on practically the other side of the world. Significantly, however, it was mentioned almost immediately after it happened on every news station, and it was on the front page of pretty much every major newspaper the following day.

The above story is actually an unusual one for the books, because it was a fairly accurate prediction made by a peculiar synthesis between human intuition, language, and a machine. Could a mysterious force in some dimensional field that we are mostly unaware of be able to send us glimpses of the future like that? Perhaps to a skeptical disbeliever, seeing as this wouldn't have been able to solve any problems, it may seem irrelevant, but what if there was a way to get a more accurate picture? What if there is an area within this realm that inspires more scientists to come and see what's going on? It is, indeed, interesting when we can observe how some things that we don't initially understand can be seen to correlate to something significant in the future. What if we knew how to better interpret such things like weathermen?

When mystical or cosmic connections are experienced, is it an illusion, a delusion, or is there something more that is giving us the chance to reveal its presence?

PART THREE

MIND OVER MATTER

CHAPTER 14

MEN OF MYSTERY SPEAK

THE INCREDIBLE URI GELLER

Recently, I was able to speak with my friend, Uri Geller. The term, the "Geller Effect," was originally coined by the media as well as some scientists in order to explain the eerie property of metal bending inexplicably and/or broken watches suddenly and mysteriously made to work fine again, as if by the power of one's thoughts, energy, and intense desire.

This strange power that Geller was known for was witnessed many times on national television. He would not just bend spoons on TV, necessarily, but in fact would tell the viewers at home that he will send his thoughts through the television set and affect the cutlery, keys and watches in the TV viewers' own homes! In other words, those watching from their own homes would be able to see proof of his powers by witnessing it themselves while in front of their own television sets. Without him being there, a spoon or key would be made to bend in a TV viewer's own hand or even be found inexplicably bent while still in its own silverware drawer. Broken watches were coming to life while energy was being sent through the TV sets, as people held them in front of the image of this incredibly powerful and gifted man. That was what started the terms "Gellerism" and "The Geller Effect."

Most everyone who hears the name Uri Geller immediately forms in their mind a mysterious man who has paranormal powers. His fame and success at his craft has literally made "Geller" into a household name. For over forty years, he has remained a public enigma. He is known for being able to manipulate metallic objects with what appears to be purely mental (and much of the time, even remote) energy. He has a natural openness to how life can work wonders through the power of positive energy while he spins miracles that will amaze and inspire anyone he meets. He is a genuine bona fide "International Man of Mystery." He is trilingual, and speaks English, Hebrew, and Hungarian fluently. He has been on television all over the world consistently since the 1970's, showing enormous "staying-power," and has authored more than 15 books. To this extent, he's like *The Rolling Stones* of mentalism...

In just the past seven years, Uri Geller aired his own reality/contest shows in (so far) fifteen different countries including: *Phenomenon* (USA, co-hosted by Criss Angel), *The Next Uri Geller* (Germany), *A Kivalasztott* (Hungary), and *The Successor of Uri Geller* (Greece). These were all the same format as the original, called *The Successor*, which started the entire idea in Israel, back in 2007. For a man who is approaching seventy years old, as of this writing, anyone must agree that this is a man with true energy and stamina. Try looking up photos of him online. It would be a fair estimation to say that he looks hardly fifty. This is a man who is in shape, looks young, and never ceases to encourage a strong positive attitude.

Uri Geller is known for not only being a mystifying showman, but also for having become a self-made millionaire, a close friend to many famous celebrities, and a collector of strange antiquities of mysterious origin. On the subject of his paranormal-level of eccentricity that he has cultivated over the years, the most flamboyant might be his 1976 Cadillac which has been completely covered with over 5000 bent and twisted assorted silver cutlery, each individually riveted to its entire body, yet still technically allowing the vehicle to be drivable. There is a very long and impressive list of famous personalities who have used, owned or touched many of the individual pieces, making his relationship to each separate piece of cutlery adorning it meaningful. I first had a chance to see his car in person, as it was exhibited at the American Visionary Arts Museum in Baltimore, MD about 15 years ago. I remember thinking how it must be a real chore to keep polished, but it is a truly magnificent piece of drivable "visionary art." My (no-longer) secret wish is that he might one day drive me to Burning Man in it. Of course, only time will tell, for now...

An even more mysterious acquisition of his was that in 2009, he purchased a small island in the Firth of Forth, known as "*The Lamb*," or "*Lamb Island*." This is a 300' X 150', uninhabited island of volcanic rock that sits off the coast of Scotland. The Lamb is the middle island of three, the other two named the "*Craigleith*" and the "*Fidra*," which are positioned nearby. Interestingly, these Scottish islands have been noted to uncannily mirror the layout of the three pyramids at Giza. Uri told the UK's *Daily Mirror*, that "Scota," who was the half-sister of the Egyptian pharaoh, Tutankhamun, arrived by boat 3500 years ago and buried a "huge haul of treasure" there. I feel fairly certain that the early Templars who fled to Scotland would have noticed this intriguing configuration of the three islands as well, since they were said to have early connections to Egyptian knowledge. Treasure or no treasure, perhaps there are mysteries yet to unlock about the three islands? One wonders what Geller plans to do with this interesting piece of real estate?

Before moving on to introducing you to him, allow me to throw in just one more, of (probably still) several other things about him that might astonish you, psychic powers aside. At Geller's wedding, in 2002, Uri's best man was none other than Michael Jackson. Therefore, if the amazing Uri Geller is not eccentric enough for you, do consider his *best man*, the (now deceased) King of Pop. Of course, however, Michael Jackson, the icon, will live forever.

Uri is an amazing international public figure, an entertainer, an entrepreneur, and a promoter of strong positive feelings as a way of creating miracles in one's life. Part of this is he is a very good storyteller. He always has the most far-out thing to tell you. I think it drives skeptical people a little batty because they don't know what to believe when it comes to this thing called "Gellerism." Uri, on the other hand, seems to have either consciously (or unconsciously) developed (or evolved) a manner of *pushing just the right buttons* which send skeptics and naysayers into torrents of outrage for the public claims that he makes and has made. Unquestionably, though, he is a man around which miracles have happened. Perhaps, Geller believes that he has some control, or maybe it's that he has a *faith* that consciousness and reality can be molded (or bent!) by having a strong and *positive will, conviction* or *intention* that one finds within oneself.

"The bending of the metal is only the 'visually-communicated expression' of how amazing, and genuine, the process is to 'transform' or 'shape' one's reality for real." The Man Who Knows

That is how I see it, at least. Although I cannot speak for Uri, I can speculate that Uri's mastery, and thus, ultimately, his particular "art" is in consistently defying the laws of logic by combining a large element of showmanship, a gifted story-telling skill, a true belief in himself and the extraordinary things that seem to manifest around him. Then, there is his contagious ability to transfer this belief into other people. He gets instant rapport with most everyone he meets by exhibiting his excitement, focus, and powerful kindness. In truth, the paranormal qualities of *just who he is* quickly come into sharp focus as one realizes how remarkable the results are that he gets. Could it just be luck of the draw, or positive intention? Not just anyone can achieve the "higher frequencies" that Uri seems to get to so effortlessly. These are, after all and allegedly, the very things that made him successful.

Some skeptics will be quick to point their fingers and cry out "Charlatan!" but Uri tends to ignore them. Simply put, what Uri loves to do most is amaze people. He amazes people with his demonstrations of mental power, his intense conviction in himself, his wild stories, and by just being Uri Geller.

Although primarily a public figure and a showman, during the 1970's, when he first stepped into public perception as an *international phenom*, there was also, simultaneously, a "secret race" going on between the United States and the Soviet Union to gather up as much intelligence as possible about the inner mind's ability for military reconnaissance and other spy-related missions.

Just recently, in a 2013 BBC documentary, *The Secret Life of Uri Geller-Psychic Spy?*, Oscar winning director, Vikram Jayani, reveals a lesser-known, and far more covert aspect to Geller's relationships with key world leaders since those days. A question is raised as to whether it might be possible for Geller's psychic abilities to influence other world leaders to make certain decisions. Could his mental powers help to restore balance between nations? Has such a thing secretly happened, or more so, happened successfully? The idea that it might even be a possibility—that the mind of Geller would possess such an infinite, albeit immeasurable ability is part of the intrigue, here.

You must believe in Uri Geller, to appreciate what he can do. In fact, quite dynamically, he still continues to add to his ever-growing list of remarkably notable accomplishments. True, a few of his attempts have not been successful, and skeptics might be quick to point these out. In the case of military strategies, however, they already know that perfection is not always the outcome. It is in the *overall successes*, the meta-analysis of his success-rate, which (he claims) cannot go ignored. He tells me that oftentimes he is not told what the mission is for, or even if a mission was successful. But so long as "they" keep calling on him, and so long as the missions involve positive energy, he says he will "remain active."

His BBC documentary begins with Geller, himself, showing us around his estate near London, off the banks of the river Thames, starting in his yard. Uri points to an ancient-looking stone lantern, and tells us how it came from Mt Fuji. He reminds us of his friendship with John Lennon and Yoko Ono with a story of how years ago, John said to him "Find spirituality," followed by Yoko saying to him, "Go to Japan." So he did.

Leading us through his garden, he brings us to a red-colored *Torii* gate. These simple structures represent the gateways to the Japanese Shinto shrines. Legend has it that the Torii gates divide our world from the spirit world, since Shinto shrines don't actually exist in "our world." Leading us through his gate, Uri stops, and says dramatically, "Imagine... we are in spiritual realms now."

He pulls from his pocket, a small golden egg, telling us that John Lennon had given it to him and that John Lennon had told him that he had gotten it from an alien! That, "An alien hand stretched out, and dropped this into the palm of his hand. And he gave it to me. It's heavy, it's unexplainable..." Uri says.

Allow me to pause here and dissect this beautiful and mysterious moment. Just now, you have entered the *spirit world* with him, as you felt the camera cross through the symbolic Torii gates. Now, Uri tells you the story of his friend, John Lennon, and how he was given this impressively mysterious golden "egg" *from an alien*. Your mind races to reach for something stable to hold onto, but you are already in the spirit-world and your spirit must now decide if you can believe what he is saying, or is it that you should believe in what *John Lennon*

157

told Uri... Welcome to the world of Uri Geller, man of mystery and intrigue.

Before you are left for too long floating in this spirit-world, however, Uri continues his story, revealing that after carrying it everywhere since, he has gotten thousands of e-mails from friends and associates asking him if he ever had the golden egg tested by scientists to determine the possibilities of its true origin. His response to this question is nothing but pure Geller. He says, "I don't want to test it. I don't want to find out that it's made in Taiwan. I want to believe John. I want to believe his words. I love it. It's been with me since the day he's given it to me. And yes, I do believe in UFO's." He now puts it back into his pocket, turns around, and then leads you further into his latest documentary. That, in my opinion, is Geller's lesson in belief.

I wanted to give you a glimpse into the thoughts of someone who has lived a full life as an enigmatic man of mystery. A man whose history is rich with television and media appearances, controversy, friendships with world leaders and other high-profile celebrities, but also a man who knows who he is, what he has become, and what he stands for now...

NU: So you are planning to move back to Israel?

GELLER: Yes, the world is like a small global village today, so it doesn't matter where I'm based. I'm everywhere, but my base will become Israel.

NU: As someone who has been targeted by critical thinkers as being someone who doesn't think critically, is there anything that you would say to the world about your side of the story?

GELLER: (Originally), I thought that controversy like that would destroy me. I felt, when the skeptics came out and attacked me, that that would be the end of Uri Geller. But very quickly I learned. My biggest lesson was on the Johnny Carson Show (*The Tonight Show with Johnny Carson*). I walked into a trap, and I sat there for 22 minutes feeling humiliated by Johnny Carson. During those 22 minutes, I felt that Johnny Carson was sneering at me, mocking me, and the spoon that bent wasn't bent enough for him. When that interview was over, I thought: That's it, Uri. Go back to the hotel, pack up and fly back to Israel. You are finished. Everybody told me that to be on Johnny Carson meant that you made it in America. So I went back to the hotel. I was devastated and drained. I fell on the bed, and fell asleep. The next morning, the phone rang and it was the operator from downstairs, saying, 'Mr. Geller, I have a Merv Griffin on the line for you.' I said, 'You mean, *the* Merv Griffin?' It was Merv Griffin, himself, and he said to me, 'Uri, I saw you last night on Johnny Carson and I want you on my show this week.' That's when it dawned on me; there is no such thing as bad publicity. Soon after that, I learned that no matter what they write about me, as long as they spell my name correctly, that's what I want! *I started measuring the length of the articles* that came out about me rather than reading them. Oscar Wilde was famous for saying:

'There is only one worse thing in life than being talked about, and that's not being talked about.'

Inspired by those words, I was able to take the debunkers and skeptic's attacks, and make it so that basically they became my unpaid publicists. I'm a master publicist myself, and I'm saying it shamelessly. I took their attacks and twisted them to boost my career. In the grand scheme of things, for Uri Geller, they were the best things that could have happened to me. Throughout my career, the skeptics created the buzz and the curiosity that fueled the controversy around me.

NU: Skeptics are now probably really upset with you claiming 40 years later, that you had any relationship with the US Army's *Project Stargate*, (which experimented on ways of applying meditated mental consciousness to the military spy program). I am a friend of Colonel John B. Alexander's, and I know that you and he go way back, so it doesn't surprise me much to hear you finally admitting to having some involvement in such programs. But you were mentioning about how these things still happen to this day...

GELLER: The governments that need to extract information by remote viewers will still use remote viewers. There are still programs everywhere in every big intelligence agency around the world. I believe they actually contributed to the debunking of parapsychology. This way, they can continue to work without any worries that there will be a big story in *The New York Times* or the *Los Angeles Times* that the Pentagon is still using psychics and so on. Everything went 'deep black,' yet there are still remote viewers, in fact, hundreds of them, still working. Parapsychology, like medicine or science, advances sometimes in slower steps but sometimes in very big leaps. There's no doubt in my mind that sooner or later, extra sensory perception will be validated in laboratories scientifically. I consider my tests and experiments at Stanford Research Institute, under laboratory-controlled conditions, pretty conclusive. In the future, people will be able to use their mind telepathically, and even use psychokinesis, mind over matter. As you know, they are already able to teleport things, little tiny protons. So teleportation, dematerialization, that's all around the corner.

NU: Yes, exactly. If people, for instance realized that the mind has such scope, maybe they would even just embrace life more fully...

GELLER: I think if you take into account the worldwide population, you find that skeptics (and, generally, people who don't believe) are insignificant by comparison. Most people believe in angels, in life after death, in God, in telepathy, in mind over matter... most people are believers. Look at how many people around the world believe in God. Atheists are a tiny minority. Also, look at how many horoscope columns there are in serious newspapers. I'm not talking about gossip newspapers, such as the *National Enquirer*; I'm talking about the serious newspapers. The very fact that they have a horoscope column tells me that people are interested, people believe, they believe in the stars and the forces of the universe. So there is an open mindedness all around the world. Movies about the paranormal come out more than ever. Robert De Niro played Uri Geller just last year in a movie called, *Red Light*. You also have the *X-Men*. So, on the contrary, there is a huge surge of belief in the mind, consciousness, extraterrestrials, and the paranormal.

NU: Tell me a little bit about your theories of how you think we are all gifted in ways that we don't fully know.

GELLER: I have a few theories. First of all, let's make it clear that I do believe in extraterrestrial life. I've seen UFO's. I've never seen an alien, but I have witnessed and seen UFO's, so that makes me a believer. This opens the gate for me to accept the theory that we are perhaps 'star children.' I don't quite buy the Darwin (evolution) theory, that we crawled out of the muck, and then from amphibians, we became monkeys, and from monkeys, humans. Possibly, the ancient Egyptians derived their information and their know-how from an extraterrestrial intelligence. One has to go deeper into the atom to discover other universes and inner space. Our minds are infinite. There's no end to inner space and there's no end to outer space. It's infinite out there.

NU: Can you elaborate, to our readers, a little bit more, regarding any of your personal UFO stories?

GELLER: (My earliest experience was) when I was about five or six years old in Tel Aviv. I saw a sphere of light and (before I could do anything) a 'laser-like light' hit my forehead. I fell into the grass, it was so powerful. My mother, when I ran home to tell her, didn't believe me. But I wrote about this encounter in my first book. In fact, I talked about it in hundreds of interviews and television and radio shows, but I actually never had any concrete proof. It was therefore hard for anyone, including my own mother, to believe my story. Then, after the BBC documentary about me back in 2009, *A Life Stranger Than Fiction*, (by Simon Cowell) it happened. In that documentary, again, I tell this (UFO) story, but this time, a day after the documentary aired in Israel, I got an e-mail from a retired Air Force captain who said to me, 'I saw your documentary last night, and I must tell you, I saw that same light which you saw in that garden.' So I jumped on the phone, called him up, and he said he was walking on the way to his parents' home, in Tel Aviv, and he saw a little boy, with a white shirt, black hair, curly hair, (which I had at that time), and this huge ball of light chasing him towards the apartment! This man had no interest to lie to me. He was actually a very serious person. So that became my personal validation of what actually happened to me when I was five... I now know, for sure, that it was real, and not a dream.

NU: Well, you were indeed in the Holy Land, could there be any connection there? I've come to the point in my life where I have become hyper-aware of recognizing anything that might be either significant or seen as inexplicable by normal standards. Each time I have an unusual experience, I try to enter it into a journal, as if to create a strange collection. Some of them are just in my memory, but almost like little blessings—each one becomes a part of my own little collection of strange stories to tell. By doing this, I also can't help but make new connections out of them. Do you have any recent stories of something inexplicable or something fantastic that happened within recent times?

GELLER: My life is riddled with inexplicable and interesting phenomenon too numerous to mention here. I view my different experiences as aspects of the paranormal and the mysteries of the universe. I have to say that I am an open minded individual and I tend to believe in elements that bring magic into our lives.

NU: 'Energy work' is obviously part of what you do, but then there are also other types of paranormal things that you are involved with, remote viewing, being able to read minds, etc. Is there a particular thing that you personally enjoy doing over the other?

GELLER: My most favorite 'missions,' these days, are the ones that yield something positive. Like trying to influence world leaders, or meetings with politicians to convince them to sign certain documents that help advance peace negotiations. I think this is what brings me the greatest satisfaction because I can sometimes see whether the results work or not. Most of the time, when I put my hand on something, it works. The smaller things, like psychokinesis, and mind reading, those things, I can't say that I have lost interest in it, because of course I live in this world, but these days, other more important, secretive work has overtaken (my interest in the more trivial aspects of) paranormal phenomenon.

NU: There has been a recent popularity of mediums and mediumship, at least here in the United States. Do you have any personal views on mediums and mediumship?

GELLER: When you bring up the word 'medium,' the first thing that comes to mind is 'Are they real, or are they charlatans?' I don't go to mediums. I don't talk to the dead. But I do believe in the afterlife. I have experienced certain things in my life that led me to believe that, as Albert Einstein once proved, energy cannot be destroyed. One must ask the very simple question, 'If energy cannot be destroyed, then what happens to our body, our soul, or our spirit when we die?' I believe that it travels elsewhere. It enters different dimensions. That's why I believe in life after death. But concerning the mediums that sell their services, it's hard to know who's legit and who's not.

NU: Well, on cable TV, we now have 'cable TV mediums,' and 'cable TV ghost hunters.' They have actually become quite a popular re-useable programming format. As you said, there's a horoscope in practically every newspaper out there. So now that there are about four hundred channels to choose from, there are at least nine or ten ghost shows and psychic medium shows.

GELLER: Ghost shows go way back fifty years and more. There are ghost stories written by famous writers and there are ghost movies produced all the time, the interest in ghosts and the spirit world never ebbed away. Which one is real? Who is cheating the public and who is doing it genuinely? I cannot say. Maybe there are people who are very intuitive who can contact the other side, and that's why there is such a huge interest in these television shows and movies. Of course, then again, who wouldn't want to talk to their deceased loved ones?

NU: True... Didn't you mention having spoken to your deceased loved ones in your dreams, or something like that? Do you believe in some area of consciousness that has to do with spirits?

GELLER: My mother told me that she had eight abortions before having me. I said once that I always feel that my brothers and my sisters are around me, and are kind of protecting me. Again, however, it's a field that I didn't really study deeply because I believe that it exists. So, if my belief system says that one does not die, we just go over to the 'other side,' then that is where it ends. What else is there to prove? If I believe in it, I don't need any proof.

NU: Well it's interesting that your belief in yourself has led you to so many incredible things, like being able to find oil in mineral deposits for energy companies! What did that procedure for you entail?

GELLER: I just got into helicopters and airplanes with maps and I made an "x" with a marker on the map. In many of the instances, oil came out, and that's how I actually became a Mexican citizen. The president of Mexico was so impressed that I found oil for *Pemex* (which is a Mexican national oil company), that they honored me with a Mexican passport. You've got to be always motivated and inspired to be successful. You must not allow any negative thoughts into your mind. And that's what happened to me when I was six, seven years old. I wanted to stop my mother from working. I wanted to buy her a television set. I started fantasizing and visualizing about how these amazing things will happen to me. I knew how to take the demonstration of bending a spoon, and create something mammoth out of it, and I immortalized it into world culture. That's how I made it. I attribute much of my longevity to the skeptics who

163

created a myth about me. They created, in a way, a legend, but I bring it down to the uniqueness, the weirdness of what I do. I bring it down to my charisma, my personality, to my character, to my chutzpah, and to the right people who were around me. That is my success story. It doesn't matter what you are aiming to be or become. You can make your dreams come true if you remain focused and positive-minded. The secret of success is originality.

NU: Thank you, Uri. I expect that this will offer something meaningful to any of those who can read this without judgment. What I see in you is an amazingly strong human spirit, and that is what the world is always looking for.

Learn more about Uri Geller at UriGeller.com

CHAPTER 15

SEEING WITH SCIENCE

To be accepted by western science as a part of reality, the concept of mind over matter will first need to enter the mainstream public's perception. Western science will not fully accept mind over matter as a reality until it becomes obvious that the public perception at large has intelligently shifted or evolved its understanding. Science fiction books and film have already begun to more recently offer their own interpretations of certain conceivable technologies. Usually, however, the very first question most people will ask themselves when contemplating such extraordinary notions would be:

Is it real, or is it impossible?

My feeling is if we begin with that first question, it quickly brings a majority consensus to believe such a thing would be *impossible* right at the outset, since through most people's practical experiences, this appears quite the case. Around the 4th century BC, when Plato first proposed the idea of a spherical world, most everyone else around him was quite satisfied that the Earth was flat. By 1960, the idea that nine years later, a couple of men would be walking on the moon (and staring at our own spherical planet for the first time from a lunar terrain) was still completely unfathomable to most people. These are only two of the more obvious leaps that mankind has made by allowing ourselves the desire to explore and persevere in the direction of our crazy ideas.

Perhaps rather than asking if it's impossible or real, it would be better to approach the notion more inquisitively. Maybe we need to focus on a more specific way of thinking about just what it is and what it can do. So let's ask a few questions that may help us define, in more exact terms, what mind over matter, or psychokinesis, really is.

1)   Is it possible to move things by using only the power of our

minds?

2) How are things affected by our mental thoughts?

3) Can we heal illness or injury by somehow using energy, intention, or the power of prayer?

4) Where can such energy come from?

5) How might we access it?

6) To what degree can it be used?

As I first contemplated the above questions, I was reminded of what the late Carl Sagan had once mentioned about the idea that "thought alone" might possess a minimal power to affect "random number generators":

"At the time of this writing, there are (reasons to consider) that by thought alone humans can (barely) affect random number generators in computers." Carl Sagan, from *The Demon-Haunted World*, 1995

Sagan was one of the truly great critical thinkers of history. He was not saying that he believed that this was possible, but that he felt it required further investigation. Something made me wonder what exactly Sagan meant by putting the word "barely" in parentheses when he wrote that sentence (was that even him?). I wondered if he had ever taken part in an experiment that involved thought projection on random numbers. What made him, as an incredibly critical thinker, feel even remotely confident enough to say this? Maybe he was referencing a study given by someone he knew and trusted? Or was it an educated guess that he made by an inner understanding that he may have intuited? Most would not believe that it would be intuition, but how probable could it be that he would trust someone enough to believe in such a remarkable claim without having taken part in an actual study?

It was hearing about amazing or fascinating things that stretched our limits that always piqued my curiosity. I knew that the mystery that surrounded them would never be fully understood by me unless I immersed myself, headfirst, into answering such questions on my own. I did already have some ideas of how to consider and experiment on what I personally interpreted as mind-over-matter. I thought of it as a rudimentary understanding, and used it as a mental game that I would play in my own head. It did not have to do with controlling *matter* necessarily, but rather controlling the *outcome of circumstance*, like a coin flip. I would find myself privately experimenting on this "heads or tails" idea on all sorts of events and outcomes throughout my life. No point in doing it with a coin, when there were far more important issues to consider that I could see had a "heads vs. tails" element. It was what eventually led me to the philosophy and science of Yin and Yang. Some would be quick to call this "magical thinking" or "woo" but I just saw it as a game, like a video game, except that it was happening in real life and didn't cost me any money to play. I would make jokes later of how it might have been the only thing that allowed me to graduate from high school.

Just like Sagan suggested, it seemed (to me) that I *barely* did have some control over something, hence my continuing to run this game in my mind. Oddly, there appeared to be an aspect of precognition attached to this concept as well. It always began, by my simply trying to predict how an outcome would occur. Most interesting, however, is when the odds are completely against you, and what can only be described as "force of will" takes over (usually seen as "luck" or "fortune"), and your mind ultimately appears to somehow control reality, as you know it. I know, again, I am thinking magically here. I've accepted this notion partially into my reality simply because of the few times when I have had no other option but to use my force of will in this manner, "something" worked. Maybe, there are "spirits" that hear my cries and come to my rescue. Maybe, it's an extraterrestrial intelligence. Maybe, it's God. Maybe, it's my grandmother; or maybe, I'm just getting better and better at fooling myself. It would take me years before I found something that I thought was consistent, easy and accessible to experiment on, but I was about to...

THE PEAR LABORATORIES

In the summer of 2010 I took a trip to Boulder, Colorado, where the Society of Scientific Exploration was holding their annual conference. This is an amazing meeting where university professors, scientists, and researchers of cutting edge studies come together in order to share their most recent findings. Scheduled speakers have 20 minutes to deliver their presentation and each fascinating topic is discussed at an academic level, one right after the next. It was there where I had the pleasure of meeting Robert (Bob) Jahn and Brenda

Dunne, the two founders of the PEAR (Princeton Engineering Anomalies Research) laboratory at Princeton University. Bob, now retired, was once the Dean of Engineering at Princeton. Brenda has been his longtime partner and co-author of the many books and articles they have published together about their unusual experiments.

PEAR was a research facility at Princeton University for 28 years, whose primary interest was to study the possibilities of the mind's potential ability to affect highly sensitive physical random processes. If it could be proven that this was possible, it would clearly be a matter of engineering concern worth further investigation. Most of their experiments were conducted using microelectronic random event generators (REGs) but one of the more dramatic devices they used in their studies was a specially made, ten feet tall and six feet wide, giant "pachinko-like" machine that used multiple metal balls, which they lovingly called "Murphy."

Imagine a frame, ten feet high and six feet across, mounted on the wall in the reception area of the laboratory facing a comfortable couch. In operation, 9000 precision-cast polystyrene balls, ¾" in diameter, trickled downward from an entrance funnel into a "quincunx" (similar to how bowling pins are staggered, except the pegs remain stationary) array of 330 nylon pegs, also of ¾" diameter, mounted on 2 ¼" centers. The balls bounced in complex random paths through the array, colliding elastically with the pegs and with other balls, ultimately accumulating in nineteen parallel collecting bins across the bottom. The front of this peg chamber (as well as the collecting bins below it) were made of transparent plastic sheets so that the cascade of balls and their developing distributions of bin populations were visible, as feedback, to the operators. After considerable empirical modifications to determine appropriate combinations of peg spacing, ball-inlet arrangement, and material properties, the resulting distribution of ball populations in the collecting bins could be tuned to a good approximation of a *Gaussian* (bell curve) distribution. It was the research findings by observing the distribution fluctuations of instruments like Murphy that inspired PEAR to take a turn in their interests towards the greater field of consciousness.

INTERNATIONAL CONSCIOUSNESS RESEARCH

The PEAR Lab explored the effects of intention on many different random physical devices, looking for evidence that conscious intention could influence random chance. Chance, by nature of the very word, is unpredictable. If it is proven that our minds have free will to affect chance, even on a minimal level, a whole slew of breakthroughs and new understandings will begin to surface. Since size is no obstacle and somehow, the energy that is at play is not affecting the *object* but the *chance odds themselves*, and we all begin to understand this, there could be far-reaching implications for any system or process that involves a random component.

Of course, there will always be the question of whether any random outcome, if correct, was destined, willfully intended, or synchronous with mere luck. However, many prestigious universities, including Duke, Cambridge, Princeton and Cornell, have invested years of investigation into such studies. The overall consensus seems to be that conscious intention does have some sort of inexplicable non-local way of interacting with randomness, in much the same way that it appears to interact with subatomic particles as in the laws of quantum mechanics. This is still currently a much-debated issue in mainstream science, and perhaps it needs further investigation, yet the scientists who have studied the evidence all seem to agree that something interesting is going on that is worth taking seriously.

International Consciousness Research Laboratory (ICRL), the successor of the PEAR Lab, is in the process of installing a PEAR Museum in its Princeton headquarters that will display many of their unusual experimental devices. These look a lot like something one might expect to see on an old Star Trek episode with William Shatner as Captain Kirk, nonetheless, they are both quite impressive and attractive at the same time. I have gone there to visit ICRL a few times as one of my corporate clients is based in Basking Ridge, which is only a short drive away. It is always a delight to speak with them.

Robert Jahn and Brenda Dunne have published the results of their studies at PEAR, along with their implications, in many scholarly articles that are available online, and in two books: *Margins of Reality: The Role of Consciousness in the Physical World* and *Consciousness and the Source of Reality: The PEAR Odyssey*, both published by The

ICRL Press, a division of ICRL.

PSYLERON GAMES

When I first went to meet with the people of ICRL back in 2010, Psyleron was just a sprouting business that shared space in the same office complex. I met with Dr. Roger Nelson and Adam Curry, who were also both there at the time, and Adam was eager to have me try out one of their interactive REG-based games. I was a little more apprehensive, as I suddenly had visions of being outted as a phony, if I was found not able to succeed. The REG, a device, conveniently about the size of a cell phone, plugs into your computer's USB port. The game I played, which was only one of several that were Psyleron-designed, worked like this:

At the beginning of the game, you are looking at a simple circular track on your computer screen, at the top of where there is a ball, which represents "the action of the thing" you want to try to consciously interact with. When the game starts, the ball will ultimately decide on choosing a path either to the right or to the left of the circular track that it moves along. The way you get the game started is that you had to first decide which path (to the right or to the left) the ball will ultimately decide to travel down before it stops by arriving at the very bottom. Then by depressing either your R key (for "right") or the L key (for "left"), you let the game know which direction you've committed yourself to, so that if the ball ends up taking the path you chose, it lets out a triumphant sound of victory. If the ball does not choose the direction you predict, however, it gives you a sound that signifies that you lost that round.

Before being able to appreciate a game like this for what it may actually be able to develop within us, however, it is actually best to first appreciate the "true random" nature of electron tunneling.

For a long time, even random number generators were not truly random but were only as close to being random as scientists were able to configure into a program. Before using electron tunneling for this purpose, other algorithms were used that mimic randomness, like that of radioactive decay, which was one of the closest patterns to being random that could be applied.

At a subatomic level, however, it is much more difficult to get anything that is absolute or certain. Imagine a coin constantly flipping. Sometimes it's heads, and sometimes it's tails. Sometimes it distributes between heads and tails fairly evenly. Sometimes it comes up on just heads, or just tails, repeatedly for no particular reason. One way of putting it, which is the way Adam tried to explain it to me, would be to try and "steer" the pattern of electrons by "believing" in your ability to have some control over this.

Somehow, if what was happening was actually what he said was happening, the experiment would be to either predict the direction on the track that the animated ball decides go down, or to *psychically direct* the movement of the animated ball using one's power of intention, so that it will be seen pushing against its own already randomly-chosen natural course. The ball will begin at the top, and once you start the game, it will begin shaking back and forth starting at the top of the circular "track" until it chooses a side to run down to get to the bottom. Left on its own, once you start the game, the ball will jerk this way and that, eventually choosing one side of the circular track to travel down.

The interesting thing is that at any point, the ball may change directions based on the random signal. This means that it could theoretically get very close to the bottom on one side, but then, any fluctuation in its random signal could send it back in the other direction, where it may end up on getting to the bottom by means of ultimately choosing the opposite side. Regardless, the game automatically ends once the ball finally reaches the very bottom (six o'clock position) of the track.

It does appear quite possible, that using just conscious intention, or ESP (or both!), one could learn to use willful intention or possibly even predict the direction of an animated ball on your screen without touching or being connected in any way to your computer. If that were possible, however, would that not be considered "mind over matter" or "psychokinetic"? How might this be applied so that it could be also used in a more powerful or exacting capacity?

Adam put me in front of the screen and explained to me what I was to try to do. I must admit, I felt a bit put on the spot. After all, I had just played the role of this powerful and mysterious enigma on four hour-long television specials for the TLC network called, *The Mysterious World of Alain Nu*, and I had a reputation to uphold.

Adam made it easy for me, however. All I had to do was choose either left or right and hit my key to commit to the direction. I wanted the ball to move down in. So I chose left, and hit the L key.

The ball started to shake rapidly along the track this way and that. Then it started to move to the right. "You chose left, right?" Adam asked. "Right, I chose left." I said back. "Well, then you better start making it move to the left." Adam said. The ball continued to shake itself to the right until it got to the three o'clock position. It was frustrating. I continued to stare at it thinking, "Just move to the LEFT, move to the LEFT!" It wasn't working. Suddenly, I thought, what if I just closed my eyes and started sending emotional energy at it while visualizing the ball moving to the left? So I closed my eyes and took a deep breath, I started to send as much emotional energy outwards as I could and kept my eyes closed the entire time. After about twenty seconds, I heard Adam's voice say, "You're doing much better now." I opened my eyes, and saw that the ball had moved itself all the way back to the ten o'clock position, but was rapidly deciding whether it wanted to continue in that direction or not. So I closed my eyes again, and tried to put myself in a similar state of mind. Within another twenty seconds, I was excited to hear the triumphant sound of electronic victory music. My reputation remained untarnished; I now really needed to buy one of these things.

THE AUBURN TIGERS vs. REG GAME

I started bringing my REG to all the universities and colleges that I performed at that year. Usually by the end of my shows, I would have about a dozen or so students who would stay afterwards wanting to ask questions or relate personal stories, and I found it to be a fun opportunity to have them try the REG game for some "psychically interactive show and tell." During that time, it was easy enough for me to bring the REG unit, which is about the size of a cell phone, and just connect it to my laptop, in order to show people the game.

I went to seven different colleges and universities, where I was able to show small groups of students, including Mount St. Mary's University, Rochester Institute of Technology, Siena College, University of Minnesota, University of Rochester, and Villanova University. There seemed to be one consistency that occurred each time I tried to demonstrate this concept for a group.

The task I gave them was as follows. We would make 10 predictions arbitrarily, but in advance, and so that our intentions were set prior to starting the game. Since the game we were playing was simply the REG-based game of "Heads or Tails?" the idea would be to allow the "Ball on the Track" to freely move to our predicted side, if that's what we could see was happening. However, if we saw it moving towards the unintended side, we would then try to use the force of our will to move it slowly back to the side which we originally chose despite its seeming desire to go in the other direction.

Let me note that many college students have a limited attention span, and that made it hard for me to conduct the experiment all the way through on any but one occasion. So although we did always make ten predictions, it was rare that they stayed past five tries, with the exception of one incident. This is also because, as it turned out, the experiment actually takes a bit of energy to take seriously.

What was interesting was that *all of the above schools* were able to predict or persuade the ball to move to its intended goal on the *first two tries*. Two in a row isn't that bad, and does show something interesting, considering that at seven out of seven schools, the first two tries were always successful. Three out of the seven schools failed on the third and fourth prediction before coming back on the fifth. Those three schools all lost interest after their fifth try success. They wanted to quit while they were ahead. Three more schools failed on the fourth prediction and fifth prediction, before again, losing interest, but that ultimately gave me a score of four out of seven schools tested, who were successful on their first three rounds. I found out from Brenda later, that, similarly, the PEAR experiments repeatedly demonstrated the best effects on their first and second trials as well. After that, the effects tended to diminish, but when operators persisted in generating data the succeeding efforts showed positive, but more modest results. Beginner's luck, anyone?

The seventh school I went to was Auburn University in Alabama. At Auburn University, the crowd that greeted me after my show consisted of mostly boys from the football team, The Auburn Tigers. Six of the ten people present were members of the football team. I always felt the need to convince the students first, that it was possible to either predict or intend a circumstantial result. I would always mention to the students how I believed that feeling a *strong emotion* seemed related to the success of the intention before getting them started. This group impressed me as they got the first *seven in a row correct*. They lost it on rounds eight and nine, and came back on round ten. Eight out of ten does significantly beat the odds. We were all drenched in sweat, just from concentrating, by the end of all ten rounds.

My friend, Hale Brownlee, a 1993 alumnus of Auburn University's Engineering Department (by coincidence), recently developed a similar "mind over matter awareness app" that is designed to play a similar game on one's smartphone called *Mind Race*. He conjectured insightfully to me that it was not surprising to him that a group which consisted mostly of football team players would be better at playing such a game under those conditions because they are already used to working with one another. Despite the fact that the game they ordinarily play is a physical contact sport, it can also be considered equally as mental. Because they were already trained to work together, their minds theoretically were already entangled. Unfortunately, as time has been limited, I have not had a chance to follow up on any of these experiments, although it is something which I plan on getting back to in order to create stronger conditions, more detailed notes and a larger number of replications.

THE INCREDIBLE MINDLAMP

Dr. Roger Nelson was a part of the PEAR staff and research team, and as the ICRL began to take shape, John Valentino and Herb Mertz formed a sister manufacturing company called Psyleron. Psyleron's mission is to manufacture REG-based machines, games and novelty devices designed to be experimented with in the privacy of one's own home, leisurely with family and friends.

When I first met them, Psyleron had only three "consciousness testing products" that they were marketing. Now, there are quite a few more and they are getting quite interesting. Their most decorative device that they carry is their *Mindlamp*. This is a shapely frosted glass lamp that sits at about 18" high and individually emits eight or nine varieties of soothing colors in varying intensities. The idea is to try to interact with it *non-locally*, so that even though there is no connection between you and the lamp whatsoever, it oddly seems to be able to be able to interact with your thoughts, personality and emotions.

It was in 2010 when I acquired a *Mindlamp* and their *REG* that can interact with game programs. The *Mindlamp* that I have has two settings. One goes through the color wheel spectrum cycle in either one direction or the other, eventually settling to remain on a color for longer periods of time. From there, depending on the random event generated by the measurement of random data it is collecting, it will move at different speeds in either direction or decide to remain stationary on a single color. Each color also has a variety of hues that it may end up lingering on, from very faint to the deepest, richest, and most brilliant intensity. I remember thinking of how much it reminded me of a color-changing hippie mood ring, which in the seventies became popular to wear. But as I continued to own it, it became far more interesting than any mood ring I had ever owned, even back when they were in style.

Back in the 1970's, mood rings became fashionable as they were sold to the "hippie consumer" as a ring that had set into it a "special stone" that changed color to reflect one's mood. To enhance this concept, the rings were often sold with a small instruction sheet that correlated certain colors that the ring would change to with a basic set of human moods and emotions. The secret ingredient to those mood rings was liquid crystals. Invented by Josh Reynolds and Maris Ambats in 1975, who originally figured out a way to bond liquid crystals with quartz. They marketed the idea as "mood rings," that if worn, were supposed to reflect the mood of its wearer. Liquid crystals react to heat, and thus will change its color depending on the temperature that surrounds it. As soon as the wearer puts it on, the body temperature of the wearer's finger activates the liquid crystals.

In some ways, one could easily make the incorrect assumption that the *Mindlamp* is the same thing. One can perceive it in exactly that way. Just a mood lamp; like a mood ring, except it's a lamp. However, one only has to spend a short while in front of it to realize the connection it seems to have with how you think or feel. You can also choose whether or not to have it change colors on its own. The most noteworthy distinction is that the *Mindlamp*, at no time touches any part of your body, nor do you need to wear anything special to connect with it. Once you get used to how it interacts with you, it becomes easier to conclude that you may actually be

175

connecting with it through some kind of conscious field.

There are other similarly categorized "mind control" novelty items out on the market, like the made-for-children (and George Lucas fans) *Star Wars 'Force Trainers,'* made by Mattel. Here, a ping pong-sized ball is made to float within a clear plastic tube that lets out air currents that are essentially controlled by the electrical impulses that your brain can learn to interact with. The big difference here, however, is that one must wear a "special helmet." The helmet is battery powered and is held onto your head by comfortable smooth metal sensors. These sensors pick up on electrical signals that are felt through galvanic conduction caused by one's brain, so that in a bio-feedback manner, one can interact mentally with the movement of the ball, as the air streams allow it to float at different heights, or even drop, based on your level of concentration and focus. With the *Mindlamp*, however, the interaction is completely *non-local* and the lamp works whether you are close to it or several feet away. The most astonishing about the *Mindlamp*, is that one needs not be connected to it, or anything at all, in order to interact with it.

After spending a few years with this device, I have tried a number of different experiments with it and have noticed many different behaviors that it seems to have which I do find peculiarly inexplicable. It's funny, after observing one for a few years, how one develops an odd kind of relationship with the device by just watching it. As I mentioned above, there are two settings in which the *Mindlamp* will function.

1) The first setting is simply "color-to-color," so the colors predictably move in either one way on the natural color wheel cycle, or it may also change course and decide randomly to cycle in the opposite direction. For instance, if it were on Orange, it would either move in a cycle that would change it to Red, followed by Pink, Lavender, Indigo, Blue, Sky Blue, Aquamarine, Green, Yellow, etc. When it is moving in the opposite direction, you will see those colors change in reverse. It will occasionally change to white as well, but this will happen only when the built-in REG is registering what it would consider a *highly improbable* signal. In such cases, it will turn white for as long as it continues to register that level of improbability, and then will eventually choose randomly to fall back into any one of the colors in the

spectrum.

2) The second mode is a "white-to-color" setting, for those practitioners who want to experiment with trying to make the lamp go from white into any chosen color that it can select using the same randomizing process. I have only tried the second setting more over this past year. Sometimes I find I am better at it than other times. Oddly, I do feel I am better at it than when I first got started with testing myself on that setting. The way I like to practice demonstrating control with this setting, however, is to see if I can keep the lamp on "white." By doing this, the lamp can be seen to stay in this "state of limbo" as you can observe it trying to fade slowly into a color, but then get pulled back into becoming white again.

The second setting can initially feel more frustrating than the first setting, but amazingly, since my daughter turned seven she seems to have developed a hit-rate that is quite impressive, and to the extent that she is willing to show anyone who comes over to our home how she is capable of changing it to "orange" which happens to be her favorite color. It is actually extraordinary how well she is able to do this.

The other day, it was on green, which is the color it tends to rest at when I'm around it. My daughter was trying make it change to orange, and found it would move from green to almost yellow, but then would pull back to green. She told me to leave the room because she believed that my energy was interfering with it. So, I stopped doing the dishes, and walked into the living room around the corner. Within only a few seconds of doing so, she cried out, "I changed it to orange!" Sure enough, as I rounded the corner, there it was. Somehow she was right. She became successful after I left the room.

I leave the *Mindlamp* on all the time, twenty-four hours a day, seven days a week. I usually have it set on the color-to-color setting, although I have experimented significantly now on both settings for four years now. If I were to choose one machine to publicly endorse out of every one mentioned in this entire book, it would be the *Mindlamp*. When you're not interacting with it, it just sits around and looks beautiful. Once you realize that it seems to use color to interact with you, I believe that is when you start to really interact with it. It is oddly "alive" in the way it reacts and responds to the environment. Like a glowing mechanical sea anemone, it appears to communicate with its environmental surroundings by using a brilliant spectrum of both color and intensity.

MINDLAMP EXPERIMENTS

One thing about the Mindlamp is that they are a bit high in price, but not unreasonable, in my opinion, especially for what you are getting. The following consists of my personal notes of playful do-it-yourself experiments one can try with the *Mindlamp's* color-to-color setting:

1) The easiest thing to try to do to interact with the *Mindlamp* is get it to change color. By just playing around with a few different ways of getting yourself into different modes of thinking, one is able to eventually find a way that seems to change the color that the lamp is currently on within a few seconds to about 60 seconds of focused concentration.

2) Once you feel fairly confident at being able to change the color of the *Mindlamp*, the next step, would be to see if you can not only make it change color, but to also make it change to the precise color that your intention directs it to (for instance, if the lamp is orange, and on the color-to-color setting, your goal might be to change the color to red instead of changing it to yellow).

3) You can also try to get it to move through the colors in a continuous pace until it changes to the color that you want it to be. Try then to change the "frequency or wave" or whatever you believe you did to make it change colors, so that it stops on the color you selected, instead of moving past your selection. Sometimes, if I give a mental "push" at the color that my *Mindlamp* is on, I will find that it will cycle through the color wheel in a direction similar to that of a roulette wheel, so it is possible to, at times, choose a color to land on the other side of the color spectrum. For instance, if it is on Blue, I may aim for it to turn Pink, and see if the "mental push" that I give brings the lamp to land on that color. This allows me to feel as if I am also practicing my

ability to stop the continuing movement of the colors as it moves through its cycle. To me, it's a little like steering a boat, in that you will want to try to anticipate sooner to exert your "counter-energy" before it moves past the color that you want it to stop at. I tend to start exerting my counter-energy as soon as I see it changing into the color of my choice. Truthfully, however, that may not even be it. It's not very easy to know exactly what controls it, but it is possible to interact with it, in a seemingly meaningful way.

4) Another game is to test how long you can continuously and consciously intend for the lamp to remain on the same color that it is on. Should you see it just barely start to shift out of your chosen color, try to shift your concentration, and make it move back to the color you wanted it to stay on. Time yourself. On a good day, I can keep it on the same color for up to 8 to minutes, when I am alone with it.

5) Take note of other people, plants and animals around it, and the colors that it appears to choose for them. Take note of how it also behaves during electrical storms and unusual weather conditions.

6) Take note of how it behaves around larger groups of people. Note the difference between how it behaves when the energy of a group is dispersed, as opposed to when it is focused and engaged.

7) Notice if children can interact with it differently than your adult experimenters.

8) Perhaps it is possible to summon up a special mindset or thought pattern that enables one to interact with the *Mindlamp* more easily. Try different thinking patterns by experimenting with it after stretching, yoga, meditation, exercise, breakfast, etc. On those days when you notice that you are feeling stressed out or emotional, consider sending your thoughts as interactions in the direction of your *Mindlamp* just to see what happens. If anything, the soothing color it radiates will help to wind you down.

I have tested the *Mindlamp* in all of the above ways (and some). It can sometimes be temperamental with listening to me, but I have made it run through the above tasks on enough occasions that I am quite convinced that there is something unusual happening. I have the most ease with getting it to change color when I want it to, but I'm not as good at making it move in the direction I desire. I find that whatever natural laws cause it to choose a direction, makes one have to put a stronger focus on breaking the pattern it had already chose to move in (that is, if your desire is to make it take the opposite direction that it originally chooses for itself). As I continued to practice, however, I found that I was able to stabilize it so that it will stay on one color for up to 10 minutes, sometimes longer, and I have discovered I can (on several occasions) encourage it mentally to move back to its present color if I focus my intention on it just as I see it beginning to shift away.

I have also noticed that it tends to stay on one color for longer periods when several people are around it, but can still change color when the entire group directs focused attention at it. Animals seem to be able to affect it as well, and so does unusual weather. There are plants in the room that we have our lamp in, but I mostly pay attention to how it acts around our animals, our interactions, and our environment. During Hurricane Sandy, I was watching it and it was racing from one color to another. I had saved a praying mantis from being outside and had it in a jar right next to the *Mindlamp*. To this day I am not sure if the spastic color changing of the *Mindlamp* was due to an energy field created by the hurricane, or perhaps by the insect's brain pattern reacting to the storm. I took some cell phone video of the constantly changing lamp during the storm, and posted it shortly afterwards on Facebook with praying mantis in the background.

Working with kids through the process is always fun. I have noticed that if you can brief a youngster on how it works, younger kids normally find they can interact with it pretty easily up to a point. Boredom or apathetic thinking is the easiest way to lose interactive connection with the lamp, so it will depend slightly on the youngster you work with. One of my daughter's 9-year old friends was really demonstrating amazing control over it one evening while at a party we were having. It could've been beginners luck, but it was amazing to all of us who were watching. He was playing on the advanced white-to-color setting and managed to get three or four colors to come up by either predicting that they would or just willing them to surface. He was starting to get really good, but then suddenly, it stopped working for him. I find it interesting that keeping up a controlled connection with the lamp does appear to stop at a certain point for some reason. It does appear to be a consistent observation. I'm not sure if it is from losing interest, becoming skeptical, or just not being able to hold the connection easily, based on the very nature of unpredictability. It does seem to be a frequently recurring effect of the anomaly. So in a weird way, at least that too can be predicted...

One day, my friend- Hale Brownlee, who also owns a *Mindlamp,* and I decided to video-chat over Skype so that our respective lamps would be able to be seen in both of our monitors. I remember it being a little frustrating at first, as each of us tried to do what we are normally accustomed to doing, but in front of each other, we had absolutely zero response from either of the lamps. We focused on both the lamps that we owned as well as the lamps that were in our monitors, but nothing seemed to work. Mine remained a faint pink and his, a light blue. However, as we began to lose interest in our being able to demonstrate any control over our *Mindlamps,* both of the lamps suddenly started rapidly shifting colors.

It was odd, because the topic we started to talk about, just as the lamps both began to go wacky, had turned to our mutually bizarre encounters with a psychic woman who we had both met in Colorado on separate occasions. The fact that she claimed to possess enormous psychic ability was only part of her package. She was, at the time, convinced that she was being followed by "Men In Black," did not divulge her last name (or real first name, I am sure), and used a pendulum to answer questions for herself faster than I have seen anyone ever use one. The pendulum that she used, and that she would dangle only about 4 inches under where she held it, would immediately and quickly begin to swing to and fro, as if she knew the answers to the questions she was asking even before using it. She claimed to be able to channel up to fifty or sixty different spirit entities from animals of all types to extraterrestrials in different galaxies. My friend and I felt that there was something that she was tapping into, if not through her own psychosis. It was at that point in our conversation about her that we noticed that both of our Mindlamps started to very rapidly change colors. Is it possible that our suddenly finding a funny story to ignite our conversation with started to cause our respective lamps to behave like this? Could they have possibly even been trying to tell us something about her?

Maybe it was her trying to tell us to leave her alone! Unfortunately, we have not heard from her since.

Perhaps the most unusual thing that my *Mindlamp* seems to do is actually act as a genuine mood lamp. It is for certain the truest mood lamp that anyone could ever own, in that I have come to be quite convinced that it is able to actually tell what mood one is in, among all the other experiments I have tried. I have heard other owners of the lamp give similar testimonials. For instance, my wife's favorite color is purple. I have noticed more often than not, when she is within visible eyesight of the lamp, it tends to be purple. If I am washing the dishes in the kitchen and no one else is in that part of the house with me, the lamp tends to move to my favorite color, green. If my daughter is in the room, drawing on the dining room table (her favorite past-time), I will notice that it tends to be orange, her favorite color. Am I only noticing these correlations when they occur and not noticing them when they are not occurring? If the change of color is only dictated by random signal, how would it know which color is which? Why would it care?

One of the more unusual things tends to happen, usually only at those times when feelings in the room are tense, or someone gets upset or angry. My *Mindlamp* turns *red*. I have no idea if this is true for other *Mindlamp* owners, but it is certainly true for me. Once I realized that this happens, it became a habit of mine to take note of every time the lamp turned red.

As hard to imagine that a lamp would be able to interpret a mood or a person by the color it changes to feels highly unlikely, and yet, this is how it appears to be behaving.   I am only the messenger.

JOHNS HOPKINS APPLIED PHYSICS RESEARCH LABORATORY

For a few years, I had been performing for an annual fundraiser for friends of mine at the Johns Hopkins Applied Physics Research Laboratory Theatre Department. The head of the Theatre Department had his own *Mindlamp* and he decided to include it as part of the décor of the set, to make it look like a "weird science drawing room." Since I would be performing two shows on two consecutive nights there, it became impossible for me to not take a moment of my program to involve the audience with this strange machine, just to see what would happen.

I had to think fast, as I didn't know beforehand that it would end up being there, decorating my stage set. Knowing that I had to focus the audience's interest on the lamp in order to make it work, I suddenly came up with a plan. If I could get the lighting guy to dim the lights so that the only visible light was the *Mindlamp* itself, that would make it easier for the audience (as a single entity) to focus on it. I also decided to incorporate a small child, because I figured that having the audience all focus on one person might help to channel the energy to the one thing that is happening as they observe an unadulterated young mind trying to do something so far-out for the first time.

Midway through my show, I announced that I was going to try something that would demonstrate a true potential for mind over matter. Calling attention to the lamp, I described its background based on the work at Princeton University, and explained briefly the quantum theory regarding the concept of what made the lamp change color and posed the question, "Can anyone do it? Let's find out!"

I instructed the lighting man to lower all the lights and had a young boy who was about 7 years old, wearing a green soccer jersey and shorts, stand up at the back of the theatre. I walked up to the row at the back where he was sitting and from there, I instructed him to walk slowly towards the lamp and then, once he got to the edge of the stage, I told him to acknowledge the lamp and it's color, and then to slowly walk up to the lamp and put his hands near it. Truthfully, I was making the whole thing up on the spot, and really was just hoping that if the boy was in the audience's focus along with the lamp for long enough, that maybe it would change color for him.

The funny thing was, until that point during my show, the audience never saw the lamp change color at all prior to my calling attention to it. It had literally stayed light blue from the moment people started walking through the door, and had acted as if it didn't change color at all. I hadn't realized that was a fact until everyone was suddenly looking a lot more curious after I mentioned how the lamp was able to change to that many colors. When I asked the audience what colors they saw it change from, no one spoke up. Then several people mentioned that it was light blue the entire time since my show began (this would be about midway through an hour-long program). Sigh.

Feeling insecure, I remember wondering if there were just too many minds that could possibly be affecting it simultaneously. Remember what I said earlier about experimenting with seeing how many people around will affect it? Well, one thing I have noticed is that it does appear to change color less frequently when there are many people present. Perhaps with 250 people in my audience that night, it might have somehow gotten jammed? Plus I was working with a *Mindlamp* that I had never worked with before. I had no idea if this mattered in the least or really even what was about to happen. The young boy did as I had instructed, slowly walking down towards the lamp and then to the edge of the stage, where he stopped and waved at the lamp before walking over to it. The entire time the lamp did nothing but sit there as light blue as the sky. Beads of sweat forming on my brow, I asked him to go ahead and try putting his hands around the lamp. As soon as he did this, the lamp quickly turned from blue to green, as if purposely shifting in the direction to match his outfit! The audience looked pretty amazed. I had been convincing enough at explaining that this was not my own lamp but one that belonged to our host. As far as I was concerned, this gave me the perfect excuse to take all the credit.

The truth was, I was not only terrified that nothing was going to happen at all, but rather profoundly startled to see it do pretty much exactly what I had set up to have it do. Perhaps it would have been more impressive had it started to rapidly change color as the boy approached the stage, but the single change of color seemed to elegantly prove the point. The boy looked amazed, and the audience gave him a round of applause. That night, I ended up being just as amazed as everyone else. Maybe my host, the owner of the lamp was equally amazed, but I had more at stake.

At first I thought I had an interesting group experiment with this effect, now that it appeared to be somewhat demonstrable using the *Mindlamp* in front of a larger group. But as in most mentalism effects, the method to create the phenomenon is not exactly the same as the phenomenon. In other words, just because the boy was able to make it change color, doesn't mean that anyone can do it. By specifically using a young boy, from the back of the room to help focus the audience's attention, while getting a little extra time out of the distance the boy would need to walk before reaching the lamp, and combined with the extra time it takes to get the lights to be lowered in order to focus attention also towards the lamp, I was essentially doing everything that I could to tilt the odds into my favor. Therefore, even though the lamp worked in the manner that I hoped it would, I was regardlessly increasing the odds so that there would be a greater possibility that something significant would happen as the boy approached the lamp. Nonetheless, I still impressed myself.

The lamp does take some getting used to in order to understand just how to affect it (or grasp the idea of how it can potentially be affected). One would find it frustrating if they thought that all they would need to do is think of the word "change" to have it change color on command. It is, after all, a little more than just that. After the show, many people (who were all part of the JHUAPL scientific community) were curious to see what would happen if they went up to it and put their own hands around it. No, it was not the heat from the boy's hands that did it, nor was it as easy as they thought to make the lamp do as they wanted. But I hope they didn't completely lose interest. It really doesn't take that long before you start to notice some unusual correlations between your focus and it changing color. I have a suspicion that an understanding between you and the lamp organically forms as you continue to own one. You just eventually figure out how to interact with it more and more, kind of like having an "electronic pet." In fact, the second show I did the following day worked just as successfully and in much the same manner, but with a young girl.

I remember thinking- if this were actually something that we could learn to control, one day we may utilize a part of our brain that can potentially cause things to work just by our thoughts. Within time, a whole new part of our thinking will be revealed. I still feel that this will one day be possible. However, this idea of using our mental energy like a circuit breaker switch (in an "on or off" sort of way) is not something we often think about. I believe this is why people might find it difficult, at first, to understand how we might use our thoughts to affect REG-based mechanisms like the *Mindlamp*. I feel, however, that as time moves us forward in evolution, an understanding of this on/off (1/o) nature could conceivably come about, which will set off an explosion of innovations, and quite probably the next wave of information culture.

OTHER IDEAS

Back in 2010, when Psyleron only had three products that they were just beginning to launch, the REG and Mindlamp were their only two physical products, but they were also just starting to offer an online service called *Sync TXT*. This uses a random text-messaging feature so that you will get random texts in which you can program what you want it to say. I was both enchanted, as well as a little creeped-out by the concept, so up until now, I still have not yet tried it. Basically, you would be sending specific text messages to yourself at random times, as dictated by a master REG. However, because of how quantum entanglement mysteriously connects things, the idea is to see if you notice any of the random messages you "put on rotation" coming back to you at profound or meaningful times.

For instance, you could program a series of messages to be sent to yourself, like "WTF! Caution... Oh my! Dear Lord. LOL!" so that randomly throughout the week, you would be getting those texts to see how meaningfully they correspond to the moment that you are being texted, or the few moments that follow. Can something like that actually work? I believe that at worst, they have created a far superior Magic 8-ball, but at best, they might be onto a wholly new area of discovery: "Mind controlled apparatus" and "quantum reasoning." If it can be figured out that these apparatus are in any way controlled by using emotional energy generated by our mind, then who knows? Maybe we all really do need to get more in touch with our emotions.

DO I BELIEVE?

All right, allow me to try and ground this discussion for a moment, just so you can trust that I am not completely eligible to be taken away and put into a psychiatric ward. These are, but personal, notes as I continue to experiment my way through this adventure quest. I came in to all this with crazy ideas already in my head. However, I can also tell the difference between when I am thinking magically and when I am being rational, at least most of the time. Quite honestly, it really does appear to me as if something strange, and possibly even consistent is happening. Later, I will leave you with some exercises, so you can try some of these ideas yourself, and see if you can witness any of your own results.

Why wouldn't I believe? I am both an artist and an entertainer, so why wouldn't I want everyone to be included when I say that you can manifest your own destiny for good? I believe you can even make completely improbable outcomes manifest just by continuing to practice and observe your awareness and ability to use conscious intention. Whether you use meditation, contemplation, incantation, prayer, song, exercise, breathing or all of the above, do so with a vibrant loving energy, and observe as ordinary events and situations swing to your favor. In the words of John Lennon, "Come together, right now, over me."

Alain Nu, The Man Who Knows™

PART FOUR

MYSTERIOUS FORCES

CHAPTER 16

QI GONG, THE CHAKRAS & THE FISH

I was introduced to the idea of *Chi (or Qi)* when I was very young. My Chinese mother used to try as best as she could, in English, to explain to me that our bodies are made up of these tiny things called cells. Our cells, can multiply, especially in the stages while we are growing up. If we are happy and healthy this *chi* can strengthen our cells. However, our cells can get sick and even die, if we get too stressed, angry or find ourselves getting upset too easily. This was her simplified, Theory of Everything, suggestion that mysteriously good health can be achieved by maintaining a happy and positive disposition whereas the opposite effect can potentially happen with equal but wrongly applied thinking. As I got older, discussions with different people about this would start to sound even more mystical than ever. There were all sorts of things about chi that both seemed to make sense and not make sense at the same time.

When I was 11, my mother took Chinese watercolor lessons from a *Chi Kung master practitioner*. It was difficult to truly connect with him, as he only spoke Mandarin, and I hadn't spoken Chinese since I was a toddler (back when my Mandarin was perfect). From what I could gather at that time, chi had something to do with controlled breathing, meditation, and controlling our heart rate and blood flow.

189

As the New Age was upon us, I remember much being said about how this universal Life Force energy can even be *felt* and is also said to possess incredible *healing* qualities. Could any of that be true? When I was younger, I found all this quite hard to believe.

Later, I realized that there were actually a lot more people than I thought who subscribed to the underlying philosophy of this energy, and I found these people to be pretty genuine and intelligent, yet down-to-earth. From them, I learned that the idea that it could be spelled "Chi Kung," has been modified over the years. The syllable *kung*, or *gong*, means "hard work and labor put forth in the study of." So kung fu, which would be more correctly spelled *gong fu*, is usually translated to mean "hard work and labor put forth towards the study of the martial arts," but this is not entirely correct. Gong fu is essentially hard work and study put towards the mastery of *any art or skill*. Qi gong is essentially, "the study, contemplation and inspiration put towards understanding *qi*, or *energy*," specifically in the sense of the Universal Life Force. Wikipedia mentions that the study of qi gong could go back as far as 7000 years ago, but has at least been around since roughly 400 BCE.

I performed at Caesars Palace between 2000 and 2004, about three times a year, where I would spend about a month to six weeks during each contract, living in Las Vegas. It was there where a very knowledgeable teacher instructed me during classes that I would take at the Shao Lin Temple, located on Spring Mountain Rd, in their three-block "Chinatown." From what I could gather while I was there, qi gong is a combination of controlled breathing, movement, balance and stillness (much of which is influenced by eastern numerology, the study of energy centers in the body, and early traditional martial arts practice). Mantras and visualizations, based on eastern medieval mythology or philosophy, were also incorporated.

What I found interesting was how the importance of every aspect of human awareness, balance, breath, control, exercise, movement, positive intention, energy and healing were all contemplated in one form or another in *every session*. Simply going through the motions of qi gong, even for only 30 minutes per day-- done in the manner I was instructed to practice, (which involved learning the names of each posture and movements, the corresponding visualizations and precise number of breaths), one cannot help but have all of that automatically absorbed into one's psyche. By the end of each session, one felt energized, fully aware, and ready to move effortlessly through life. Qi gong everyday will provide you with an extraordinarily healthy and meditative low-impact exercise program.

What is it about the *mysterious healing properties* of this qi energy we are said to possess within us? For centuries, eastern medicine has cultivated an entire study and philosophy of our anatomy based on how it uses and refines its internal energy by understanding ways of directing the flow of one's qi, or *universal life force*. Practitioners in yoga, tai chi, acupuncture, acupressure, herbal remedies, martial arts, and meditation all study the properties of raising, lowering and directing energies that are visualized to be mysteriously guided by us within ourselves. Of course, there are many ways of motivating ourselves to feel better... The Old English phrase, *"It's time to gird up your loins and sally forth!"* comes to mind.

The reason why the idea of simply "pushing ahead" or "plowing through" is not the same thing as qi gong is because, although the average human being's strength of will alone can be surprisingly powerful just by itself, the underlying philosophy of "gong" is that *betterment* comes in the form of an increased spectrum of function, control and overall ability. Emphasis can be put on concentrated study and contemplation of any subject, whether it be energy, the martial arts, calligraphy, or cooking. Literally, anything can be studied to the point of esteemed mastery- even breathing- and, in fact, that would be considered an important aspect of qi gong.

With regards to our minds, on a basic level, we generally know when we have had too much or too little nourishment or sleep. Some of us have very regimented ways of living around our meals and our sleep needs, others are more free form, and still others, who are more adventurous, will try different things. Gong reminds us that there is no single correct way between methods of which to master. Gong also reminds us that there can be mastery within any method if one resonates with and strives towards such mastery. As we learn more to appreciate the exploration of mastering our thoughts, we might also begin to appreciate the importance of continued contemplation and continued mastery.

Remember how by just creating a ritual that is followed, one will begin to manifest immediate changes in one's life? Partially from personal perception and expectation, but also in quite mysterious ways, one can put an end to life-long habits, reinvent oneself completely, adopt a desired skill or a mindset that you never thought achievable and allegedly can even activate healing processes within yourself as well as in others. All of this is gong fu.

This simply reignites all the questions that have always made me wonder:

1) Early eastern mysticism is filled with traditional rituals, mantras and prayers. Could it really be possible to direct and refine intentional energies, through these acts of a traditional ritual, mantra or prayer? Rational science would not call this plausible, and yet, it is a tradition that is still alive today, and it is as old as the earliest documents of man.

2) If it were possible, how would we best direct such intentions? Would there somewhere be (within one of the ancient texts) a list, which might have a spectrum to choose from our own wellness to the well being of our family and community network, of what priorities would be best to focus on?

3) Are there deeper secrets to possessing or magnifying this mysterious wisdom that generates from these ancient "energy centers" within us in useful or other creatively applicable ways?

There are, indeed, many, many levels of ancient secrets, mysterious teachings and profound wisdoms that come from the Far East. Taking on the subject of ancient Chinese mysticism, just by itself would need to include the histories of Buddha, Confucius, Lao Tse, as well as understanding the I-Ching, Oracle Bones, and ancient Chinese mythology. It could potentially offer you more than enough for a lifetime's worth of study and experimentation, if one were to try to get to its deeper meanings and genuine applications.

YOU ARE WHAT YOU GENERATE

What is known as *Qi* in China is known as *Ki* in Japan, *Ashe* in Africa, and *Mana* on the Hawaiian Islands. In ancient Egypt, it was known as *Ka*. In ancient Greece, it was known as *Pneuma*. In India, it is known as either Prana or Shakti. It is interesting how such a concept was spread so worldwide since the beginning of man. Everywhere, no matter what the name, this is the same Universal Life Force energy that is known throughout most every culture to both "animate" as well as "manifest" any situation and every physical form that we can sensorily experience in our reality.

In Chinese culture, there are known to be three "energy furnaces" within the body, at three different areas of the spine, known as *dantians*. The lower dantian is positioned near the base of one's spine, centered in the lower abdominal region. The middle dantian is located within the heart. The upper dantian is positioned within the brain between the eyes and the top of one's spine. More commonly, however, energy centers said to be found within the body are known as an ancient knowledge from India called the *chakras*. To revitalize yourself internally, by forming energy that you can direct using your hands, try the following.

ENERGY AWARENESS EXERCISE

We are all energetic beings. We can feel energy and refine the energy we have within us, and we can even offer energy to others as well. Let us now try to feel it. The first thing that we must do is refine that energy within us. Try this simple exercise to get a sense of how one might actually *feel* this energy.

1) Close your eyes, so that they are almost closed but you can see some light. Take a few slow deep breaths, and allow yourself to feel centered. Make sure that both your feet are flat on the floor, and your head is aligned with your spine perpendicular to the floor.

2) Hold your hands stretched out in front of you and shake them as if they are wet, and you are flicking water off of them. Now put your hands together and rub them palm to palm for about 3 to 5 seconds.

3) With both right and left fingers aligned, very slowly separate your hands about an inch apart. You will feel a warm energy between your palms and possibly connecting your fingers. Visualize this energy to be a "Golden Healing Ball of Light."

193

4) Move your hands a little further apart and you will actually feel very subtly that this ball of energy can slowly be made to grow between your hands. You can also feel it pushing your hands apart as you expand that energy.

5) Now, imagine yourself pushing this energy back into a more condensed ball, feeling that energy beginning to feel more solid as you slowly bring your hands together. As the ball ever so slowly gets smaller, visualize the energy from the ball being slowly absorbed by your hands, the energy travelling up through your arms and into your chest as you take a nice deep breath. Continue to hold this condensed ball as if you are holding onto a bright star.

6) Keeping your hands extended out in front of you, touch the tips of your fingers together, but now move your wrists away from each other as you feel the ball immediately take the shape of the entire circle that is now formed by your arms, like you are hugging the trunk of a large tree.

7) As you take a final big deep breath, bring your two hands towards your heart, while imagining yourself absorbing all the energy into yourself. Once your lungs are filled with oxygen, exhale hard, stretching your arms up and out, while imagining this energy flowing into all parts of your body and mind, with any excess resonating outwards as positive energy being given back to the universe.

8) Slowly bring your hands down and towards yourself, feeling the remaining energy that continues to pulse through your palms, and with your left hand, place it over your heart, slightly above the center of your chest, while your right palm is placed over the center of the abdomen. Close your eyes and take a few deep breaths as you feel the strength of the healing sensation begin to manifest within you.

This visualization should help you refine and revitalize your inner energies and motivation. It is interesting to me how it demonstrates the uncanny idea of how it can be refined and transferred using your hands.

ENERGETIC ENLIGHTENMENT

In most Vedic/Hindu systems, there is mention of seven significant chakras. In today's urban society, one will tend to hear the term "chakras" bandied about particularly by yoga practitioners, as well as people who practice meditation. Is there any scientific evidence of chakras at all? Is there a special X-ray, sonogram, or MRI device that can measure the flow of prana or qi energy along one's spinal column? Could it be a "secret principle" taught only to natropaths, acupuncturists, hypnotherapists and yoga instructors at their special training seminars and retreats?

Originally introduced to western culture in the book, *The Serpent's Power*, translated by the Englishman, Arthur Avalon, the chakras were a part of the *Vedas*, a written text from India that is said to have originated at sometime between 2000 to 6000 BC. Then, the texts known as the *Sat-Cakra-Nirupana*, written by an Indian pundit in 1577, and the *Padaka-Pancaka* that was written in the 10th century, contains more specific descriptions of the chakras. The *Gorakshashatakam*, which was also written in the 10th century, gave instructions on how one can meditate on the chakras. The above texts form the primary basis for the understanding of chakra theory and Kundalini yoga (which visualizes a mythical serpent, representing the flow of energy that travels slowly through the chakras) in the present time.

For mastery, the chakras are used to attain enlightenment. This is done through meditation and raising one's energy levels so that one's consciousness is also lifted. In yoga, meditation, qi gong, and hypnotherapy practice (among others), the visualization of such spinal energy meridians has been used as an effective tool for relaxation, but also for summoning up energy for motivation, self-empowerment, and to stimulate naturopathic healing and wellness. Mindfulness, which is a form of hypnotherapy that tends to draw upon the chakras for mental visualization, is currently used to treat obsessive-compulsive disorder (OCD), depression, anxiety, and other similarly related mental behaviors and conditions.

The chakras are energy points that are said to reside at seven (and in some systems, more) specific points from the crown of the head and continuing on down a central channel (with two, twisting, side-channels of energy) to the base of the spine. They are generally visualized as energy meridians where the two side channels twist around the central channel, and where it is said that energy can be refined through one's inner visualization. This is said to vitalize and adjust the mind-and-body's emotional, spiritual and physical balance.

THE SEVEN BASIC CHAKRAS

Imagine yourself, in meditation, sitting in a cross-legged Lotus position. The Muladhara Chakra resides at the base of the spine, and is considered the "root chakra." From there, the chakras are found at ascending positions along the spine to the top of the head (the Crown Chakra). Each chakra is associated with a certain color and other characteristics, which are said to aid in one's meditation and guide one towards personal enlightenment. The basic meditation happens by merging one's visualization with one's breathing, and then to visualize a "Kundalini" (serpent) energy that rests coiled up at the root chakra (tail bone), to gently awaken and be slowly guided through each chakra until it reaches the top (Crown or Shasrara Chakra). As this serpent energy slowly ascends, the knowledge that is associated to each chakra is said to connect you to the universal life force. This ascension is said to guide one to the experience of enlightenment, while simultaneously clearing your energy channels as you contemplate the depth of each chakra and its relationship to you.

Regardless of what one believes, knowledge of the chakras provides us with possibly the oldest energy wisdom that is still practiced today. Meditating on them offers an effortless way to focus on control over one's self through one's energy. Fulfillment is gained as other potential uses of this energy is applied, practiced, and understood. For now, allow me to introduce you to each of the seven basic chakras along with aspects of them which I believe are worth meditating on.

1) **Muladhara** (Root Chakra): Generally associated with the color Red, the geometry of a Square, the element of Earth, but also the fire signs of Aries, Leo and Sagittarius. It is also associated with the sense of smell, and is said to represent the nose, the teeth and the bones, kidneys, the immune system, adrenal glands, bladder, the prostate gland (in men) as well as the legs, feet and toes. Mostly, the organs and anatomy based in, and lower, than the tailbone. This Chakra

is at the base of the spine and tailbone, but while sitting in lotus position, also rests close to the legs and souls of the feet (the roots). It is also seen as the resting place of the serpent Kundalini who is visualized as laying coiled up and dormant, but can be awakened as breath, attention and energy is focused on it. The Muladhara Chakra recognizes our physical existence, the elimination of our insecurities, and the development of self-confidence to learn new things. It is said that feelings of insecurity come from an underactive Root Chakra, whereas arrogance or greed may be the result of an overactive Root Chakra. It is visualized that the serpent Kundalini can be slowly made to travel up, from its resting place at the Muladhara, through the energy centers of all the major Chakras, and finally coil itself to rest at the Crown Shasrara Chakra. It is during this state that one reaches true and complete enlightenment.

2) **Svadhishthana** (located two finger widths below one's navel): Usually representing the color Orange, the symbol of a Crescent, the element of Water, and the astrological water characteristics of Pisces, Cancer, and Scorpio. It is linked to the sense of taste and appetite. Focusing attention to this Chakra is said to bring energetic healing to the spleen, reproductive system, gonads, and lumbar plexus. It is the Chakra that connects us to others through feeling, desire and sensation. Meditating on the Svahdishthana Chakra puts attention on flow and grace, a feeling of being 'at one' with one's sexuality, and helps to develop a deeper understanding to accept both inner and outer changes and transformations.

3) **Manipura** (Solar Plexus): Known as the Navel Chakra, it is actually located about two or three finger-widths above one's navel at the *solar plexus*. Associated with the color Yellow, the sense of Sight, the geometry of a Triangle, the element of Fire, and the astrological earth signs of Taurus, Virgo, and Capricorn. It is said to influence the stomach, liver, digestion system, pancreas, and skin. Known also as the "Power Chakra," this is understood to govern our personal will as well as our metabolism. Meditating on the Manipura Chakra focuses our energy, effectiveness, spontaneity and a non-dominating power. There have been many claims of receiving clairvoyant messages while meditating on guiding the

Kundalini through Manipura.

4) **Anahata** (Heart Chakra): Associated with the color Green, the sense of Touch, the geometry pattern of a Six Pointed Star (two interlocking triangles with one inverted), the element of Air, and the astrological air signs of Aquarius, Gemini, and Libra, it is said to affect the heart, lungs, thymus, blood pressure, breathing and the immune system. Meditating on guiding the Kundalini through the Anahata Chakra puts focus on developing compassion and empathy for others. It also is said to bring balance and harmony to the opposite dualities that exist within one's mind. Feelings of anger, jealousy, impatience, laziness and other negative conditions are reconciled by understanding the nature of their duality to achieve an improved state of conscious balance. Unconditionally offering love and respect, a calming influence on others and having a deep sense of peace and centeredness, are qualities that are manifested by accepting the gifts of the Anahata.

5) **Vishunddha** (Throat Chakra): Located at the base of the throat, this Chakra is associated with the color Blue, the sense of Hearing, the geometry of a Circle, the element of Ether and the higher expressions of all astrological signs. It is said to influence the thyroid, neck, and ears, as well as the respiratory system. The cynicism that may come from an overly analytical or material mind may be balanced with one's more intuitive and creative side by focusing on this Chakra. The Vishunddha Chakra most importantly represents the power of one's voice, especially through creativity and intuition. The evolution of mankind with all of its civilizations could not have been so great, had it not been for our ability to communicate from this higher place, and ultimately raise our own intellectual vibration through our art, our culture and our creations. This is our voice. From this state of consciousness, we may find the answers and solutions to our most complex problems.

6) **Ajna** (Forehead Chakra): Also known as the "third eye" and positioned at the center of the forehead, this Chakra represents the senses that are extrasensory, telepathic, precognitive, and clairvoyant. Telepathy suggests the power

to tune-into, as well as send, thoughts to others. Precognition is the potential to determine something before it happens without physical clues. Clairvoyance allegedly picks up on the appearance of an unknown energy or object and/or its location in time and space. Ajna is associated with the color Indigo (deep blue), the geometry of a Pyramid, the element of Thought (or Awareness) and, similar to Vishunddha, the higher expressions of all astrological signs. Meditating on the Ajna Chakra is said to relax the forehead, temples, pituitary gland and the carotid plexus. As we do, we begin to recognize the deepest levels of our subconscious and even unconscious thoughts while working on them from within. The most profound questions may be answered as we contemplate them at this energy level and state of consciousness. The feeling that one may experience in this state is that of absolute bliss and complete detachment from ego as we relinquish to a more *embedded intuitive knowledge* of ourselves.

7) **Shasrara** (Crown Chakra): Associated with the color Violet, the sense of Knowing and Oneness, the geometry of a thousand-petaled Lotus inverted onto one's head, the element of Light, and physiologically affecting the head, hair, pineal gland and central nervous system, it is not, however, represented by any astrological sign. This marks the final stage of the Kundalini, when it reaches the very top of the head and coils up to rest in this highest state of consciousness. This is the place of complete enlightenment. An extended moment of complete clarity will be reached in this state of mind.

Many believe that meditating on the path of Kundalini can bring one a newfound awareness of all things. Some have claimed seemingly supernatural powers to command nature, control one's destiny, and even leave one's own body. The Hindu sage practitioners consider all of these "vritti," Vritti is essentially anything that represents a conscious distraction from the path to achieving *true enlightenment*, for as one becomes enlightened, all else becomes quite unimportant. As such, very little is actually known or been scientifically documented about the phantom properties of *vritti*. Exploring a path towards enlightenment, on the other hand, is an awesome experience and well worth it. I am positive that focusing on the

Chakras will lead you towards unique, gratifying and, in many ways, supernaturally enlightened feelings.

May the furnaces of all your energy centers burn brightly...

LOVE: THE ULTIMATE ENERGY

It appears, even from understanding the teachings of such ancient texts as the *Yoga Sutras of Patanjali*, that the best way to connect ourselves with our energy levels is to practice directing them through our breathing by using our visualized thoughts to magnify the spirit of joy and love. This would be distilling it down to its truest level.

1) Breath is what nourishes our blood, and keeps our brain, as well as all of our organs, in syncopation and harmony. Breathing is perhaps the most basic and yet most important life-giving activity.

2) Our Mind has limitless creativity, reception and processing capabilities, even as we know it. Its ability to store untold amounts of data and then figure out useful or creative ways of applying such information might be infinite. Its expression towards visualization and willful intent potential (for good or for bad) works at perhaps the highest level when compared to any other animal on Earth.

3) Our ability to feel compassion for our human race, our planet, and all living creatures, along with our ability to recognize and create beauty, joy, and love *through art*, could be seen as an energy that represents the infinite Universal Life Force. Or it might just only be a fingerprint of its existence. It certainly may be such an integral part of it, that if it is not being generated in a way that keeps the Earth stable, ongoing focus on negative energy will continue to damage our collective reality even further than it already has. More people, communities and nations must recognize the growing importance of "planetary sanity" so that we may continue reconstructing a stronger and healthier eco-biosphere.

TRADITIONAL FOLK RITUAL WORKS IN 21ST CENTURY

Christmas Eve, 2002, my then eighteen year old cousin, Diana, was driving her Chevy Blazer to spend Christmas Eve with her parents (my uncle and aunt) and the rest of her brothers and sisters and their families. While on the Florida Turnpike, she was run off the road by another driver and ended up in a high-speed, high-impact car crash. Her Chevy Blazer rolled over sideways into a ditch, before crashing and immediately burst into flames. Miraculously, and for no reason that anyone could solidly piece together, she was somehow thrown outside of the vehicle before it burst into flames. By the time the ambulance came and the paramedics saw what had happened, they were in the process of pronouncing her dead, when a witness who saw the accident, suddenly saw her take the slightest breath. She was alive, but barely, as she was in a coma.

There is a lot of uncertainty that takes place around a person who is in a coma. No one is ever sure just when they will wake up, or even if they will wake up. There is simply a lot of time spent looking at a person lying motionless on a bed while surveying their blood pressure, heart rate, brain waves and breathing patterns. The days of watching over her turned into a week, with no real changes. By the 10th day, it wasn't looking good. People can be in comas for months to years.

As a sudden last resort, my aunt started to unquestioningly perform an ancient Chinese folk ritual called *feng sheng*. My aunt and uncle are devout Chinese Buddhists in Orlando, and she and my uncle have given unconditional support to the local Buddhist temple there. This sudden act of desperation for her youngest daughter through her devout faith caused others within the community to also act on their own, in similar such acts. Much like in sacred magical rituals, the act of sacrifice is sometimes used to establish karmic balance. In this case, however, as opposed to making a sacrifice by taking away someone's life, feng sheng is the ritual act of *saving a life in exchange for a wish*. It is the poetic act of saving one life in exchange for another, despite its irrational-sounding outlandishness.

Feng sheng (as practiced by my Aunt):

1) Go to your local fish market or pet shop.

2) Purchase as many live fish as you can. (Do not kill)

3) Quickly bring them to a tranquil place of their natural habitat.

4) During this time, consciously connect hopeful and positive vibrations with the fish.

5) Set them free into their natural habitat, and then take some time to clear your mind.

6) Meditate on your wish while in the act of freeing the fish from quite certain death.

Feng sheng could be one of the oldest and most basic rituals of applying the ancient principle of *sympathetic magical thinking*. This can be seen as being made up of two basic laws: The *law of contagion* and the *law of similarity*. The *law of contagion* merely suggests that once two people have met or an object is interacted with, a mysterious link will persist between these things. The act of *psychometry* is the alleged ability to sense characteristics of energy (human or otherwise), that are either possessions which people have owned or have worn for a long time, or it may even be something that they just recently touched or came in contact with. Psychics who offer their help to the police in order to gain an intuitive direction for hard-to-crack cases and violent crimes most commonly use this alleged ability.

The *law of similarity* is the law that pays attention to the affectations of "like causes like," or "appearance equals reality." The law of similarity is the law that recognizes that there may be a mysterious connection between situations, directed thoughts, and their outcomes when focused applied symbolism is used. The way to explore such a ritual is to make careful personal observations of things that resemble one another, even on a superficial level. With faithful belief and focus, it is theorized that the ritual activates the transformation or change within one's consciousness in order to actualize it upon a physical body.

The most basic understanding of feng sheng is that the act of freeing the life of animals or fish that are destined for death makes it more reasonable for one to request that Buddha negotiate with the divine cosmic intelligences for consideration to grant one's wish. The usual custom is to go to the market with a bucket, so that an easy purchase of the fish can be made while keeping them alive. This was, in fact, what my aunt did. She really meant business. Members of the Buddhist community who wanted to participate, but who did not want to spend the exorbitant cost for market fish, simply went to the local pet store and purchased a dollar's worth of feeder goldfish. The term "feeder fish" implies that the fish are destined to become food for pet frogs, snakes and larger carnivorous fish. Since, technically, to many Buddhists, no single life is worth more or less than the next, feeder goldfish may be the most affordable option, should you ever decide to try this yourself.

For those who see themselves as skeptics, a natural first-reaction to hearing such a theory would be one of extreme dubiousness. However, when the person is someone you know, and she has been in a coma for over ten days, suddenly the act of doing *something*, anything at all, feels better than nothing. I remember back then, hearing about my aunt and her valiant trips to the market, only to release these fish into their nearby lake. I remember thinking how absurd it would seem to any rational person if they were to know that the decline of available fish at nearby Orlando markets and pet stores had something to do with an ancient Chinese folk ritual of freeing them into nearby lakes and ponds. Only a day or two later, my cousin miraculously awoke! She had been in a coma for fourteen days.

Of course, there are many things that would contribute to her ultimately coming out of her coma, including her own courage, strength, and desire to live. The most rational way to think would be to believe that the act of feng sheng would have hardly any relationship to my cousin's regaining of consciousness. Many of the goldfish may have even been eaten by larger fish just after freeing them or died suffering from the harsh adjustment to the new water they were suddenly put in. On one hand, it would seem to be a big waste of time and money for anyone to contribute to such a superstitious belief. The fact that any positive change happened just after the ritual of feng sheng, would be considered a complete coincidence, at best.

True, it could have just been good timing. Two weeks, however, is a long time to be in a coma. I don't even want to wonder if she might have been stuck in the coma for longer, had there not been as much focus, concentration, and prayer towards her strong recovery. Incidentally, my cousin did have a truly remarkable recovery. She is married now, has a beautiful family with two kids and still lives in the Orlando area.

Fish, particularly those found in the carp family, in Chinese culture, have always been seen as an important symbol. They have been thought to be transformations of dragons. The Asian carp, that are known to leap out of the water, have been thought of as "wishing to transform into dragons that fly into the sky." There is a Chinese story of an account at Longmen Falls on the Yellow River at an actual place known as, "Dragon Gate." As the story goes, there is an annual competition held for all the carp to try to jump the falls. The carp that were able to successfully leap over the falls were seen to transform instantly into dragons that would immediately take to the sky.

Also, when the Chinese accent on the pronunciation of the word "fish" (pronounced, yu), is said slightly differently, the same word also means "abundance." There are theories that since the words are homophonically sympathetic, that perhaps, so are their meanings.

Retrospectively, my family members, with the exception of my aunt, did not take the act of feng sheng very seriously, although I have not spoken directly to my aunt about it (my Chinese is about as articulate as her English is). Regardless, I am forever impressed by what an interesting, creative and oddly humane way this was for dealing with the stress of having no other options. It is strange, mysterious and beautiful, no matter, and those are three of my favorite things.

FREE FLY

For the past year and a half, I have created a similar little "ritual game." I began to meditate on the healing and well being of certain people I know each time I free an insect from my home or studio. According to Tibetan philosophy, *no single life is greater than the next*, so if I helped to set free any moth, bee, wasp, or fly that gets trapped in my home, in honor for those who I know, who need assistance, I wondered if I could spiritually hold off, for any length of time, what they may sometimes believe is the inevitable?

The truth is that our general household rule has always been to not kill, and instead free unwanted insects that we find in the house. The best part was that the ritual of remembering from a list of names that flash through my mind, each time I release an insect, added nothing but the idea to an already existing habit. Incidentally, none of those people know that I have been doing this at all, least of which, for them. It would not matter, even if they did. Because it's just a silly game I play with only winners (the insects). So far, the experiment has been going well, however, and this has made me feel nothing but grateful.

I will, however, smack a mosquito dead on my arm in less than a heartbeat, if I am able to.

Alain Nu, The Man Who Knows™

CHAPTER **17**

TO DIVINE, DIVIDE & DECIDE

FUTURE BY FIRE

C hina's earliest-known significant body of writings can be seen to contain the most important historical data of its time-period. Because of the discovery of such documentation, there is now complete confirmation of an entire royal genealogy, as well as thousands of dates and concerns regarding most all of the important battles and significant moments that mark other turning points during the Shang Dynasty Period, approximately 4th millennium BCE, in the middle of the Bronze Age. Many scholars even doubted that the Shang Dynasty existed until there was evidence marked by these writings. It must have, at first, seemed odd, to find out that these notations (which were found specifically marked, either on tortoise plastrons and carapace, or on the scapulae bones of a water buffalo), were mainly used during the Shang Dynasty period for divination rituals, that involved what is known as *pyromancy*. Pyromancy is a truly strange Homo Sapien practice, found to be used all over the world during ancient times, and is considered one of the earliest known divination techniques, which used an oracular process of interpretation.

Pyromancy is a divination technique that involves the interpretation of cracked lines that form on animal bones or turtle shells, when put over fire and heated until expansion causes it to crack. Once the ritual was complete, instructions were carried out and/or major decisions were made. It was always the Shang Dynasty custom to make written record (on the shell itself), of the advice that was divined, the people present, the date and the results of the divination. Thousands of these oracle bones, which have been excavated and found to be from this time period, helped to piece together the lost history of the Shang Dynasty.

It seems that both the *soothsayer and their specific* interpretations of pyromancy during the Shang dynasty, was eventually replaced by the older trigram system (which was said to have been originated by Fu Xi), a few thousand years *before* the Shang dynasty's popularity of oracle bone divinations. It wasn't until after King Wen, in the following Zhou Dynasty, created the more complex interpretation using the 64 gua that the *I Ching* began to really take shape. If Fu Xi was only a made-up legend, then where could the first 8 trigrams come from? It isn't surprising to find speculation to the legend of Fu Xi's authorship of the eight original I Ching trigrams. Could King Wen have *made it all up* and then decided to give partial credit to Fu Xi to give it more historical importance to the people of his time? Even that notion seems disputable. The *I Ching* continues to be studied, not just as a divination system, but also as a system of profound philosophical wisdom that is embraced by an amazing mathematical relationship.

Moving back to the subject of pyromancy, it was well appreciated that a record of the prediction results were inscribed onto the bones, after each event as well, so we have historical record of not only the divine decision of the paths chosen, but also the outcomes of each decision. Through the pyromantic documenting system, however, they were also successful enough that they were able to piece together practically the entire history of the Shang dynasty by reading literally thousands of these divinations. If such a divination process was closer to the Law of Averages or didn't work most of the time, one probably wouldn't have found so many of these oracle bones lying around all over the place. It seems that during this time, we also discover that there is some experimentation with more than one path that might lead us to the same cosmic place.

FOUR FATHERS OF THE I CHING

"In the beginning there was as yet no moral or social order. Men knew their mothers only, not their fathers. When hungry, they searched for food; when satisfied, they threw away the remnants. They devoured their food hide and hair, drank the blood, and clad themselves in skins and rushes. Then came Fu Xi and looked upward and contemplated the images in the heavens, and looked downward and contemplated the occurrences on earth. He united man and wife, regulated the five stages of change, and laid down the laws of

humanity. He devised the eight trigrams, in order to gain mastery over the world." Ban Gu, *Baihu tongyi,* 56 CE.

Not too far upstream from Dragon Gate, the legendary cultural hero, Fu Xi, was born in a province off the lower middle area on the Yellow River. Fu Xi is said to have lived more than 2000 years before Confucius, around 2800 to 2700 BCE. He is credited, by Chinese legends and folktales, for repopulating humanity after a huge flood killed everyone. He was known as the inventor of writing, cooking, and hunting. After becoming inspired by watching a spider catch a fly in its web, it is said, he also became the inventor of fishing by using a net. Fu Xi, his sister Nuwa, and Shennong, who was said to have invented agriculture, were considered in many Chinese cultures as *The Three Sovereigns.* Fu Xi is depicted by most as a demigod who ruled peacefully among men, and who lived to be a ripe 197 years old before he died.

Fu Xi was also the man credited to be the author of what is known as the *I-Ching.* In many ways, considered as holy to the Chinese as the western Bible, if the authorship is truly ascribed to Fu Xi, then this takes the *I-Ching* as far back as 5000 years into history, making it certainly one of the oldest and most complete divination systems (not to mention text) still being read and practiced today.

Taoist Master, Alfred Huang, author and historian of *The Complete I Ching* (1999), makes an important mention, that although the *I Ching* credits Fu Xi as its original author, the complete history was most likely that Fu Xi created the first eight primary gua (sequence made in three lines). King Wen, of the Zhou dynasty was the one who arranged the sixty-four gua and wrote what are known as the *Decisions of the Gua.* This work was passed down to his son, the Duke of Zhou, who composed what are now known as the *Yao Texts.* Confucius apparently then wrote his own "commentaries," known as *The Ten Wings.* It wasn't until after Confucius wrote *The Ten Wings* commentaries did the systems of wisdoms become known as the *I Ching.* Thus, four legendary men, all of who added their own knowledge and wisdom to complete the system, actually wrote the I Ching.

Huang puts particular importance in what he calls the *Tao of I.* Since I have read this in his book years ago, I have not heard this principle spoken about, not even online, and yet it continues to resonate within me. It is one of the most eloquent ways of expressing the *I Ching*. I am including this entry of his here, as I strongly believe one can gain much from understanding this, whether they are interested in the *I Ching*, or not. I hope this also ignites an inspiration for those interested in learning more to explore the wisdoms of this most revered ancient knowledge. For now:

"Many Westerners know the I Ching, but they do not know the 'Tao of I.' Of the numerous treasures in the I Ching, I value the Tao of I the most. The main theme of the I Ching is that everything is in a process of continuous change, rising and falling in a progressive evolutionary advancement. Although this is the main theme of the I Ching, it is never mentioned in the text. It is revealed only between the lines, and in particular is embodied in the succession of the names of the gua and the sequences and structures of the gua and the yao (lines). The 'Tao of I' discloses that when situations proceed beyond their extremes, they alternate to their opposites. It is a reminder to accept necessary change and be ready to transform, warning that one should adjust one's efforts according to changes in time and situation. The Tao of I also says: In favorable time and situation, never neglect the unfavorable potential. In favorable time and situation, never act abruptly and blindly. And in adverse circumstances, never become depressed and despair." Taoist Master, Alfred Huang, *The Complete I Ching, The Definitive Translation, Inner Traditions* (1999)

Coming to an understanding with the *I-Ching* is best done as a longtime study. Once you get past learning the meanings of the 64 hexagrams and their interpretations, along with the Yao Texts and Confucius's commentaries, you will be quite old and wise whether you understood any of it, or not. The most important thing to understand about the *I Ching* is that it is a divination system built upon the nature of duality.

So divining is simply dividing and then deciding. It's the "getting it right" that is the tricky part.

THE MYSTERIOUS POWER OF YIN & YANG

As mentioned by Huang in the last section, all things, energy and otherwise are in a constant state of change, which are continuously in a cycle of interacting with both positive and negative elements. He also mentions how the Tao of I teaches that *"when situations move beyond their extremes, they alternate to their opposites."* It is good to think about this as we go into a brief history.

It was just after the time of Confucius (476-221 BC), and during the era of the *Contention of a Hundred Schools of Thought*, that Chinese scholar, Zhou Yan, became the founder of *The School of Naturalists* (also known as *The School of Yin Yang*).

His theory was that the concept of Yin and Yang exists in all things. Some more subtle than others, in which deep understanding can be gained. Some more obvious (i.e.: day and night), which is only but the constant reminder of its existence. He is credited for being the one who first synthesized the concepts of Yin and Yang with the Chinese Five Elements (Wood, Water, Fire, Metal, Earth). Zhou Yan's model is quite impressive, actually, as it is represented in diagram by a five-pointed star with a circle drawn around it. It becomes clear that the dualities are springing out of each point of the star in two directions, each of which interact with only two other specific points in the star. These are seen as dualities regarding "change" or "overcoming." The circle, which each of the five points touch, represents the continual cycle of dualities between "generation" and "creation." Through the sacred geometry of the Circle-Pentagram, each distinct point is seen as significantly connected to each of the other four points. Reflecting on this symbol can give one a very thorough understanding of the Yin and Yang with its relationship to the five stages of change.

Most people, however, recognize the Yin and Yang as a less intimidating symbol, known as a *Taijitu*. This is a circle, divided by an S curve that runs evenly through its middle that form a pattern of two rain drops intertwined within a circle. One side is black and the other is white. Finally, there is a smaller white circle spaced evenly within the black side, as well as a smaller black circle, equidistant from the other, in the white side. This is the symbol of *dualities in complimentary motion*. The laws of positive and negative, day and night, man and woman, fire and water, Above and Below...

Yin: representing the female counterpart, has been ascribed a vast assortment of characteristics that can be associated with anything feminine, birth, the moon, darkness, secrets, sacred knowledge, sadness, intellect, community, agriculture, inclusiveness, earth, water, wood, zero, giving, night, north, shady side of hill... value of negative.

Yang: representing the male counterpart, associates with anything primal, the warrior-spirit, the sun, fire, metal, lightness, laughter, openness, obviousness, love for risk, testosterone, battle, wood, one, wealth, day, south, sunny side of hill... value of positive.

The underlying concept of Yin and Yang is to illustrate or equate how opposite or contrary forces can be seen as complimentary, interconnected, and interdependent in, what would end up being, a limitless variety of creative and useful ways. It would symbolize an entire culture with its meaning, and be recognized as one of the greatest principles of mathematics, not to mention binary and computer sciences. There are three main aspects to the relationship between Yin and Yang:

1) Yin and Yang are opposites. They are always found on the opposite end of the other's cycle. Both Yin and Yang are always in a state of perpetual movement and change, and are most importantly seen as being in a perpetual state of changing levels of *balance*.

2) Yin and Yang cannot exist without each other. Nothing can be completely Yin or completely Yang. Just as a total state of Yin takes over, Yang begins to grow. Yin and Yang both can be seen symbolically in the *Taijitu* to contain the "seed" of one another.

3) Yin and Yang have levels that are also changing and in continuous motion. Healthy and balanced creates a healthy functioning system, but if one side becomes too strong the other will become weaker.

THE TAO OF TWO

The understanding of the nature of dualities can be seen at the origins of classical Chinese philosophy, science, and traditional medicine, as well as the different martial arts styles and wellness/energy exercises like Qi Gong and Tai Chi.

Taoist philosopher, Lao Tzu's classic, *The Tao Te Ching*, piques the reader's interest with the knowledge of the complimentary nature of opposing forces from the very beginning in its first chapter when it alludes to the divine duality:

The Tao that can be spoken is not the eternal Tao.

The name that can be named is not the eternal name.

The nameless is the origin of Heaven and Earth.

The named is the mother of the myriad things.

Thus constantly without desire, one observes its essence.

Constantly with desire, one observes its manifestations.

These two emerge together but differ in name.

The unity is said to be the mystery.

Mystery of mysteries; the door to all wonders.

In the last three of the first nine sentences, glimmers of the Yin and Yang principle already begin to emerge. By Lao Tzu's second chapter, the concept of complimentary contrasts, are set in full motion, where he shows specifically the laws behind the dualities of beauty and ugliness, good and evil, being and non-being, difficult and easy, long and short, high and low, etc:

When the world knows beauty as beauty, ugliness arises.

When it knows good as good, evil arises.

Thus being and non-being produce each other.

Difficult and easy bring about each other.

Long and short reveal each other.

High and Low support each other.

Music and voice harmonize each other.

Front and back follow each other.

Therefore the sages:

Manage the work of detached actions.

Conduct the teaching of no words.

They work with myriad things but do not control.

They create, but do not possess.

They act but do not presume.

They succeed but do not dwell on success.

It is because they do not dwell on success.

That it never goes away.

Now you only have 79 more chapter verses to go. To learn the philosophy and metaphysical nature of Yin and Yang, the *Tao Te Ching* will guide you through its verses in a profound and poetic manner. Just try not to think of Yoda.

THE MYSTICISM OF ANCIENT WISDOM

After a more thorough look at something as simple as the concept of Yin and Yang, it becomes far easier to understand, at closer range, how one can carry this formula into other realms of understanding, for instance: *Wood, Water, Fire, Metal and Earth,* might replace *Living, Enjoyment, Art, Strength, and Science,* and be understood at a greater depth just by using the Five Elements template (of Zhou Yan's) to study the comparisons? *Rock Paper, Scissors, Lizard, Spock?* Never mind... It is first important to go into some detail, to emphasize the infinite levels of profound wisdom and philosophical understanding that one feels, when internalizing the Yin and Yang, because knowing its depth is the beginning of seeing it from a more metaphysical perspective.

We can now take this discussion back to the subject matter of the divination system known as the *I Ching*. As mentioned, there are 64 gua, each with a separate visualization, characteristic, interpretation, and representing the *balances and imbalances* of duality. If you are interested in further investigation of the *I Ching,* I highly recommend reading the Alred Huang translation.

An important thing to realize is that the depth of the Yin and Yang is profound, but for the sake of duality, it is also simple. Knowing that duality exists in all things, and understanding how it flows, gives us extraordinarily useful information about many solutions to help us

214

out of some quite difficult issues, such as anxiety, depression, bad eating habits, pain, sleep issues, and that's just the beginning.

Therefore, in theory, the Yin and Yang, which also represents *matter and energy*, can allow us to receive an impression (energy) made by someone's thought (matter). This would be an especially valid point if conscious entanglement was proved to be occurring at all times. In most forms of Hindu meditation, these moments of potential entanglement are seen as *ripples of distraction* that will lure you away from achieving enlightenment. As mentioned earlier, in the *Yoga Sutras of the Patanjali*, this is known as *vritti*. Sometimes the distractions make no sense and may never completely make sense. But much of the time, it will seem to make complete sense in precognitive, telepathic, and clairvoyant ways. Sometimes, these unusual *distractions* can be found to be quite interesting, and other times uncanny and profound. It is, after all, human to explore what possibilities may be found in such non-linear messages, even if it is a completely immeasurable mental experience. Perhaps, one day, it will be possible to use such a technique to receive thoughts from the field of consciousness, similar to how a radio picks up waves of coherent reception... Only ongoing experimentation will provide a true answer, so for now, it's interesting enough, just to conjecture the possibilities.

Might we, through our wisdom, learn how to unlock the greatest of all mysteries? If so, what directions do we take? This is the best time to use your intuition. Close your eyes and allow your qi energy to flow...

Alain Nu, The Man Who Knows™

CHAPTER **18**

CRASHING NUMEROLOGY

THE MYSTICAL NATURE OF NUMBERS

Earlier in the book, I brought up the notion that perhaps the most complex "intelligence system" used from the dawn of civilization up until today, and which contains a code that is beyond most anyone's ability to comprehend, would be the infinite systems within the laws of mathematics. There is so much to learn about the sacred relationships between numbers. Perhaps it can explain, through measurement, virtually anything that can be measured? What I find so curious about such a logic-based system as *math,* is its relationship to its less-used mystical counterpart, known as numerology.

Originally developed by one of the great fathers of math, the Greek philosopher and mathematician, Pythagorus, the idea behind this system of thinking was designed to express every stage of human experience, not just through mathematics, but through *wisdom that had been given to the numbers themselves.* Everything in the universe, (it is believed), can be experienced as reduced to ten basic virtues that are connected to the numerical characters that range from 0 through 9 (as well as the numbers 11 and 22, which you will see later). Interestingly, however, according to the studied *arcana* (or secret teachings), these sacred ten digits need not only to be expressed mathematically, but also characteristically and experientially.

From the days of Pythagoras (570 BC – 495 BC), numerology has had a long and rich occult history. There is evidence in fact to suggest that it indeed goes back long before even Pythagorus. Those researchers will point out how, since the idea of numbers refers to cycles and measurements that can be naturally observed and agreed upon, that numerology, which is the idea of characterizing numbers with tenet virtues, technically goes back as far as into early Egyptian and Babylonian civilizations. The conclusion that there are characteristics of their gods that can be distilled to numerical values that played an integral role in Egyptian astrology and architecture should seem obvious. The significance of characteristics ascribed to numbers may even predate those times in man's own history. Compelling, isn't it?

Through the continued studies and explorations of dedicated generations of practitioners since, the tenets that were given to the 10 digits have been streamlined and elaborated upon. According to modern usage of numerology, since we now live in a world among numbers, it is possible to derive numerological inspiration from any numbers that you see as you walk through life. The secret to serendipity is that there are no accidents.

The way any multiple digit number is quickly distilled to a single digit number, is by first separating the multiple digit number into single digit numbers and then simply adding them all up. It really is that simple. If the sum ends up as a two-digit number, simply break it apart into two single digits again and add them up so you are left with only one single-digit number. The advice or wisdom that one can receive from the "divine" is numerologically always represented by the final single digit that remains.

The single digit that remains becomes the number that represents your *oracle*. The wisdom you receive from contemplating the characteristics of this number (oracle) is the advice that is given to you from the divine, spirit world, or universal life force. Of course, you want to try not to be obsessive about it, but technically speaking, each time you look at the digital clock and date on the lower right hand side of your computer screen, you could quickly add up all the numbers and distill their order to derive spiritual advice any time you want.

My very good friend, Richard Webster, from Auckland, New Zealand, who has been dubbed as "probably New Zealand's most published author," and writes mostly for Llewellyn Worldwide, which is perhaps one of the largest (if not the largest) publishing distributors to book stores, of spiritual and new age books, is the man most responsible for my interest in numerology. While growing up, I have taken note of my own family members having odd superstitions based on the number of things, days (or what-not) regarding this or that and how it could be interpreted, but it was learning from Richard that made me realize just how easy it is to incorporate this unique way of seeing things into virtually anything we do.

Your personal "Life Path Number" is the single digit that is the distilled number formed by the above process when used with the numbers that comprise your full birth day, month and year. So since my birthday was on, August 21ˢᵗ, 1965, it is a simple matter for me to just add 8+2+1+1+9+6+5 that equals 32. Once you have the sum total of any remaining two-digit number separated and then added, you will be left with your Life Path Number. So, for instance, 3+2=5, so my Life Path Number would be a 5. Some of the characteristics of someone who has a Life Path Number, 5, would be sociable, though sometimes temperamental. Impulsively creative, free-thinking, adventurous, a captivating conversationalist, and good at taking on problems as challenges... That does sound a lot like me, but I don't know, maybe everyone has those qualities in them?

See if *your* Life Force Number describes you! Just tally up the single digits that comprise your full birth day month and year and then compare your natural demeanor with the characteristics listed below in order to see how accurately your Life Force Number describes you.

NUMEROLOGICAL CHARACTERISTICS

(Corresponding to each number)

Zero (0): is never factored in to anyone's Life Path Number since the human experience will only span between the numerals One (1) and Nine (9). The numeral zero is seen in everyday life, however, so its image can be used as an oracle, just as in all numbers and symbols. Zero can be seen to symbolize, the ancient Ouroboros, the image of the snake (or dragon) eating its own tail. Representing all things that are outside of the human experience, Zero is the reminder that all things are connected, that the connection is eternal, and with movements of ascending and descending, rotating, spinning, and reincarnating. Zero is our reminder that all things large and small can be seen to move through patterns and cycles. Often times, you may see multiple zeros in a row. Generally, Zero signifies the completion of an episodic period or the start of something new.

1) Men have a tendency to be somewhat competitive, goal oriented, and set on personal success. Women have high personal aspirations, but are also impulsive, and have youthful, playful characteristics. You are confident, ego-driven, responsible, and generous and will give yourself to the point of spreading yourself thin. Playful, you love to see things in an original way and are good at coming up with useful or practical ideas. You are attracted to those who show you loyalty and you enjoy the attention of others. As such, you work best as a leader to others as opposed to following other people's instructions. You enjoy absorbing lots of knowledge in small bites, and you put great value on the time that you have for yourself. Despite feeling self-conscious at times, especially with so many interests that you have that will take up much of your time, your strongest traits are your courage and your drive to keep pushing forward.

2) Strengths in being cooperative and diplomatic, you also have a love for art, music, and an aesthetic to your own vision of beauty. Generally understanding at seeing things from other different perspectives, you provide great comfort for your friends and close family members. You seek balance in all aspects of your life. You are a deep thinker, but you are also prone to be threatened by things that test your sense of security. Your emotions can be blinded by jealousy, for instance, if you are not careful. Though you may travel far away from home, you are always looking forward to your return trip. You are extremely loyal and take your relationships very seriously.

3) Self-expressive and creative, you are talented and unconventional, with specialized interests. You also exhibit a clever and/or witty rapport with people. Sometimes you are a bit of a perfectionist. You have a friendly demeanor and are attracted to attractive people. You are also seen as attractive yourself. You are well versed and have a diverse set of interests. You tend also to seek that passion in others. You find that your need for a serious relationship is not necessarily of prime importance in your younger years, and you are prone to eventually find a partner within the field you have chosen as your domain. As a creative person, you

will sometimes   delay things until the last minute, and you often will leave a cluttered workspace.

4) You are thoughtful and you apply your knowledge and wisdom in effective ways. This is especially true with those things that you believe are most important. Nature loving and down to earth when communicating with others, you use these skills to enjoy living life to the fullest. You like taking part in personal creature comforts, like having your dinner come with dessert and other fancy and exotic things. You also have a need to experience new and exciting things. Sometimes fours might appear insensitive. Women find they are most comfortable in their own home, surrounded by the people they love and work hard to keep their family close. Men may find themselves on their own, but are thorough when being adventurous and are extraordinary at planning things out. Fours excel the most with those things that they have developed and learned in their own way.

5) Freedom, variety and independence are your creeds. . Optimistic, sociable, and comfortable when at the center of attention. Sometimes you can be quite temperamental, sensitive to your own feelings, and if not careful, may be prone to depression. Impulsively creative, freethinking, and always adventurous. Not always tactful, as there is a tendency to speak one's mind too quickly, you are nonetheless a captivating conversationalist and good at taking on problems as challenges. You make a loyal and supportive partner, but you tend to also be restless. You are energetic, enthusiastic, and endlessly passionate for those things that interest you the most.

6) Though you may not be as close to your family as you would like, the connection to your family holds significant meaning to you. Specific family traditions tend to be kept up, and higher importance may be put on gatherings and occasions. Men might indulge themselves and develop self-destructive habits, if too stressed. Organized, hardworking, careful with how finances are handled, but will not be shy of spending when feeling abundant. You will not let too much get in the way of your being able to handle it. Women especially, will feel it is important to stay active. Both tend to find

themselves being naturally talented when trying new things. Quick witted, and can be cuttingly expressive at communicating thoughts succinctly, especially when written.

7) Charismatic and displaying a personal and unique ability to be charming, you are nonetheless always supportive of those you hold near. You are powerful and strong with a unique and stylistic sense about how you approach life. Graceful, philosophical, and savvy, by surrounding yourself with the people who you admire and who you learn your many gifts from, you also find yourself able to be supported by their devotion to you. Much less time or patience tends to be given to anyone who is not in your corner, backing you up. Otherwise, you possess the gift of being precise and communicative when staying in touch with others. Unless extremely fortunate, you may have difficulty in finding a life-long partner who can match your energy.

8) You have a strong drive and ambition, and are impressively efficient at fortifying yourself with everything you need to accomplish anything that you need to do. You pride yourself on your efficiency, and when you are organized, you are able to get extraordinary things done. You are pretty good at self-motivating and are able to handle quite complicated tasks. You are gifted at coming up with ideas to earn money and moneymaking ideas intrigue you. You have a side that you mostly keep to yourself, and some people might find it hard getting to know you as a result. You may be perceived as someone who is egocentric and superior acting if not careful. Your sophistication and sharp intellectual sarcasm can sometimes get you into trouble with people who are more down to earth. Travel is no issue for you.

9) You are a sociable humanitarian and have no problem giving of yourself to others around you. You love animals and love to travel and see new places whenever you have the chance. You are most comfortable, however, when you are at home. Movement, excitement and activity are accomplished with little effort on your part. It's in your blood. You find that you can do all things you love to do, more or less effortlessly. Always surrounding yourself with people who love you for who you are, you are seen and admired by them for your

genuineness. You love the merits of being healthy while surrounded by nature and exotic places. Later in life, you will be seen by many as a compassionate teacher, advisor and person of recognition. Putting the needs of others before you is one of your greatest strengths, although it can wear you too thin if you are not careful.

Aside from the ten digits discussed above, in numerology, there are also two other numbers to seriously consider. Eleven (11) and Twenty Two (22) are both two-digit numbers that are considered by numerologists as *Master Builder Numbers*. This means that, if while distilling your numbers, you find yourself arriving at either of those *two-digit* numbers as a sum total, they are seen as particularly significant. At those rare times in which you see those numbers, they are considered "old souls" by numerologists. If one believes in reincarnation, these numbers indicate having been here before, and since having already learned the easy lessons in life, these people are now facing the more challenging ones. Usually they end up becoming quite successful later in life, but most of their lives are spent teetering on potential self-destruction and uncertainty. A lot of nervous energy and/or a wide range of emotions may be felt as coming from people who possess these as their Life Path Number.

MASTER BUILDER NUMBERS

Eleven (11): Sensitive and showing skills at being precognitive, you will best use your skills by seeing ahead in the future and using the present time for planning. You have much of the characteristics of 2, but it is super-charged. You will find people are expecting you to lead them. Feeling what other people are feeling can sometimes give you stress and anxiety. As someone who is empathic, you are best suited to working with other people and in healthy social environments. You abound with inspirational ideas, but can often be caught in a daydream. Helping other people or animals through your creative energy is where you may find the most fulfillment in putting your energy towards. Finding balance in your life that supports your personal sense of flow is paramount to your success. Trust your intuition.

Twenty Two (22): is the most powerful Master Builder number. It represents the fully formed Master Builder. Understanding how to integrate all the organizational and applied-structure characteristics of the number 4, as well as the creatively inspired foresight ability of the number 11 is your ultimate task. This will take up much of your early life, but when you are finally able to bring those elements together, you will find that you can move through life effortlessly. Every time you reach success, you are philanthropic of your earnings. Money is not as important to you as connecting with others and finding ways of helping them. You are artistically creative and motivated by your own inspiration. It probably feels, at times, that supernatural forces guide you. You will learn many lessons throughout your life, but once focused and organized, you will find that you are a strong leader for whatever is your cause and you will become highly recognized for your position.

There is, indeed, a lot more that you can learn with regards to numerology, but the above ought to give you a good start. There is a chance that, while reading the above descriptions, you may have found that you appear to match the characteristics of a different number more than the one that is your own Life Path Number. If this is the case, it might be because you have a master number secretly embedded within your birthday numbers.

Try to add up the numbers of your birthday in different configurations to see if it adds up in any way to either 11 or 22. Ironically, my birthday (8-21-1965) gets to 11 by adding just the first three digits, and then the last two digits also add up to 11, which sort of makes me both an 11 and a 22... Sigh. I was excited to just be a five.

From having just a basic understanding of numerology, you will form a deeper understanding with how it relates to Astrology, Tarot, Palmistry and much more. Don't be afraid to experiment. Take special interest in the numbers that you see around you. It is strange to know that many successful people who play the stock market (or even the lottery) will use numerology or astrology, to help them make their choices. Some have even used REGs (random event generators) with successful results. How can that be possible? Is it, that they are just lucky? Could it be that they are lying about it to misdirect others from what their actual game strategy is? It was fairly well known that Nancy Reagan was very close friends with and consulted an astrologer. The things that happen behind closed doors...

CHAPTER 19

THE OUTLAW OF ATTRACTION

THE CONSCIOUSNESS GAME

Once you know what to do, this takes no more than 60 seconds to make some of the craziest things happen. Most effectively, start by focusing your thoughts on any subject, but it should best embody the most ideal thing that you would need for yourself.

Your concentration on any subject matter that you find important is best dealt with clearly and one at a time. In fact, it is usually the times that there are too many important tasks which need to be dealt with, that it becomes the most stressful and confusing because your priorities have not been properly sorted for you to begin using any mental or subconscious ability. I developed the following experiment, have used it myself, and have received amazing results from it. Try it out, and see for yourself how remarkably effective it is. Most importantly, if your mind is open, an answer will soon come and your subject matter will be reconciled.

1) Take your first 10 seconds to imagine literally having within your mind, a "search bar," just like you would see on Google. Mentally type into that search bar anything at all, but most effectively, the subject should best embody a single most ideal thing that you feel you need in that moment.

2) As you imagine it there, take approximately the next 20 seconds to try and imagine that search bar as being surrounded by the spirit of every person, place and thing that is most loved and most important to you. Imagine being happy with all of these things, symbolic or tangible, but together in one single body of thought. All of our thoughts

225

are a kind of energy. That shouldn't be too difficult to believe. Allow that feeling of happiness, love and empowerment to grow within you. Then press ENTER.

3) For the next 20 seconds, allow a list of related "links" to automatically form on your mental computer screen and focus on only the top link. Remind yourself, as you imagine clicking on this link, how many levels there are to manifesting what you want the most, so the greatest importance should be placed on what manner to approach your subject matter that you feel the most comfortable with. All you need to do here, however, is take a moment and meditate on (preferably) just one or two words that this top link will offer you in the form of advice.

4) Since this word (or words) that you visualized from the top link will come as some sort of advice, hold onto this piece of information as something to be later taken into consideration. With a deep breath, feel the entire experience being absorbed into your heart. As you exhale, open your eyes and visualize everything that you have taken time to process, integrating into all that you see now as becoming a part of a new reality around you.

It shouldn't take longer than one minute, and one should strive for it to take even less time, since really, the time spent will not make any difference, so long as one can follow the steps as above. All that needs to be done is for you to be aware over the next 24 hours, in case you receive any significant messages, especially if you want your wish fulfilled. If your wish does come true, take a moment to be grateful to the universe. If your wish does not come true immediately, it is most likely because what you wished for takes longer to process. Keep looking for messages and take the advice that came to you from that top link.

Also consider all the people you meet, during that time, as potentially somehow being connected to the destiny you have summoned, especially chance occurrences. They don't need to know what messages you are looking for. In fact, it is better that they don't. This is the rudimentary basis of "magical thinking." Essentially, anything that is being worked-on or worked-out can be wished for by thinking about it, and then one can simply keep an eye out for messages on how to carry on using the timing and inspiration of the moment regarding whatever is being thought about.

Try it. Test it and you will find that it is uncanny when it works... Take careful notes of when it does and when it doesn't work. For me, although I am about to explain why it probably shouldn't work, in the few times that I really needed it to work, and I had no other choice but to use it, quite miraculously, it worked for me. Even though the more scientific side of me says that this is outrageously suspect, the magical thinking explorer within me continues to get excited each time I note when it succeeds for me.

THE STRANGEST SUPER POWER

In case reading or trying the above test makes you insecure that this could end up becoming your first step towards clinical insanity, you can try what I do. Each time you think about it, simply think about it as a game or just a personal experiment for fun. Technically, it is a creatively visualized *call-to-action ritual process*, and would normally be used as a *wishing-ritual*, of or relating to that of a *Law of Attraction.* This premise is better known today as *The Secret,* originally made as a film in 2006 by Rhonda Byrne, which essentially re-packaged (and re-named) the premise. What is interesting to me is that the strange powers of The Law of Attraction takes the concept of "the Force" from the movie, *Star Wars,* to a whole new level. It would be stranger than Transcendental Meditation's claim that coherent brain frequency can affect its surroundings. It would be stranger than consciousness' effect on computerized random number generators. It would even be weirder than spirit apparitions or extraterrestrial contact, if one thinks about it. If you need something, just wish for it, and see what happens. In 1904, British Judge and New Thought proponent, Thomas Troward, is quoted to have said:

> *"The action of Mind plants that nucleus which, if allowed to grow undisturbed, will eventually attract to itself all the conditions necessary for its manifestation in outward visible form."*

The entire Law of Attraction concept sprung out of what would be called the *New Thought Movement* that began in the late nineteenth century and early twentieth century. In 1906, a man named William Walker Atkinson (1862–1932) wrote and published *Thought Vibration or the Law of Attraction in the Thought World.* Wikipedia cites him as the editor of *New Thought* magazine, but he was also the author of more than 100 books on an impressive variety of religious, spiritual, and arcane subjects. The following year, Elizabeth Towne, who was the editor of *The Nautilus Magazine, a Journal of New Thought*, published Bruce MacLelland's book *Prosperity Through Thought Force*, in which he summarized the "Law of Attraction" as a New Thought principle, stating:

"You are what you think, not what you think you are."

I love that one. It's a good one to Tweet.

The Law of Attraction, which is based on the tenet that "Like Attracts Like," has somehow convinced many people into believing that it possesses *uncanny summoning characteristics,* in so much that the mere focusing on something positively or negatively will bring about positive or negative results. All of our thoughts are made up of energy. Along with our voice and bodies, projecting and acting on the many levels that it does towards the creation or manifestation of our dreams and desires, it is said to make the idea open up and reveal itself as a reality. One has to admit, however, it is quite beyond belief, even for something of that sort to makes sense...

Based on MacLelland's quote, I was inspired to create a new female super hero (so many are men already) who uses Law of Attraction as her super-power. Has anyone done this, yet? She lives an ordinary life going to high school and dealing with teenage issues, but also knows that she has this weird power to wish things to come true. Thus, she keeps finding herself constantly working on saving the world, though nobody else knows about it. They see the world as just typical reality, while she quietly shifts it, by using her powers. Her weakness, obviously, is that she has to deal with knowing how to have this gift while adjusting to high school classes and friends. Of course, there are also just too many horrible things that are happening in the world simultaneously that it becomes a challenge to decide whether today it's going to be controlling the spread of some new disease, or helping Uri Geller successfully arrange an important peace negotiation. There would never be an end to what people would want or need to wish for, so this idea certainly has the potential as an ongoing series. At any rate, when this screenplay idea manifests, my prediction, (if I may) is that it will be a smash hit.

NEW THOUGHT: SCIENCE OR SPIRITUAL?

When one looks past what people know today as the *Law of Attraction*, we find that many of its philosophies stem from what, at the time, was called the New Thought movement. Authors like Atkinson and MacLelland were only two of what was a movement largely created by a booming market for *self-help*, *will-to-power*, and *get rich quick* books. New Thought authors such as Israel Regardie, Wallace Wattles, Napoleon Hill, Frank Channing Haddock, Perry Joseph Green, and Thomas Troward have all been quite popular and successful men who have perpetuated the notion of New Thought ideals over history. Rhonda Byrne of *The Secret,* credited having read Wattle's book, *The Science of Getting Rich*, as her original inspiration for creating the film documentary, during an interview with *Newsweek.*

After the success of the film, *The Secret*, in 2010, Oprah Winfrey devoted a whole two episodes of her show on examining the Law of Attraction and its amazing hard-to-believe claims. Around that same time, on *The Larry King Show*, in a discussion with Bob Solis, the talk show host had pointed out several issues he had with the premise of the Law of Attraction in relation to world suffering and his concern for global issues, saying "If the universe manifests abundance at a mere thought, why is there so much poverty, starvation, and death?"

Wikipedia cites the chief tenets of New Thought as being:

- Access to Infinite Intelligence

- An omnipotent and omnipresent God

- That spirit is the ultimate reality

- That true human self-hood is divine

- That divinely attuned thought is a positive force for good.

- All disease is mental in origin.

- Right thinking has a healing effect.

With just a quick look, it's not hard to see how quickly the idea turns spiritual. This is because the idea was spiritual from the beginning. The idea here is simply, that one must believe in the power of oneself as having the potential for godly powers if one were to expect such otherworldly connections to manifest. However, just because you have godly powers, doesn't mean that you won't have godly struggles.

If you want to see angels, angels appear; but if you start seeing monsters, monsters appear. Give yourself the power, and you will have that power; so be careful with that power.

GAME OVER LAWS

Mary Carmichael and Ben Radford, writing for the *Committee for Skeptical Inquiry*, commented that "neither the film nor the book has any basis in scientific reality," and that adopting such a philosophy has "an ugly flipside: if you have an accident or disease, it's the universe that is trying to teach you something." Many others, both skeptical and investigative, have criticized how New Thought ideals reference modern scientific theories in misleading ways. Digging a little further, it is common to also hear of how the The Law of Attraction misrepresents concepts regarding electrical activity of brainwaves, among other examples.

Skeptics mention frequently how the use of quantum mysticism to explain any seemingly implausible effect is a common trait of modern pseudoscience. Critics have asserted that The Law of Attraction cannot be fairly studied, that the evidence provided is usually anecdotal and that, because of the self-selecting nature of the positive reports and the subjective nature of any results, that reports will always be susceptible to confirmation bias and selection bias. Physicist, Ali Alousi, has criticized it as immeasurable and questioned the likelihood that any thought can affect anything outside the head.

All of the above does make quite a bit of sense as well. This is why, in the end, I have always felt that it is best to be played like a *game*. If I had to choose, however, between a world in which I can find ideas like the Law of Attraction available to experiment with, or a world who believes such thoughts should be banned, or ridiculed if interacted with, I would want more the world that believes in reaching outside possibilities. Otherwise, it would seem a little harsh. Despite Alousi's skepticism, the notion that thought can affect things outside of the head, may be more possible than would seem immediately obvious. I do believe that something more is going on with regards to all this.

Just because it's impossible to measure, doesn't make it impossible to play. The (now old) New Thought tenets, by virtue of its own nature, if deconstructed, will tend to fall apart. Is it better to try to figure out how or why something is not true, or to try to figure out how or why something might be seen as curiously possible? The Law of Attraction concept is much simpler when said in the following manner:

As energy, I am the creator of my own destiny whenever I choose to initiate it, with all that I have, physically, emotionally and spiritually. With a clear mind, when I summon, using my faith in the universe of all things possible, my reality will shift towards that summoning.

In my opinion, that would be the most basic up-to-date perception for the Law of Attraction. It is your motivated and heartfelt call to action. Everything else is just reality unfolding, revealing the nature of everything else that is happening at the same time. As for the darker side mentioned earlier, regarding unasked-for misfortunes, it is still best to see them as tests and challenges. Grief and loss, for instance, is experienced in such a way in which knowing that the irreplaceable will never return again, and cannot ever be changed back to the way it once was. It then challenges one to regain the feeling of completeness by integrating the most meaningful aspects of whoever or whatever was lost into becoming a part of oneself. We are born into a world that expresses itself in all ways, and this includes feelings of confidence, joy, abundance, neediness, nurturing, pain, loss, regret, triumph... everything in all ways. Therefore we take what we are given, and we use our mastery of whatever faith we have in of ourselves, and whatever skills we possess. We use these to the best of our ability so that our stay on this planet is good for ourselves, those around us, and ideally, for the health of the planet itself.

WATCH YOURSELF...

By connecting ancient eastern philosophy to the spiritual tenets of New Thought, perhaps achieving harmonious inner balance and strength can be seen as the first steps towards becoming more aware of one's ability to shift reality to one's favor. To achieve a state of feeling completely balanced, in control and aware, just follow these seven easy steps:

1) Inhale deeply, and as you exhale slowly, take moment to become mindfully aware of the space you are in, paying particular attention to the nature of the climate, objects, plants, animals, and people that are around you. One may need to readjust one's own energies, depending on the energy of others who are nearby. Your mind should be alert and paying attention to everything that is present and immediate.

2) Next become aware of your vision and ability to focus your vision. Eyes should be able to move up, down, and side to side without feeling discomfort.

3) Check nasal passages should be clear so that breathing through the nose is easy and without feelings of any blockage or discomfort.

4) The jaw should not be clenched and all muscles in the face should feel relaxed but vibrant and ready to cast a sincere smile to someone who, normally, you wouldn't.

5) Be aware of the condition of your lips. Tongue should not be coated and mouth should not be dry. Simply drinking more water will heal the mouth quite quickly.

6) Body should feel as loose, limber and as flexible as it can. Diaphragm should be able to draw in a deep breath and blow out hard without discomfort.

7) All joints should feel functional to their best ability. Hands and feet should be able to clench and release to the best of one's ability. Movement should feel as effortless as possible.

Once you have gone through this mental checklist, close your eyes, and try and reach a state of mindfulness. This will help you to be more physically and mentally prepared for whatever happens to be your next task. This can be seen as the beginning of your ability to shape your *subtle reality* in some very interesting ways.

Becoming more and more aware of your chakras as energy centers and how well you feel they are functioning, (relative to their individual meanings and characteristics), will allow you to more easily identify which areas seem a little off (i.e.: imbalanced). Learn how to counteract the negative things in your life that need attention, in order to pull yourself back into balance.

DUALITY GAME

The idea of treating it as a game, makes doing this more fun, and less disappointing, especially if you have convinced yourself that something you tried didn't end up manifesting. Plus, it allows you to practice without feeling attached or like you had to do anything with any sense of urgency.

This is also why one must use such cosmic inquiry, such as *summoning or wishing*, with good intentions. It also works with negative things, hence showing that it plays to *no-one's-favor*. If there is any imbalance or disharmony whether it is intentional or unintentional, even if it feels as if everything is working perfectly, know that *equivalently contrary aspects* can be born as a result. Focus carefully on what feels like the most balanced choice, even if it is not the most desired choice, and especially when you feel you are in these situations. As energetic beings, it is easy to see that we are most healthy when we represent balanced aspects of our planet and ourselves. The body will conquer a night of heavy drinking with a throbbing hangover the following morning. However, if you live as one who strives to achieve balance, one can simply meditate on the Tao to help conquer:

1) Anger with Forgiveness

2) Pride with Humility

3) Deceitfulness with Straight-forwardness

4) Greed with Contentment

5)   Sarcasm with Virtue

As you can see, with just a desire to understand and acquire greater knowledge using key philosophies, simple mathematics, and strong intentions, we have mortal access to gain control and power which, when we are most balanced, gives us the most contentment and ease, while keeping the energy of our surroundings healthy as well.

Of course, situations will occur sometimes, wherein although we may feel as if we are following our basic natural tendencies, we have, in fact, actually pulled ourselves into making a wrong decision or choice. That would be similarly equivalent to making a "foul play." One must become both naturally vigilant and aware, but also playful, with these balances and imbalances. As the mystical nature and philosophical wisdom of these subtle forces are better understood, I believe we will continue to find more power in them.

PART FIVE

THE POWERS OF OUR MINDS

We began this book with a bite-sized sampler of how mentalism can be used as an anytime and anywhere demonstration which, if anything, can amaze and astonish the senses and sensibilities of those around us.

We then took a turn into the real world of mystery, mysticism, and manifestation. The reason why it was important for me to write this book was to give you a glimpse of how it is quite possible, if not easy, to appreciate those things that we understand the least, by getting to know them in more depth.

I think it would be wonderful and amazing for us to one day understand how to manifest world peace, and suddenly, it becomes real... The Chinese believed that there was a time, during the days of Fu Xi that this was so. There was, apparently, a time of complete peace and harmony back then. Perhaps, one day, we will cycle back to a similar such time.

As we continue to find out just how much further our conscious ability extends beyond what we know it to, we will also move forward to break ground and gain new insights towards answering, to a more specific degree, the following questions:

1. Could there be deep mysteries about our ability to build or cultivate our past civilizations that we may one day suddenly rediscover, remember or re-invent?

2. Is there a connection that our minds have with a field of consciousness that interplays between other existing energies? If so, how can we better interact with it? What is the extent of our applications, remotely or otherwise?

3. Do we have, within us, a method or technique that allows us to communicate with cells in our bodies that can correct health, heal disease and/or prolong life?

4. When our brainwaves are made to become "smooth and coherent" through meditation, can that really make the temper of other people's brainwaves respond in sympathy?

5. Can thoughts become entangled so that two persons might communicate with one another through the ether of consciousness?

6. Can the spirits of people no longer alive be connected to consciousness in such a way that their energy, characteristics and wisdom can still be communicated with or connected to after death?

7. Can the continuing development of consciousness experiments, games and research equipment be the beginning towards the development of more complex devices, like mind-controlled computers or Internet?

8. Could some ancient, sacred or evolved knowledge of our minds be rediscovered by some kind of learning, understanding, finding, or even by accident through "play"?

9. Is there a way to believe a certain aspect of one's reality in such a way so as to shift it from one existence into another by thought, wish, or prayer, when needed?

10. Is numerically based math, and all of its profound equations and interlocking laws, an aspect of nature which man discovered, as an aspect of man himself, or an aspect of God?

Who knows what the future may hold? If I may make one final prediction, it would be: *There is greatness yet to be discovered by man in the understanding of our consciousness.* That understanding doesn't have to come from anywhere but from within yourself. I think that there is an answer to be found for each of the above questions, and for many of them, the answers may be more incredible than the average human being is currently willing to imagine or believe.

CHAPTER **20**

ESP MADE EASY

I n this last section, my aim is to offer you a number of suggestions, demonstrations, and experiments which you can try yourself that may open your mind, just a little more. There are amazing possibilities that we still have yet to discover about ourselves in relationship to our consciousness. In fact, you don't need random event generators, Ouija boards, or even tarot cards to experience some pretty profound, strange and spooky effects. By just looking a little deeper, while enjoying the journey, you can interact with your own telepathic, intuitive and precognitive senses, and possibly exhibit a more acute ability to interpret subconscious cues and oracular symbols as "hidden languages" within reality!

I will also be introducing you to a few other friends of mine who have helped to shape my current understanding of the extraordinary path I have chosen. Like myself, my friends also share a common interest in understanding the powers of our thoughts, our consciousness and all its possibilities. These are people who come from many different backgrounds, from palmistry (palm reading) to hypnosis models of transformational therapy, neuro-linguistic programming (NLP), shamanic and pagan practices and even the neurosciences. All of these people are extraordinary people in their own right, (and so are you!), thus, by learning these things, you will be able to try for yourself, and experiment on just how effective they may or may not be, for you. You may have more of a resonance for doing one thing over another. However, you should find all of the following contributions to be quite fascinating. If nothing else, they will remind you of peculiar clichés, superstitions, and even old wives tales to give you a chuckle.

The similarities that Part I has with Part V, are that both contain demonstrations and presentations that enable you to experiment on friends, family, classrooms, training seminars, formally or completely casually, all the while being more or less impromptu, with nothing to prepare, of course, except yourself. Rehearsal, practice and experience are all you ever need. The difference between the two sections, is that although the first section consists of methods that use mathematics, language and word anomalies to cultivate a manner of engagement that may catch your audience by surprise, the following consists of experiments that are designed more to amaze yourself as you attempt to interact with consciousness or the universe in creative ways. Sometimes you will find that doing so will require other people to help and be witnesses. After all, appreciating the extraordinary is so much more fun when done with a group. With other demonstrations, feel free to try them privately and by yourself. Stay committed. Stick with repeating and adjusting each exercise a good five times before making final conclusions.

It does take an open mind to play games of *magical thinking*. However, there is little, if anything else, to invest (besides having an open mind) to play the games I am about to illustrate. It is best that you consider the following exercises and demonstrations as "games and experiments" as well. The more detailed notes you take, the better you will get. Remember to date, describe the conditions, trials, results and the people involved. There is no better way to experience this for yourself, and I personally believe that if you do decide to record your experiments, to get ready for some interesting things to start occurring for you. Try to change your thinking patterns to improve your abilities. I am quite certain you will get some pretty remarkable results by just having enough of a curiosity to give it a try. You have nothing but to gain.

COMPLIMENTARY MAGIC WORDS

Yesterday afternoon, I was having a conversation with my friend, Dr. Richard Restak, who is a prolific neuroscientist, neurologist and author of more than 20 books on the human brain. We were creating a game plan with one another, before giving a joint-lecture regarding mental illusions and delusions as a special program to be held at the American Association for the Advancement of Science, in Washington, DC. I was mentioning to him how easy it is to see how science has always embraced both language and mathematics to impart its theories, results and knowledge. Yet when you take the two, that is to say both math and language, far back enough in time- it is then interesting to see how quickly both are found to be naturally and intrinsically linked to magic and mysterious powers

A well-placed compliment, for instance, given at the right time and place, just like *magic words*, will award you with an assortment of unexpected perks. It might seem obvious at first, but give it a little more credit than you would ordinarily, and you will see some interesting things begin to happen. Here is a little game that is easy to play regarding just remembering to say nice things to people. Compliments should always come spontaneously, so it is equally as important that you do not start to fall into a groove of always saying the same thing. Be creative. Try and make it a habit to say between *one* and *three complimentary things* to any person you are in front of, during the duration of time that you are with them. You don't have to fawn all over these people either. Compliments are most effective when offered with subtlety. The less you know the person you are complimenting, the more concentrated the joy is that you are giving them.

If you forget to do this- and I often do myself, just from getting caught up in my own crazy world, you won't lose anything. However, if you just try to make a natural habit of giving only up to *three compliments* of the most sincere kind, to anyone you see during however long the duration of time that you are with them, you will have anything to gain without even needing to expect it.

A couple of things are at play here, besides the compliment itself. One is not being asked to be insincere about the compliment that is given, so perhaps the most important thing is that a genuine personal appreciation for the person you are with must be made, and regardless of the kind of person they are, in order for the compliment to be given. Appreciation is one of the greatest positive-energy initiating qualities that one can have. If you can appreciate someone for any quality that they may have, their gratitude is returned to you automatically. When this happens, you are immediately off to a good start and chances are greatly lessened that things will turn against your favor from there, so long as balance can be maintained. If you find that you are successful with manifesting anything positive in return, it is then perfectly fine to graciously thank them and take another moment to appreciate them.

To be materialistic about it is really not the point at all, but just from regularly complimenting people in passing, I have received upgrades into first-class seats from coach, upgrades in rental cars and limousine service, free entry into music clubs, free desserts with meals, getting the student-rate to let me into museums like MOMA, etc. More importantly, pretty much all of my best friendships and relationships have begun from just a nice exchange of words. Establishing a positive connection with people you meet by offering them a compliment sparked from a genuine appreciation of them is simply a nice character trait to have. In doing so, a personal "entanglement" is formed, and the prospect of either individual fulfilling the needs of the other is automatically opened.

THE SMALL TO LARGE COFFEE

With Craig Browning

One such way of experimenting with visualization was recommended to me by my friend, Craig Browning, who is considered an intuitive counselor that hails from the New England region of the U.S. He recently dropped an interesting idea into my brain while in conversation with him. This devilish technique can be done while ordering coffees any place you might be in which you must order your coffee *before* someone pours it for you.

What you will do (while placing your order), is specifically order and pay for a *small coffee*. You don't need to feel like you have to downplay your ordering a *small*, though do try to psychically up-play your desire for a large coffee without just blurting it out. Since you are just experimenting, and certainly not wanting to pull anything over a profit-driven business, you can always give whatever your financial difference (and more!), as a tip, back to your barista. Of course, if you really must use your Jedi powers in time of need, "Do what thou wilt..."

After paying for the small coffee, engage the person who is making your coffee in a friendly conversation, while visualizing strongly the thought of them making you, instead, a *large coffee*. Compliment them in some way and say something positive about the day, all the while, visualizing them making a *large cup of coffee* for you. See if they can pick up on your visualization while they make your coffee. If you buy coffee often at a specific place, see how many times it takes before it works for you. It's a simple experiment, and complimenting people is a nice habit to have, even in passing. It is not 100%, but the odds are good enough to try, and so long as the scenario is similar, it can also work with other kinds of food and drink orders.

One might question if it is the compliment that causes the other person to show their appreciation by providing you with the larger drink, or if your visualization of the larger drink is what puts the thought in their head. It is only a game. It could be both, just one, or neither. Put it to the test. Try doing it without complimenting the barista first, to see if only visualizing it will work just by itself. Visualization is a powerful thing. When Craig Browning does it, it is a psychic test, using only visualization... and yet, he will tend to get a larger drink more often than one would expect!

TIME AND (PARKING) SPACE

Many ideas are born out of people who want to be known for having come up with that idea. I know that it is mentioned in the movie, *The Secret*, but I remember hearing this idea long before that film was released. My estimation is that this idea of "manifesting a parking space" would have been created sometime between the 1950's which was a huge decade for the construction of parking garages and the 1980's, as that is when I first started hearing about this exercise. So during the thirty years in between, somehow a parking space manifesting ritual took shape. Although it's mentioned in *The Secret* as well as in other places on the internet, the author of the original idea is unknown.

I find the "authorless" ideas to be interesting in their own right. Not because I want to take credit for what was created, but because they are mysterious. The fact that no one knows who he or she is gives rise to a further delusion that the *authorless idea* may have been somehow born mysteriously from the cyber-organism of an *Internet collective*. There may be innumerable anomalous entities of knowledge just like this one out there (similar to the one I described in Part I, regarding how adding numbers to six causes some people to think of 'carrots' when asked to think of a vegetable). Just *who* comes up with this stuff? Could such a source be one day discovered to have a non-human origin? That these were synthesized to be left as witty *cyber-clues* that lead us to the existence of a mysterious *deus ex machina*? I will leave that playful notion for you to ponder. Personally, I think it would make a great sub-plot to an Off Broadway play...

No matter its origin, this is an easy enough experiment for anyone who drives a car. Simply *imagine* that by the time you get to your destination that you will find the *perfect* parking space. Usually, it is a simple matter of just wishing or desiring an *open parking space* that is convenient to wherever you need to be by the time you get there. It's good that you begin this creative visualization just as you get into your car and enough in advance, before you arrive at your destination, so that reality is given a little time to unfold for you. Place your order respectfully in advance, and your wish should be ready for you by the time of your arrival.

That is what is supposed to happen, at least. What if it doesn't work? Well, you are not supposed to think of that in the least. In fact, if any negativity comes into your thoughts at all, it greatly reduces your chances of finding that perfect parking spot. If you start to come to expect that your wish will be fulfilled for a perfect parking spot, however, you will soon be finding yourself amazed at just how often this works. I use it every time I go to the grocery store, and I can't even remember the last time I had to take a less than perfect space in any of the three different grocery stores I regularly shop at.

Manhattan, NYC is one of the hardest areas in the world to find a parking space in. Although, for safety and convenience (and especially for long term) I will park in a garage, and there are times when I am meeting a friend somewhere and can find a parking space open at the very spot where I have to meet them. My friend, and well-respected master of mind-mysteries, Max Maven, was performing his brilliant one-man show, *Thinking In Person* at The Abingdon Theatre Arts Complex a couple of years ago in 2012, and I decided to take a trip from DC and drive a rental car. Well, what I didn't realize was that the VW Bug which I decided to rent, doesn't have as large of a gas tank as my car, and so when horrendous traffic into the city started to make me later and later to see Max's show on time, I found I was also running out of gas.

I remember being on the phone with my friend asking me what I planned to do if I ran out of gas, since I was literally stuck in the middle of slow traffic with no shoulder to even pull over on. I remember saying, "I'll just call 911, and wait for someone to save me, while getting nasty looks from everyone who passes me." I remember, at that point, mercifully making my prayer, while knowing it was way too late, to help me get to the show at a reasonable time.

Suddenly, the worst possible thing happened. I ran out of gas. I had to get off the phone now and call 911. In fact, that's exactly what I did. As I was talking to them, they connected me immediately to the Port Authority Traffic people. Then they asked me where I was. I told them that I was about a mile from the tollbooth, that I had run out of gas, but that I was coasting slowly down a gradual hill at that point. Without even realizing it, just after the moment I put in my wish prayer, I was serendipitously being taken care of. They said, "Well, just keep on coasting down the hill, and as you arrive at the toll booth, we'll have someone there to direct you to the side of the road where we can help you refill your tank." Could it be that easy? Surely, I was lucky. With a completely stalled-out engine, I coasted down the hill, and saw someone flagging me over to the left side of the tollbooths. My gas tank was quickly replenished, and now all I had to do was get through the Lincoln Tunnel and arrive at my destination. By that time, I still had a few minutes before the start of the show.

As I got through the Lincoln Tunnel, I remember wishing for a space as close to the theatre as possible. In fact, I used a technique that I often use, in which I not only wish that there will be a space open, but I add an extra thought as well. I imagine putting out a request that someone who is parked in that immediate vicinity who is planning on leaving that area will be inclined to become synchronized with my wavelength, so that by the time I arrive, they will just be pulling out of the space. That way, other fortunate people will have no chance of getting to my desired space before me. Especially in bustling cities like Manhattan, the timing has to be perfect. As I pulled right up to the theater that Max's show was taking place, a car was just pulling out of a space directly across the street! I quietly walked into his show, but I was a little late coming in. It turned out, I had come in exactly one minute late of his opening. So you see, it's not an exact science.

I know that this game, especially for a rational-minded person, feels quite far-fetched. To imagine that any of this could work, even if it did on occasion, would be thought of as "stupid" if it didn't work and "lucky" if it worked. However, since I want you to see the impossible made possible, give it try, play the game, and see what happens. It would be difficult for me to say that it will work for you, because technically, I shouldn't be able to predict the future. I will say this game delightfully surprises me almost every time I play. Since I love to drive places, so I play this game a lot. It makes me want to try it on other things. I think you should too. With some of the congested traffic conditions that I end up traveling in, this is an extraordinarily good ability to possess. It is also a good feeling to "feel lucky" and believe that you manifested it.

TELEPATHIC VOICEMAIL

How many times have you ever thought of a person, even one who you haven't heard from in a long while, when within a short amount of time after thinking of them, they call you or contact you somehow? Let us put aside, the fact that it may have just been a complete coincidence for a moment. Most of us assume that the most logical answer would be that these things just happen to be moments which appear significant, but really aren't. There may, however, be other possibilities to consider. Just because there are things that people are known to be superstitious of, doesn't mean that every one of these quirky reactions is caused by something that doesn't exist.

Here are two ideas which you can try based on this phenomena. The first thing that you must do is assume that it is actually a phenomenon that exists. Experiments like these generally do not work when the stance initially taken is that it is not going to work.

Try to put yourself in the headspace of who will be calling you today. Make a list of three names of people you feel may call you. No reason to discriminate, so anyone's name that comes to you, for whatever reason, should be whom you write down. Basically, any of the first three names that come to your mind that you feel like "it's just going to happen" with. Not by force, but "just because." By the end of the day, simply check off how many people you were able to correctly guess.

The next experiment is better done with individuals who you are in no hurry to reach, so you can see how much time lapses before contact is made. Don't get upset if it doesn't immediately work. Sometimes it takes longer than expected. For instance, I had a close friend who lived near me that moved away, and I completely lost touch with him. He was unfortunately not that connected with anyone else I knew, and when I tried to see if he had a Facebook profile, he didn't appear to. So I put out my "psychic voice-mail" for him to call.

I waited about a month, and he never did call me. That's when I decided to see if he was on Facebook again. Sure enough, the next time I checked, there he was, now living in Portland, Oregon. I reached out, and now our friendship has been rekindled. Later, he told me how he had never been interested in being a part of Facebook, but that he decided to create a profile for no particular reason the month before. This was, in fact, just after the same time I was looking for him, but didn't see him!

Before trying to use any normal means of communication, imagine yourself (during meditation, if you wish) vividly making connection with someone who you know you would like to speak to. Make your connection as sincere as you can, and essentially you will play the *Consciousness Game* (detailed in Part 4) , but with a person in mind. Try it first with just one of your close friends, but then you can also try focusing on multiple people you know. Write down the names of those people you are mentally summoning because you would enjoy getting a call from them. Tally up your results by the end of the month, and see how well you faired.

I have two extra theories that I have put into practice as I continue to experiment. My first theory is that *how much one is mentally entangled with one's target* will determine ultimately how soon (or if) that person ends up making contact with you. Assuming that we are experimenting with mental information that is sent the moment that it is transmitted, if it exists at all, it would work as a *telepathic voicemail*. The receiver of the information (if received), will need to subconsciously process the message, become inspired to call, and then find a good time to call, just as if getting a proper voicemail. Under this pretense, the more of a need or urgency for the one who was sent the psychic message to reply, the greater the possibility that their reply will come. This notion would be my way of also including the factor that emotionally charged signals are clearer and easier for receivers (like REGs) to pick up on.

The time frame that the response takes which makes it worthy of calling it successful would be near impossible to determine. However, if there is no prior communication or expectation that the person you are targeting will call at all, for this experiment to be successful, it would require, to put it mildly, pretty terrific odds.

That is why I consider this an *advanced experiment.*

The second theory is that the more urgent or needed the contact, the better your chances of its success. Because of this, it is probably best to give a time span of a few days, and up to an entire month for the person who is contacted to initiate contact. If ESP is actually what is happening, one should allow the signal time to fully activate the suggestion that motivates your targeted subjects to contact you.

If the person who was the attempted contact does not respond before the experimenter loses patience, it's a simple matter of changing the experimental intention by asking them, once reached, if they had been considering making contact. If you had been haunting their thoughts, there is a good chance that they will let you know. In either case, this is a "high-improbability experiment" that can lead to, sometimes, surprisingly accurate results.

This experiment is a two-step process. If you are successful at sending the telepathic voicemail, and within a short period of time, your targeted-subject responds, you can also then ask what inspiration it was that made him or her call you. Of course, there is a chance that it is a complete coincidence, so finding out the time and inspiration they felt they should call can lead to useable information as you continue to experiment. It is a mystery to me that it works as often as it does.

PRACTICAL PALMISTRY 101

With Mark Sherman

I tend to run into people who work in the casino, resort, and corporate world. It just happens to be the world that I have worked the most in. Within the mystery arts, there are many different people that one can meet. We nonetheless, will tend to gravitate the most to those who work within the circles that we are most used to. I like to joke about it, but it's true. My lifestyle has definitely become a "conference club and resort hotel lifestyle." Of course, when I am at home, it feels more like an art colony, so maybe that's just part of the *yin* and the *yang* in my life.

Fellow corporate mystifiers, who hail from the Pacific Northwest of the US, are my friends Sheila Lyon and Mark Sherman, and their primary interest is in the mysterious art of Palmistry— the ability to interpret the life and characteristic tendencies of a person by simply looking at their hand, outstretched.

Mark and Sheila are co-authors of *Palms Up! A Handy Guide to 21st Century Palmistry* (2005, Penguin, USA) and have both presented and entertained using their craft for some of the world's largest corporations. Sheila would be the person most responsible for taking the concept of palm reading, "out of the tent and into the crowds," with essentially what she saw more as a "group reading" allowing for more people to enjoy having their palms read at the same time. Whereas most palm readers and psychics are used to reading for people one at a time, thereby allowing each "sitter" to donate money to them for their personal time spent, at higher-end corporate events, the vendors are already "prepaid" and not expected to accept tips or donations. At these events, the psychic becomes a "psychic entertainer" and is expected, especially at high occupancy events, to interact with as many people as possible. Sheila and Mark quickly became very well known palmists in the corporate industry simply on the grounds that they were able to move through as much as *twenty times* more people than the average fortune teller. Sheila regularly does group palm readings for as many as five hundred people at once during her corporate seminars.

Palmistry is one of those things, which if you have never tried it or had your own palm read, you probably either disbelieve it blindly, find that it is the work of the devil, or have no interest in it. Those who have had their palms read at fairs, amusement parks and holiday events will sometimes end up with someone who has absolutely no idea of what they are talking about. But for those who are curious to get a good glimpse and find out just how much there is to know about a person by knowing what the lines on their hand mean, I have included this section here. That way, you can make it an experiment for yourself, while entertaining your friends in the process.

I have met many people who read palms, and know some of the world's most prolific (and accurate) psychic palm readers, and Mark, is a master of presenting his knowledge in a fun and entertaining way. After more than thirty years of studying and putting himself out there in front of thousands of people, Mark is a natural. The first time Mark ever had his own palm read, was for twenty five cents, by a Creole woman in New Orleans' Jackson Square, when he was just a boy. That's actually where you will, still today, see many palmists, card readers, crystal healers, and occasionally, a voodoo priestess... From that first time, Mark became a devoted student of the craft. What I personally like about Mark is that he is also an enthusiastic historian of New Orleans culture as well as Zydeco and Cajun music. It ends up "going with the territory," for him to also be a master of interpreting palms.

All my life, I have performed at various social or corporate business events where there would also generally be a palm reader stationed somewhere. At these events, usually you will find people mingling and sipping scotch and waters not long after the cocktail hour begins... never late for drinks. A jazz trio is heard playing standards on the far side of the room, drawing you in. A caricature artist sits at her easel near the front, as you walk in. At these events, as you look around the tables decorated with elaborate floral centerpieces, one can generally find a very long line of curious people waiting. These people are all waiting for their turn to find out what can be interpreted about themselves by opening their palm and letting the psychic see what can be read...

Fortunes and predictions of coming business deals or relationships, can always be topics to psychically consult with, but skeptically, I have always felt as if it probably wouldn't have mattered if the psychics just gave the same spiel to everyone they met, or just rotated between four or five already-memorized monologues that are designed to appeal to 90% of those recited to. Lyons' and Sherman's "open palm" approach lets you be extraordinarily jazzy, spirited and sociable, allowing for people to have whatever question they want to address be answered conversationally. Doing this demonstrates, to the group, how one actually can know quite a bit about oneself by reading one's own palm. Best of all, it allows people to get to know each other and interact with one another in a most humanly intriguing manner.

In order to do this, one really simply needs to be taught that there are a few curious aspects regarding this ancient oracular system of reading palms, which generally reveal themselves to be consistently accurate. At least, that's the way I like to look at it. It truly is an interesting discussion piece, and far more original than, "Coke or Pepsi?"

THE LIFE LINE, most people have heard, is the deep line that runs in a half-circle around the base of the thumb. The center of the palm is known as the Plain of Mars.

What Mark tries to look for are distinctions between each of your group's palms, so anyone who is interested is asked to hold their palms out, faced towards themselves, so they can see how you will make distinctions. By observing just how far each person's Life Line "bellies out" onto the Plain of Mars will generally determine a few key things that you can tell about people regarding themselves.

For instance, it is known among people who read palms that the farther the half-circle of the Life Line reaches onto the Plain of Mars, the more openly communicative and generally extroverted that person is. If the Life Line reaches out all the way to the "center axis line" of their palm, the lines are read as this being the case. This is usually a person who can stretch themselves thin with their own commitments and pressures of responsibility. This is also a person who might either feel distant from his or her parents or family, or has even moved far away in location from his or her parents later in life. Generally, the further the Life Line orbits away from the thumb and towards the center of the Plain of Mars, the more independently thinking and self-confident that person generally is. Eternally curious about other people, these people tend to turn that curiosity into a way of transforming the strangers they meet into friends and associates within their wider social network.

BASIC INTROVERT

Life Lines, which do not stretch too far out onto the Plain of Mars, indicate people who are characterized as thoughtful, introspective and sometimes, even introverted. Oftentimes, they are better at expressing themselves with the talents they find they personally excel at. They are also discriminating communicators, usually whose circle consists of a smaller group of trusted people. Considered loyal to their family and close friends, even if not blood-related, they can exhibit tendencies towards humanitarian goals. The communication they have with those people they are close to is considered an important aspect of their survival. Daily messages, ways of connecting and phone calls are usually important to these people. Generally, a person who has a Life Line that is closer to the thumb (in other words, any time it does not belly out past the center-line of the palm) will rarely go a few days without reaching out and making some communication to someone they feel close to. They are most loyal to this circle of people, and within this circle are usually more than one person who they can seek inspiration and guidance from.

Of course, instances in which these characteristics are contested will take place from time to time. No judgment should ever be placed on any palmist's interpretation. No one is being accused of having any characteristic that they feel is unbecoming; you are only interpreting what your limited knowledge of palm reading suggests regarding what you are observing. Furthermore, each side has its own duality of characteristics. You should be surprised at how much you find the "truth" in the lines' interpretations actually corresponding with what the person you are interpreting says about him or herself. It is an interesting experiment to play between wife and husband, girlfriend and boyfriend, parent and child, or just friends and colleagues. It is also a perfectly curious and interesting way of introducing oneself to the strange and mysterious world of palmistry.

There are two other deep lines that run more or less horizontally across both of your palms. The lower one is your HEAD LINE, and the one above it, is called your HEART LINE.

THE ACHIEVER REALIST

For one's Head Line, if it should cross from left to right (on one's left hand), and all the while stay within the upper half of the horizontal axis of your palm (towards the fingers), this is associated with one who is generally a realist. This is someone who values the things that represent real life over dreams and fantasies. They are pragmatists, planners, organizers, and can make great leaders as well as team players. The realist is also one who can be seen as enjoying the process of working with others.

THE DREAMING ARTIST

If the Head Line, however, should dip into the lower half of the palm, it ventures into the side that tends to be more impulsive. These are people who place great value on trying to live their dreams. They are romantics whose heads are filled with drama and ideas. Also, they tend to be artists or creative people who have strong positions about how they emotionally feel about things. These people also value personal wisdom and philosophy, and generally tend to work on things by themselves.

Note: Interpreting the Head Line on one's palm can obviously get more complex from here, as there are many subtleties and variations of interpretations which one can learn. The basic idea of including this section for palm readings, however, is to offer a basic overview, allowing you to experiment on this ancient oracle tradition, by making your own comparisons with people you know or people you happen to meet. With this bit of knowledge, you will find that you are more than equipped to give an accurate Palmistry 101 reading of the major lines on anyone's palm.

THE PASSION CONTROL METER

As for the Heart Line, the deep line that runs (usually) parallel and above the Head Line, you will also be able to make observations of it in two basic ways. With the Heart Line, the easiest way of interpreting it is by its length, whereby the Heart Line can then be seen as a measuring stick to one's *emotionality*.

With a long Heart Line, for instance, one possesses strength in how they express themselves passionately. The heart and its desires guide people with a long Heart Line. They will often find it tremendously difficult to control what their heart tells them to do. They are impulsive, will lose track of things, and can sometimes be prone to changing their mind on something it seems they were originally set on. They feel helpless to their hearts, but simultaneously, they feel that it is their heart that knows best. Spiritually, they are always curious, moving from one idea to another. Most people with a long Heart Line can also be exceptionally loyal and committed partners.

The shorter the Heart Line, the more capable this person should be at controlling their emotions. These people can range from athletes, to lawyers, to project managers, to doctors... even spies. Subtle, clever, mathematical, proud, and competitive... Sometimes cynical, discerning, and calculating, these are all characteristics that presumably describe someone with a shorter Heart Line.

THUMB WARS

In Palmistry, the Thumb is also one of the most interesting (and basic) features to learn about and understand. Here, I will give you an example of how my friend, the "Cajun clairvoyant," Mark Sherman, loves to have everyone hold up and compare the length of their thumb to try to reveal who the most stubborn person is within any particular group...

"Are you curious about who might be the most stubborn person in this group? We're going to use Palmistry to track down and identify who is the most inflexible, most 'my-way-or-the-highway,' stubborn person in this group. Anyone have any ideas or any theories?"

Mark will now look pointedly at anyone who has responded. He tends to milk a lot of humor out of this. Between husbands and wives, co-workers, or just associates, the interplay he gets is sometimes more priceless than the pay-off. "Do you know how we're all going to find out?"

Mark now gives the group a "thumbs-up" sign.

"The thumb has two 'phalanges.' Two parts... The upper phalange is about 'willpower,' and the lower phalange is about 'logic.' The top part of the thumb is either very flexible, or very stiff.

"If it is flexible, it basically means that you are a flexible person. It means you can also be an accommodating person, sometimes beyond your better judgment. You might even have a hard time saying no, if the situation felt optimal. That said, you value efficiency, creativity, and have great empathy for others around you."

"If it's stiff, it doesn't necessarily mean that you are inflexible... even though, some might call you a bit stubborn. I think it is more that you are on your own trajectory and that you somehow feel that something else, like some kind of need, guides you and is beyond your control. You feel as if you're on a mysterious mission... or that there is a driving force that makes you unable to stop yourself... Of course, I only say that because I have a stiff thumb... So let's see, can anyone beat my level of inflexibility?"

Mark will walk over to one person near the middle-front of the group, and says, "Let's see..." When he finds someone who can show how his or her thumb can bend almost to a right angle backwards, he knows he has found a flexible thumb:

"See how flexible this guy's thumb is? This is a person who has, in life, found that against his better judgment, he may have a little trouble saying no to some people... I would bet that this guy is the kind of person who will do almost anything for anyone who will ask him for a favor, so long as it's reasonable... and there is time in his schedule to do it. He might not want to admit it, but you are looking at Mr. Nice Guy, right here. According to this flexible signpost, he should also be the kind of person who says please and thank you, and is organized, intelligent, creative and fair-minded. I don't even know him, but would I be fair in saying that about him?" You will be surprised at how most will agree.

Now Mark shifts the focus to those who have Stiff Thumbs. "Both women and men whose thumbs *do not flex backwards*," he says, "are going to be people who are proud of their will power and they will visibly puff up when you identify them as having a strong will." Mark assures that it is a lot of fun to play with spectators who have Stiff Thumbs, and playing them off one another. Mark is the consummate psychic entertainer while holding these head-to-head 'competitions' between participants with equally stiff thumbs. He will start by remarking, "Ok, now show me the people who have inflexible, or what we will call, stiff thumbs, like mine." At the next corporate event you see him at, you will be sure to see him teaching others how to learn this identifying technique of checking for Stiff Thumbs. "These people believe that they have the ability to assert themselves to get what they want and they are damned good at it. They are clever, witty, and wise... their strength is in determination. Did I determine that correctly about this man?" Wait for a response from those who know him.

Whether you use your knowledge of chiromancy (or palm reading) just to make friendly conversation, or you are interested in learning more about its rich history, the sacred wisdoms of the many lines and the patterns that they make, try these aforementioned demonstrations as easy introductory experiments, if just to see if you notice any interesting correlations take shape.

THE SACRED PENDULUM

Nineteenth century French chemist, Michel Eugene Chevruel, was a staunch skeptic, who strongly detested the wave of spiritualism of that time, much of which was seen by him more as charlatanism. Regardless, many "spirit show" audience members still seemed convinced that some kind of phenomenon was happening that caused them to experience what they did.

The craze, at the time, involved tables that would inexplicably move and tip to one side as ordinary volunteers barely touched the table's surface. Interestingly, to him, the art of dowsing, pendulum readings, mysterious Ouija boards and the like, all seemed to operate with a similar function. Chevruel pointed this out in 1833, in an open letter to Andre Marie Ampere, as well as in his own paper that he wrote in 1854, entitled, *De la Baguette*. These are the earliest documented observations which first revealed that the true mystery behind these phenomena is our own human unconscious. This is where it is first announced that the mysterious acts that one can experience are nothing more than our own subconscious muscular reactions that are completely involuntary, and therefore has the ability to amaze the self while the mind is in this state. Later, this became known as the *ideomotor effect*.

A delightful hypnotist named, Marcia Proctor, was who originally certified me. She is an amazing woman who has the ability to put people into hypnosis in the easiest and most effortless manner. Her natural skills come from brilliant methods that she has learned from her closest friends, many of who are some of the most recognized hypnotists and hypnotherapists in the field today. She is both a master and self-made scholar within the field of hypnosis, and her knowledge of hypnotherapy is advanced beyond the vast majority of those practicing. In her words, *"The pendulum is a tool for communication with your subconscious, which includes your emotional mind. It knows the truth. With the pendulum, you have access to the powers of perception deeper than your conscious or intellectual mind."*

I had heard that the pendulum is the foundation upon which the polygraph was originally built, and yet, it is as simple as any swinging weight that hangs at the end of a thread or chain, which can be easily held with one hand. You don't need to go to a metaphysical bookstore to buy a pendulum, although, I must say, that pendulums are powerful, beautiful, objects that are hard not to collect. The easiest way to construct one is to just take a finger ring, pendant or charm and clip it to the end of a chain or cord, or tie it to the end of a ribbon or string so that it can hangs about 6 to 7 inches below where it is held. Even a wristwatch will work as the "hanging bob." I love pendulums because they can be seen as a gateway to our subconscious thoughts, while simultaneously referring to the classic hypnotist stereotype, swinging his shiny pocket watch at the end of its chain.

If there is a significant object (piece of jewelry, photograph, or any possession) that the pendulum can be held to suspend over, it will serve as a central resting point, and make the process easier to monitor. This may either be just someone hanging the pendulum over the center of his or her own palm, or hanging it over an object that is just placed on the table. If seated at a table, one should take care to keep one's elbow of the hand holding the pendulum off the table, but keeping the "pendulum bob" at rest, hanging stationary.

The most common way of holding a pendulum is in the non-dominant hand, securely pinching the end of the cord between the thumb and forefinger. It is then draped over the *back of the fingers*, so that the hand can hold the pendulum with the thumb pinching the cord from the top (thumbnail facing upwards).

I believe one of the reasons why the pendulum is used today in hypnotherapy, is because the "magic" that people will experience, can truly be seen as an aspect of their reality, despite the fact that it may appear somewhat fabricated by the subconscious mind. What Chevruel said was true. The subconscious will not only seem to create involuntary actions that are observable by others, when in the ideomotor state, but it will also compartmentalize the experiences, so even if whoever is holding the pendulum knows what is happening, they will still feel something that remains mysterious to them.

Therefore, rather than just feel satisfied that a fancy made-up word like "ideomotor" could end my curiosity of just how such an *ideo-motor* "ran," most hypnotherapists and people who are interested in pendulum-work will ask a few more interesting questions:

How might we better interact with this subconscious?

In what ways could experimentation in that direction be useful?

Could this concept direct us to accept a discovery that further forwards our thinking?

Anything that allows our conscious minds to reason with our most subconscious thoughts has always been extremely interesting to hypnotists. As mentioned earlier, regarding the placebo effect, even though you can tell your subject outright that it is simply your subconscious, it still can work. This is, actually, also true with a pendulum.

Chevruel originally stated that once the operator became aware of the brain's reaction, that the phenomenon could no longer be reproduced. However, it is widely known in the hypnosis community that even if one is aware that this thing called an *ideomotor response* is essentially your subconscious finding a way to communicate through your nervous system, the pendulum still manages to show successful results at nonetheless revealing one's subconscious feelings. It is also a very *permissive* approach, which never puts too much pressure on the pendulum operator. Just do the ritual. Continue to concentrate on your question or dilemma and the pendulum will move in the direction of your answer. Let it answer for you.

Before asking your pendulum anything, however, one can first make sure that one's mind is calibrated to the swinging of one's pendulum. Whether at a table or standing, hold it over a focal point, or whatever you are using to delineate a centered resting spot. Once the pendulum is completely still, in your thoughts, think "yes," and set it in motion by nodding your head. Notice how it rocks forwards and backwards, like in the direction of yourself nodding your head in agreement. This is your pendulum's "yes" response. Ask the pendulum to come to a stop and again center itself over its focal point. This time, think "no," while just gently shaking your head from side to side. Note that the pendulum moves from the left to the right, just like your head shaking or finger waving. Incidentally, if later, while asking questions, the pendulum moves in circular movements, chances will be that the answer that it is giving you is either "maybe," or "I don't want to answer."

The best way to calibrate your pendulum is to ask actual questions that have a definite "yes," "no," or "I don't know" answer, and watch your pendulum react accordingly, as you meditate on each question.

1) Did I choose my neighbors?

2) Am I a man? Am I a woman?

3) Was I born in California?

4) Is my car pink?

5) Am I single? Am I married?

6) What is the distance between Jupiter and the Sun?

Now ask yourself questions that might cause a disagreement between your emotions and your intellect, such as:

1) Am I satisfied with my car?

2) Am I pleased with where I live?

3) Do I feel successful in life?

4) Do I earn enough money?

5) Am I a happy person?

6) Should I buy another pendulum?

Continue to practice with your pendulum and you can discover more about yourself that you may not have known otherwise. It is also possible to use your pendulum to help you make difficult-to-answer decisions that require a more intuitive answer. In these cases, there are many times that the pendulum will answer a question in a way you may disagree with. This doesn't mean that you are wrong and your pendulum is right. It does mean that you need to contemplate deeper the issue. I will usually collect up the cord or chain and hold the pendulum stone (also called a "bob") in my hand to "psychically" consult with it. At that point, I might re-ask the question or ask it in a different way, in order to get a second opinion by starting up the pendulum again.

One of the first things that are taught when learning to use a pendulum is that it is really best not to dwell on letting the pendulum make predictions for you. The pendulum is best not used as a supernatural tool of this caliber. What it best does is answer questions for you regarding whether or not the timing of things seem appropriate or not, and also whether a situation or decision you make is in your best interest.

Thus, asking it things like, "Is it the right time for me to request a promotion?" or even, "Is requesting a promotion right now *in my best interest?*" would be a more practical application of using a pendulum than asking questions like "Will I be getting that promotion I've been wanting this year?" You will find that using your pendulum in a more permissive manner allows you access to your unconscious thoughts or even your "higher self." This guides you by letting you know if it feels conditions are favorable or unfavorable based on its access to the Life Force Energies. At least, that is what I am told.

Regarding the etiquette which suggests that one never ask one's pendulum for an unforeseeable prediction of the future, there is one quite well-known exception This would actually be the most commonly known phenomena regarding the pendulum as a "subconscious gateway," and it goes quite far back in history. I wondered if it truly is that, might it demonstrate an anomalous nature beyond the gender test? If so, how?

The pendulum was one of the first oracles regularly used to determine both the pregnancy of a woman and the sex of a child before birth. Doing a search online, one finds many contradicting methods which tell you what signs to look for, how to calibrate it, how to hold it, and what to be concentrating on. The idea goes far back to gypsy origins, and as such, it is hard to place just who started this tradition, what the details of the tradition were that are pertinent, and also how off base the system would become over time. Remember, as interesting as I find the mystery of the ideomotor response when using pendulums, my greater interest would be in asking the question if there is a secret understanding that we may be unaware of which we might learn to eventually put to better use?

To receive the correct answer of whether a woman is pregnant or not is, remarkably, almost 100 percent, since *a woman's body will always simply know the truth* as to if it is pregnant, whether she is consciously aware of it or not.

The gender test, however, was still quite intriguing to me, since it had an element of "hidden mystery" and also because after I had tried it over a few instances whenever presented, I started to find out that it appeared to always be correct, once I was told of the ultrasound results. Much of the time, the pregnant woman making the challenge would already know the sex of her child, but would want to know if I could somehow know for myself if her baby was going to be a boy or a girl. In these cases, I would simply give her the pendulum and I would just tell her that if it swings this way, then it is a boy, and if it swings that way, it should be a girl. Since she herself *already knows* the gender of the baby she is carrying, the ideomotor response powered by her own subconscious has no problem in revealing the truth. *It is when no one knows if it will be a boy or a girl*, while the woman is in her first trimester, that the pendulum exhibits its most amazing ability.

Since I first started playing around with this (almost ten years ago), I started noticing something else, that has still managed to amaze me, so I feel if I mention it in this book, something may come of it. My notion is that, there may be good reason to believe that there is something to this "pendulum gender game" that is truly mysterious. So far, I may have just been lucky, but it has not failed me for many years now. Could this ancient oracular instrument, have some connection to the "old wives tale" of gender divination through some esoteric form of *sacred geometry*?

Originally, I learned it from a Turkish woman who told me that this was something that her family did going back many generations. Her claim was that this method "never fails." When she did it, she did it with my (then) pregnant wife. I remember being mildly amazed that it worked. As an experiment, whenever I had a pregnant woman ask me what the sex of her child was going to be, I would make-shift a pendulum out of whatever happened to be around in the moment, and then I would have her hold it and make an interpretation. It was that easy... plus, it seemed to *always work*. Assuming that the woman who originally showed this to me was honest when she said it had never failed her (or, allegedly generations of her family past, as well), and hard as it may be for me to put more control on this experiment, since pregnant women aren't always directly in front of me to do this with, my sense is to try and begin looking deeper at this phenomena by just putting it out there. Is the urban legend really just an old wives tale? Or could we all be missing something deeper? Might *sacred geometry* somehow be playing a role?

Whether what I am about to tell you is real or just another perfect example of magical thinking, I do think it deserves looking into in the form of play. It really might amaze you. Play the game as follows, and take note, as you simply watch it unfold. The next time you are confronted with a pregnant woman, you don't need to have your special quartz crystal pendulum with you, in order play this simple game. Just tie a paper clip or wedding ring to a piece of ribbon or string, or even just have the woman who is pregnant hold a thin necklace with a pendant:

1) To begin, it is an interesting conversation starter as you hand the pregnant woman (especially if in her first trimester) your pendulum to look at.

2) Do not give her any instructions at all about what to do with it, and if someone tries to give her directions, tell them to stay quiet for the time being. Just watch her and observe what she does with it. If she asks you for guidance, have her hold it so that it hangs stationary over her open palm, and tell her to "see if it begins to swing."

3) This next part is where this game detaches from rational thought patterns. Watch closely, to see if the pendulum is swinging in any particular way. If it is motionless, tell her that in a moment she will see the pendulum swing. The pendulum will eventually swing, and when it does, you will look for one of two swinging patterns. (A) If it swings in a straight line in any direction, this can be recognized as a "yang," or male energy making its presence known through the laws of sacred geometry. (B) If it swings in a circular motion, whether it is clockwise or counterclockwise, it can be seen as a "yin," or female energy, emerging from the subconscious. Oddly, at least for me, it has proven to work 100 percent of the time. Common statistics would easily prove me wrong in the long run, but so far, to my surprise, this has worked on every I have tried this on.

The Flower of Life Model: It oddly makes sense, especially if you have ever looked into the sacred geometry mentioned by New Age Movement philosopher, Drunvalo Melchizedek, in his *Flower of Life model*. Essentially, this is a geometric pattern, which he noticed was found in ancient pictograms and hieroglyphs all over the world, stemming from (it seems) the beginning of human language and communication. The Flower of Life symbol consists of identical evenly spaced, overlapping circles, beginning with a single circle that is surrounded by six identically sized circles.

For instance, take seven identical coins, and with one in the center, you can form a basic six-petaled flower. The perimeter of each coin will be seen to barely touch each coin next to it in this configuration. Now, if more identically sized circles are then symmetrically filled in to this design, it creates a uniformed grid of *vesica pisces* that overlap all seven initial circles. A kaleidoscopic pattern will reveal smaller *six-petaled flowers within each circle* that suddenly can be seen throughout the entire pattern.

One can interpret the "male energy," as seen more as the thinner unions (the "flower petals" of the design that are formed by the multiple vesica pisces). The "motherly circles" that bring the entire design to life from the beginning represent the "female energy." Thus, the straight lines are seen as MALE "yang lines," and the circles are viewed as FEMALE "yin circles." My theory is that there might be a possibility that pregnant women will unconsciously tend to swing pendulums by themselves in a way that will reflect the gender of their future child.

Taking this "male/female" concept a few steps deeper, it would then be possible to have anyone concentrate on anything at all, before handing them a make-shift pendulum, and by just watching it swing, you will determine if the energy of their issue has a male or female vibration, and thus, you may have better insight in knowing how to balance them out accordingly. If there were a conscious connection to yin and yang energies that can be interpreted by observing the simplest geometrical swings of a pendulum, that could be be an idea worth exploring.

Even if this doesn't turn out to be true, once you explain your reasoning of why you feel this way by drawing a Flower of Life for the woman you are explaining this to, they can no longer blame you if it doesn't work anymore. Now, you can blame it on the Flower of Life. The thing to question here, however, is *what if* there was some kind of truth behind this? Wouldn't that be worth further investigation? It already has a weird way of making sense, so I encourage you to try this and let me know of your experiences. Once you have discovered how much there is to explore regarding this notion, you can begin to contemplate the possibilities of what it might mean if the straight lines swing sideways (left to right), or if the circles go counterclockwise...

SCIENTIFIC ORACLES

In the 1930's Professor Karl Zener along with his colleague Professor J.B. Rhine, who ran the parapsychology studies at Duke University, developed a simple pack of cards for the use of experimenting with (or developing) one's telepathic, precognitive or clairvoyant potentials. The deck consisted of five basic symbols, one per card, repeated five times throughout the 25 cards. The symbols were meant to be seen as classic, easy-to-visualize images:

1) A single hollow Circle

2) A simple Greek Cross (or "plus" sign)

3) A set of 3 identical perpendicular Wavy Lines (representing Waves)

4) A hollow Square

5) A hollow Star.

There were many different types of experiments conducted with these symbols and, since those days, many private researchers continue to use these symbols to explore synchronicity, clairvoyance and precognition. If researched, one will initially find a lot of critical opinions regarding the validity of these cards and symbols being used for experimentation, primarily citing the great possibility of test subjects finding ways to cheat using all the clever ways that might employ methods that magicians and gambling hustlers would use. One might also hear about how, as such, the use of ESP symbols had become discredited and is rarely, if ever, used in any serious research that is conducted today.

I find that hard to believe, since the Rhine Research Center, that is just across the street from Duke University, where all their research began, is still in existence today. Currently they still conduct ongoing classes, workshops, and lectures on various studies that are related to parapsychology. On the homepage of their website, they proudly use the five symbols as part of their logo, and they still do sell decks of 25 cards to test one's ESP in their online store. I have visited there a few times while passing through Raleigh/Durham on my travels. If you end up there, you will also see, on display, some of the randomizing machines that incorporate the visualization of the Zener ESP symbols. The Rhine Research Center is one of the country's largest libraries of books related to the field of parapsychology and the paranormal. They sell many excellent books on these subjects as well. Being there makes me feel absolutely normal.

Some, may wonder about the potential correlation to oracular meaning that such a set of cards might produce, similar to that of using Tarot Cards. Of course, Tarot is an entire field of study unto itself, but I do believe it is possible to find similar oracular principles emerge from observing the patterns of any randomly generated event. Rich in numerological meaning as well as symbolic and astrological imagery, Tarot and Astrology can also be seen as more complex divination systems. Nonetheless, they are both easy to find out about on the internet and have been written about in many books throughout history.. What I will attempt here, is to provide a useable alternative to a Tarot reading system using the five Zener symbols.. Also, using symbols with the five-element characteristics creates an oracle more similar to the I-Ching than the Tarot.

The Zener Symbols were always appealing to me. Their simplicity invokes both curiosity as well as mystery, in my opinion. The five symbols can easily be interpreted to adopt the characteristics of the Wu Xing (the Five Chinese Elements) and all of the wisdom that they carry regarding the "Five Cycles of Change." Psychic entertainer, Doug Dyment, had written about these correlations in a pamphlet which he sells on his website called, *Zenermancy*. Using this idea as a springboard to create significant correlations to symbolism makes natural sense, numerological sense, and there is no reason why it shouldn't be able to generate interesting oracular interpretations. The Circle would symbolize Wood, the Cross would symbolize Fire, Waves would represent Earth, Square would be equivalent to Metal, and Star is symbolized Water. Intuitively one might associate Waves more with Water, Cross more with Wood, or Star more with Fire, but the important thing to consider here is that the Chinese Five Elements goes through a progressive cycle just as the five ESP Symbols do, and both go through their cycles in five stages. By laying one list over the other, this is just what naturally happens. Even though the correlations that are made might feel a little obscure, the system, because of its numerical progression, provides an appropriate alignment.

In Billy Bob Thornton's, supernatural thriller, *The Gift*, which came out in 2000, the main character Annie, played by Cate Blanchett, is seen reading people's fortunes, using a set of these cards. The idea of using the symbolic meaning of the cards as oracles that can give us insight into our destinies, goes back to the use of Tarot cards, and probably beyond that into early astrological meanings and *animism*. Animism was one of the earliest human worldviews that believed animals, plants, stones, rivers and clouds are all represented by different gods of different associations and characteristics.

In fact, of the earliest items ever found, (as mentioned in Part 4, regarding the pyromancy used on bones and turtle shells), which had a systematized form of writing on it, appears to be made for the express purpose of *divination*. Nowadays, cards used for playing games maintain popularity in the gaming world, but in the beginning, the oracle that the cards provided was considered divine, hence the old saying, "I saw it in the cards." Literally, any card or truly anything, for that matter, can be used as an oracle if perceived as one.

I had worked on my own intuitive oracle system with the ESP symbols. What I wanted to construct, was a simple system using these symbols that could potentially demonstrate meaningful correlations. What I personally like about these symbols is that they were designed by scientists (as opposed to mystics), so whereas a deck of Tarot cards may be seen by some as "the work of the devil," you can explain a more potentially scientific connection by using these symbols in an oracular manner while having them perceived more as a lighthearted synchronicity exercise.

This idea uses characteristics that are ascribed to the symbols themselves. What I would like to first do here is show how the meanings of the Five Elements are relevant to The School of Yin Yang. The Chinese scholar Zhou Yan first interpreted the Five Elements, after the time of Confucius (476-221 BC), and during the era of the *Contention of a Hundred Schools of Thought*. He was the founder of The School of Naturalists (also known as The School of Yin Yang), which is based on a deep mystical meaning that regards the cycles of natural change, as well as changes through interaction.

The 5 Elements' earliest references, describes them through their movements (the order of one element to the next expresses its natural cycle, thus the sequential numbers):

1) Wood: *that which can be bent and straightened (INNOCENCE vs. BRAVERY)*

2) Fire: *that which blazes and ascends (CREATIVITY vs. ENLIGHTENMENT)*

3) Earth: *that which allows for sowing and harvesting (PRACTICALITY vs. PERSISTENCE)*

4) Metal: *that which can be molded and changed (STRENGTH vs. EXPERIENCE)*

5) Water: *that which soaks and descends (FULFILLMENT, HAPPINESS vs. SADNESS)*

As mentioned in Part 4, Zhou Yan's theory was that the concept of Yin and Yang exists in everything. He was, after all, credited for being the one who first synthesized the concepts of Yin and Yang with the Wu Xing (Wood, Fire, Earth, Metal and Water). Within a pentagram, in which each point represents one of the five elements, two lines shoot out of each point of the pentagram in two separate directions, each of which interact with *change* over only two other specific elemental points within the star. These two directions are seen as a duality regarding "change" or "overcoming." An unbroken circle, which surrounds the entire star pattern, which each of its five points touch, represents the continual cycle of dualities between "generation" and "creation" in a clockwise rotation.

In Zhou Yan's diagram, the circle represents a creation cycle which both "Creates" and "Overacts" between each element. Thus, Wood can be seen to create Fire, which creates Earth, which creates Metal, which creates Water, as per their description. Within the pentagram, one can see how the two lines which connect to each single point, rather than cycles naturally as in the outer-perimeter, demonstrates the acts of change as each of the five elements is introduced (intentionally) to the remaining two elements that it doesn't immediately cycle to or from.

Thusly, within the pentagram, for example, Fire, when introduced to Water, "insults" the Water. Water, on the other hand, is seen to "destroy" Fire, when coming from its direction on the same line. The second line that shoots out of Fire connects with Metal, and is seen to "destroy" Metal, whereas Metal "insults" Fire. Metal, likewise, has a second line that connects to destroy Wood, whereas Wood only insults Metal, if coming from the opposite direction. Wood likewise connects to destroy Earth, whereas Earth insults Wood. If this idea of elements during interaction, in the act of symbolically destroying and insulting one another, is hard to understand, it is because it is better understood through the eyes of an Eastern alchemist. Joseph Needham, the British scientist who wrote extensively on Chinese Science, defined the five elements as a *proto-science*, as opposed to giving it a pseudo-science label that was originally given to the Confucians of western scientific thought. Incidentally, Western scientific philosophy *still* does not fully embrace Eastern philosophies regarding the natural laws of traditional medicine, except through therapeutic practices.

Interestingly, I was able to discover a correlation between my characteristic interpretations of the ESP testing symbols and the Five Chinese Elements that oddly worked out in relation to the pentagram diagram. My key words which are characteristics that should be considered along with some of the other descriptions when studied below, perfectly fit over the Chinese Elements as: Innocence, Creativity, Practicality, Strength, and Happiness along with their corresponding yin/yang trait as seen in the list above.

When the five elements are layered over the five ESP Symbols along with the characteristic key words offered above, one could fairly easily see the natural cycle that leads from one to the other even in relationship with one another. Characteristics of the elements can be introduced to one another within the Wu Xing pentagram. Each element flows immediately to or from another element as it goes through its natural cycle. Therefore, there are always two elements that are seen to connect to each other by means of its depiction within the circle/star. Elements are introduced to the other two elements (that do not cycle come in contact with them) in the acts of "insulting" or "destroying." Taking the example I used above, if we substitute Fire (or Cross) with Creativity, when introduced to Water (or Star), it insults the "Happiness" of Water. In the opposite direction Water, which can also be seen as Happiness or complete contentedness, will quench or "destroy" Creativity. Fire also connects to Metal (Square/Strength) to melt or "destroy" it, much in the same way that Creativity can be seen to overcome Strength.

Strength can only insult Creativity in the opposite direction. The other line that can be seen in the pentagram connects the Strength characteristic of Metal to the Innocence association with Wood.. In this case (as Metal cuts Wood), Strength destroys Innocence. Innocence can only insult Strength, but as such the Innocence of Wood will deplete or destroy Practicality (Earth). Practicality insults Innocence, but can "dry up" or destroy the Happiness (or Sadness) of Water. Happiness can only insult Practicality. Remember, however, how it destroys (or, rather, makes complacent) Creativity?

Although it might seem a bit complicated at first, by simply drawing a pentagram with a circle around it and labeling each point as one of the five elements along with its symbolic characteristics, it should become clear how all of the connections are made. The above characteristics are fairly easy to remember in conjunction with the Zener symbols, as well as the characteristics that I have used to symbolize their meanings below. For now, let us touch upon the very basic idea for how I find it is best to use such symbols as oracles.

The first thing I decided was that I wanted to reduce the number of cards to ten. I wanted it to be both simple and "metric," basically. That way, it is only the five symbols repeated twice, (representing both the yin and yang elements of each symbol). This is easy enough to make yourself over breakfast on ten business cards that you can grab off the hotel front counter. In fact, if you are the kind of person who enjoys reading your horoscope in the morning newspaper during breakfast, this idea takes only a few extra steps and can be done just by yourself at any moment or even socially with multiple people. Use a pen to mark one side of the ten cards with each of the five symbols so that you have an impromptu set of ten (two sets of five) Zener symbol-cards. You now can do this without needing to carry anything on you. The reduction of 25 to 10 cards is perfectly suitable when used in the following manner.

The reading that will be used is known as a simple "three card reading," usually denoting the Past, Present and Future. Start by having a question that you would like to focus on. This can be any single thing at all that might have to do with the states of your various relationships, job prospects, health, or fulfillment. Shuffle the cards while mentally asking the question regarding something you would like to know most of all. Cut the cards and complete three times, however you like to do it, without looking at the

symbols on any of the cards. In a row, you will lay out three cards so
that you cannot yet see the symbols. I like to lay down the top card
to my left (if doing it for myself). Next I pull the bottom card of the
packet and place it symbol-side down next to it, and then I pull out
one from the middle and put it to my right of the other two.

Each symbol represents a different set of qualities that is associated
with each corresponding element. Below is the list of interpretations
that have been given to each card:

1) CIRCLE: Female (yin), Family, Wellness, Courage, (Family
   Circle), INNOCENCE (BRAVERY)/ WOOD

2) CROSS: Male (yang), Decisions ("Crossroads"), Change,
   CREATIVENESS (ENLIGHTENMENT)/ FIRE

3) WAVES: (yin) Travel, Excitement, Fitness,
   PRACTICALITY (PERSISTENCE)/ EARTH

4) SQUARE: (yang) Home, Career, Car, Pets, STRENGTH
   (EXPERIENCE) / METAL

5) STAR: (yin and yang) Food, Drink, Passions, HAPPINESS
   (SADNESS)/ WATER

With just a simple memory system (see end of Part 1), it is quite
easy, since you only need to know a few standard characteristics per
symbol. By contemplating, those particular characteristics while
considering the *past, present and future* position of the cards, some
pretty profound insights will be revealed. Is it supernatural? Could it
be the cosmos speaking to us? Or is it completely random and just
for fun? It can actually be seen as all three!

Simply use the ascribed interpretations as a catalyst that gives you a
direction to contemplate the characteristics that the symbols point
to. Be intuitive about the situation of which you are asking your
oracle advice. If delivering a reading to another person, feel free to
ask what his or her own feelings are regarding each symbol. Ask if
the symbol might mean something to them. Once the person who is
being read has mentioned every aspect of what their full concern or
list of concerns are, you are ready to give the reading. Use the
symbols to guide your volunteers towards a place that makes sense to

them based on the interpretations given. The most obvious answer that will surface from the reading will almost always be the truest answer.

Keeping in mind what we learned about dualities, the yin and yang, and ways of balancing our sense of energy and wisdom (in Part 4), it should become easier than ever to discover new and uncanny insights. Remember, what is considered "positive and negative" energy does not necessarily mean "good and bad." Yin and yang are best seen as the always shifting and changing, "male" and "female," counterparts to a whole. If one is experiencing a low cycle filled with negativity, usually it only means that one is not too far away from hitting a higher positive cycle. Of course, some cycles take longer than others. Using the proper mindset, the symbols may astonishingly provide insight for any personal issue or concern, and can even direct you to whether the cycle being experienced will happen in shorter or longer intervals. If duplicate symbols appear within the spread, it can be noted as significant, and emphasis can then be placed on the relationships between the repeated symbols in contrast with the one that remains in the three-card spread. Within the three-card spread, it is easy to see if the issue leans more to yin or yang, and only on occasion is seen as "balanced." (Circle + Cross + Star, or Waves + Square + Star, etc). I have found this to be one of my favorite impromptu oracles to work with.

ZENER ENTANGLEMENT EXPERIMENT

Here is another interesting synchronicity experiment that can be done very quickly with two people, using only two writing implements and some notepaper. Each person takes three slips of paper and writes at the top of each, EXP #1, EXP #2, and EXP #3, respectively. Along the left side of each slip, you will also jot down, in a single column, the five Zener symbols, repeated twice in same order, so that the ten symbols form a column that are identical along the left side of all six slips. A straight line is drawn that goes up and down somewhere to the right of the list of symbols so that there is a little distance of at least a few inches between the line of symbols and what we will call the 'finish line´ drawn on the right of your sheet.

One of the objectives of this experiment is to see how easy it is to entangle with the other person's thoughts. Take three long deep breaths while staring into one another's eyes. As soon as you've exhaled your third breath, turn away and use your writing implement to make completely spontaneous lines that extend from each symbol on the left side of the page, and criss-crosses over to the right side of the page before is passes the finish line. This can be done methodically in a pattern, randomly, or intuitively, so long as it is understood that ultimately a new order of symbols will be formed based on the line drawn from each symbol on the left to where it hits the finish line on the right. The idea here is that, with each subsequent trial, a continuing effort should be made to try to absorb something about your partner, so that a correlation manifests in the direction of improvement. A new order of symbols, based on the position of where each line ended up passing through the finish line, is simply recorded in a column on the right side of the page.

Once this is done, you will, of course, record how many symbols correctly matched up with your partner's, but that is only the first part of it.

1) Looking for the basic symbol-to-symbol correlations is the first step. Less emphasis needs to be put on whether the exact symbol moved in the exact path, but rather, relevance should be placed on only whether the order of the symbols end up matching in any significant ways. The importance of this experiment is to see if an increase in correlation, if any, can be gained during the three consecutive trials at a minimum. Increasing the number of trials can also prove to be an interesting experiment, but the "freshest" results are gained if done in three to six trial intervals, helping to avoid tediousness.

2) Although the number of *symbolic hits* that match up is one aspect of the test that can be recorded, what can also be significant will be the *two patterns* formed by the new sequence that is generated. Sometimes although the symbols do not show a matching sequence, what ends up being revealed are patterns that match by similarly formed repetitions of symbols that can be seen within the sequence.

3) Finally, the significance of having a three-phase experiment to try to improve a theoretical entanglement connection should always be treated as part of the experiment.

Although, one trial may be seen as a coin flip, the fact that two minds are at play simultaneously is part of what makes it interesting, therefore, the three-phase experiment in which two participants try to entangle should be taken advantage of, and each successive trial should be treated as a step towards trying to improve in some way.

Experimenters can also just use two sheets of 8.5" x 11," turned horizontally so four vertical columns can evenly divide the length of the horizontal sheet. The first column on the left begins with the ten symbols in order from top to the bottom. However, between each of the three *entanglement trials*, rather than starting from the initial order of symbols each time on a new sheet, you just continue to criss-cross lines towards the right, stopping at each next column, before reordering your symbols. In this variation, each time you begin, you are starting from your most recent pattern of symbols last made. Interesting correlations may take place!

This experiment is interesting as its spontaneity makes it nearly impossible to cheat and the three successive trials will either show improvement or let one know if conscious adjustments need to take place. All you need is, one willing participant, to give it a try. If anything, it will prove to be an interesting way to pass the time getting to know someone from a purely synchronistic perspective.

THE HAPPY BUTTON

With Aaron Alexander

I have a mysterious friend who can do things that most people cannot. He does not necessarily deceive you, so you cannot really call him a magician. He will, however, do things to people who he just meets that affect them in an always positively unusual manner. His name is Aaron Alexander, and it is my pleasure to share with you my take on a very interesting demonstration of his; one that I have been having nothing but a joyful time doing for people.

Aaron Alexander's special talent involves combining effective principles in a way that creates a performance filled with *impossible things happening*, almost as if by just saying "magic words." Through this demonstration, you will get to play with an idea that most hypnotists are familiar with, called "anchoring." In many ways, this demonstration feels like real magic. All it takes is for you to learn how to engage your volunteer enough to give them the opportunity to feel that sensation of something completely impossible happening. In the end, it's about how much comfort, curiosity, and confidence you can instill in your participant, but you will be amazed at how effective it is once you are confident enough to give it a try.

The idea behind this would best relate to what is known in the Hypno-therapeutic world as Neuro Linguistic Programming (NLP). This is a very in-depth study of essentially the art of effective communication, much built on top of Milton Erickson's preferred method of simply using a subtle, more subconscious manner of bringing people into deep states of hypnotic trance. Such techniques can be used both verbally and non-verbally. As opposed to the authoritative approach of the hypnotist commanding his participants to "Go to sleep now," the Ericksonian model of hypnosis was to instead explore a far more permissive approach. For this reason, it is also known as Conversational or Covert Hypnosis.

"The same situation is evidenced in everyday life, however, whenever attention is fixated with a question or an experience of the amazing, the unusual, or anything that holds a person's interest. At such moments, people experience the common everyday trance; they tend to gaze off to the right or left, depending upon which cerebral hemisphere is most dominant (Baleen, 1969) and get that faraway or blank look. Their eyes may actually close, their bodies tend to become immobile (a form of catalepsy), certain reflexes (e.g., swallowing, respiration, etc.) may be suppressed, and they seem momentarily oblivious to their surroundings until they have completed their inner search on the unconscious level for the new idea, response, or frames of reference that will re-stabilize their general reality orientation. We hypothesize that in everyday life consciousness is in a continual state of flux between the general reality orientation and the momentary micro dynamics of trance..."

The above is quoted from Erickson and Rossi's *Two-Level Communication and the Microdynamics of Trance and Suggestion*, in the *American Journal of Clinical Hypnosis*, in 1976.

I believe Aaron Alexander comes more from this specific model than anything.

So what's better, the philosophies and techniques of Milton Erickson? Or the model built on Ericksonian hypnosis, by the creators of NLP, Richard Bandler and John Grinder? Either way, if you are interested, all you need to work on is a completely conversational and comfortable manner of communicating your thoughts effectively, and you will see an immediate improvement in establishing the most present and coherent connection with others around you. You are about to see how Aaron appears to believe that this simple notion is all that really matters. Trust me, it is astonishing.

Picture this. The mood is so casual and conversational that virtually any situation is fine to try this demonstration, so long as someone is listening to you and you have his or her attention. No need to be the all-powerful "man of mystery" to make this work. It is actually better that you don't take on this character. Truly, the idea is to shift the emphasis *from power to possibility*. That is actually the first step to cracking their apprehensiveness. Just allow their own feeling of enchantment to give them the feeling of wanting more, and they will. It begins with:

"Want to see something interesting that I just learned about?

"I want to show you something called 'anchoring.' It's really simple and you probably heard about it somewhere. It has to do with how things 'mental,' like the senses, and the environment interact. Essentially, you are able to learn how your environment can trigger just about anything inside you subconsciously.

"Similar to that classic experiment where the dog salivates when you ring a bell, or how, when during that idle time waiting at an airport gate, with all the 'people movers' and TV sets, you might suddenly fall into that trancey state of just going from point A to point B. You smell the same perfume or cologne worn by your first girlfriend or boyfriend and suddenly, you snap back to that time in your life. Or, just by hearing that Facebook or text message signal, your focus suddenly diverts to wondering who's trying to get a hold of you even if the noise wasn't from your own computer or phone. That's basically the experience. When your mind can be made to naturally react to a situation... Like turning off the alarm and going back to sleep, just from hearing the sound of your alarm clock. Well, with the right mindset, I can show you how it can get even deeper than that.

"If you can tune into what I am about to show you, you will completely understand this concept of 'anchoring a thought or a feeling,' and who knows? It could even lead you to the 'secret to happiness.' So, how does that sound?

"Furthermore, we're going to see how the connection created between you and I, just from doing this, will also become kind of oddly profound in a mind-to-mind sort of way. Well, let's just see what happens...

"First, while listening to me talk to you, think of a happy memory. Go ahead. Take your time. Take a deep breath and, as you exhale, let a genuine and pure happy feeling enter your thoughts. Notice that you just kind of shifted your body in order to make it more comfortable to find a happy memory. That's perfect. I see you smile, lighten up, and then your eyes went off to the side searching for the memory. But then, when you found it, just thinking of it made you brighten up even more. You have it in your mind right now, correct?"

In these opening lines, it is obvious that your motivation is to engage someone's interest, but more so, you are *anchoring* your subject while in the very act of being in conversation with them. You are also secretly (and quite covertly) cueing your subject with rapport in the form of interest, to subconsciously prepare them to move right into an adventurous act of spontaneity with you. Verbally assessing each moment of their mental state as you point out what is happening and what you are observing in real time, will also aid in implanting positive suggestions of how their mental state will be improved by this experience.

Having seeded the conversation with ideas of what will happen if the test is successful, readies your subject to just "go with" each suggestion you make so long as a trusting rapport is maintained. Emphasis is put on their happy state just by reiterating the idea that happy thoughts lead to happy feelings, each time intensifying the experience. The more they can be made to feel their emotions and present feelings, the more real the effect will become.

"Now take a moment, close your eyes and just sink a bit deeper into that happy experience. You now can recall it vividly. Notice how your body reacts, how your smile gets a bit wider. Just thinking about it makes you feel more and more happy NOW... and you should feel that energy right here, in this area between your heart and throat..."

274

As you say "happy NOW," use your finger to poke a spot on their shoulder, arm, back of the hand, or wherever is convenient, and do it as an integrated part of the communicated gesture. Make it a deliberate and unique touch. The command should only feel slightly more authoritative at this moment.

"Here's the really interesting part. Keep your eyes barely closed, and know right now that just based on thinking about the memory in passing... or in greater and greater detail... can make you become happier to different degrees. It's like a dial that you can turn up and down. I want you to now turn that dial up, and go deeper into that memory, deeper into that feeling of happiness that you had. Turn it up and up and notice your body shifting, your smile grows as you've realized this complete sense of happiness... In fact, notice how all your senses feel happy too."

Once again you will touch them in the same spot as you say "happiness." At this point, you don't have to touch them any more. This area should be "anchored." Nonetheless, you should continue with a couple extra verbal deepeners.

"Completely and totally happy..."

And for good measure, a third time:

"Completely happy... alright, you can relax now and come back to normal." Give them a moment.

"Here's the interesting thing. I talked about how anchoring was about the physical and psychological interacting with one another. Did you notice what I did right as you were in your full state of happiness?"

No words need to be used here. Just gesture to the area, where you pressed their shoulder or hand, and say:

"Right now, just let yourself feel kind of neutral. Let it all go. Good. Now watch and feel what happens when I press right here and say the words "completely happy.""

Again you press the same spot as you say the word "happy." Let them feel that same sense of happiness radiating through them. If it looks as if they are trying to find the feeling, you are on the right path. You can encourage them at this point by saying, "It's subtle, but you should be able to feel it in this area here." As this is mentioned, point to the general area between your participant's heart and throat.

"It should feel a little strange how this area here (hold the palm of the hand over the area at the hand or shoulder where you touched them), can connect all the way to this area here (hold the palm of your hand over the area between their heart and throat). Well, it would be strange to an outsider who doesn't know about the hidden connection we made, because even if your conscious mind doesn't remember it, your subconscious mind still knows."

The convincer section in the above paragraph that you just read was something that I personally added to Aaron's formula, just to show how it is possible, through the subtle use of language, to increase and decrease states between authoritarian and permissive approaches in a variety of ways. The idea of doing this was used by Milton Erickson himself and it is plain to see, for those have witnessed him speaking in front of groups or even to individuals, just how much he really does do this. Alexander states, "Simple attention and focus changes experience. There really is nothing more to it, and it is universal."

In his writings, Aaron is skeptical of the claims and constructs of many hypnotists and NLP practitioners. In fact, he originally created this demonstration to illustrate a much more direct way of looking at the subject. My feeling is that, if anything, he certainly understands a way of getting right to the process of establishing curious rapport, which I believe Erickson would call the beginnings of a "trance state."

The confusion within the communication of quickly shifting from moments of authoritarian and permissive approaches further follows the path of what Erickson would label as another trance-state inducer. In fact, it was Erickson who pioneered the idea that Curiosity, Concentration and Confusion, are three easily found natural trance states that we are constantly experiencing throughout our days. It is during these trance states that people become susceptible to any suggestion that appears to make sense to them. Magicians, classic style clowns, street buskers, and mystery performers of all kinds take advantage of these moments to show how amazing the world can be to their audiences.

Erickson realized that this concept had much more to it than just a cheap thrill. If such ordinary things like everyday confusion, engrossment, or wonderment could actually be understood from the standpoint as being legitimate trance-states, wouldn't that mean it would be possible to use these moments for the purpose of seeding and/or suggesting ideas for personal improvement or change, or introduce any number of other ideas as well?

Anyone who has seen clips of Milton Erickson in action, or heard any of the many stories from those who have met or known him before his passing, will tell you just how remarkable a man he was during his life. Since the 1950's, Erickson furthered the understanding of hypnosis and trance, as well as influenced the therapy movement at large. He was noted for his ability to utilize anything about his subjects that would help them change or transform themselves for the better. To do this, he might choose to use his patient's strong beliefs, or words that he would notice that could be used as a trigger. He might incorporate the subject's personal history, or cultural background, sometimes even mirroring neurotic habits that he might notice. Erickson's teachings demonstrated how separate the conscious mind and unconscious mind function in the process of learning, and how the unconscious mind is able to function creatively, in positive and solution-generating ways.

The following shows us the depth of where Aaron Alexander is able to take such a concept from here. Alexander believes that by simply following the recipe that he has outlined in this very script, anyone will be able to do this. Of course, since a deep understanding of natural communication is required, it will not be as easy for some people to immediately grasp. My feeling is that so long as you are able to convey the words and simple actions taught as a well-played script, you should be surprised with the results you will get.

Technically speaking, this will work on anyone you should happen to meet, including even any random passerby, should you properly engage him or her. Let us now stay on this same line of thought, and see where Mr. Alexander might take a spectator from the point where we last left off...

"Now, you know how when the palm of your hand is slowly waved just over yourself, you become more aware of the area that you're hovering over. Like there's hypersensitivity in the area just from your attention being there? You can do that now if you want."

Here you wave your palm over any area of bare skin, and are asking your audience to do the same. Let them notice the heightened awareness, as well as the distance that one can get away from the body before that awareness disappears, before you continue.

"Now relax for a second and put your hand like mine" (this time over the *anchored spot*) and 'mirror' what I am doing."

Essentially, you are doing the exact same thing, allowing them to feel that hyper awareness, but this time over their own anchor point.

"Now what happens if we both take away our hands, and I put my mirrored hand back? Can you subtly feel a little of that same hyper-sensitivity in that area as I hover mine right here (over the mirrored hand on the table)—sometimes it's a tingling sensation, sometimes just that sense of hyper-awareness."

If they can feel the presence of anything at all through their awareness, you will have them where you want so you are able to fire off your dramatic final test using the question:

"Now... what do you feel flooding through you when I press on the same spot, but on myself?"

First, say the line, then slowly but deliberately touch the mirrored anchor-point on yourself. If their anchor point were their left shoulder or hand, you would have just touched your own right shoulder or hand with your left hand. As you touch your own shoulder, they should feel the flood of emotions as though their own anchor had been fired. Smile at them and see if it worked. You will be surprised. Plus it's endlessly amusing to do with someone at a party.

The method here is based on clever conversational conditioning. Every expectation is set as you build up each moment. By asking simple questions while slowly increasing your spectator's sensitivity during the sequence of tests, you will have given everything that is needed to very reliably create a strong experience of rapport. Continue by saying:

"That's what interests me so much about this stuff. Although you might think you have an idea of what might be happening, it could actually be something that's even more interesting, and with more possibility. It's not the same as having a dog drool when you ring a bell or a computer with clear input and output; it's something more fascinating that might even offer a glimpse of the things that we have yet to understand and discover about ourselves."

And there it is in its entirety. What Aaron has allowed us to explore here, is a casually done three-phase routine.

1) Get people to feel something just by thinking about it. This is completely normal, yet it builds comfort and shows something completely ordinary that is actually quite extraordinary— they feel genuine happiness in their body without anything necessarily truly happy that is happening at the time.

2) Create an association that manifests the concept of happiness "button." This all happens while showing an interesting aspect of the experience as well as a genuinely intriguing psychological idea.

3) Take it further and create that heightened sensation over the "button" area. This is important as it demonstrates how an imaginative mind can begin to effect reality.

4) Finally, you are now able to "play" with how near or far, from what seems rationally possible, to manifest a potentially entangled connection between you and your participant.

You are also starting with an exercise that elicits an emotion and builds comfort, which makes it hard to fail. If someone does not feel any of your suggestions during this the exercise, then they are just not into it and you can just change the subject or just simply explain what you were going to do instead of showing it. Don't give up if it doesn't work the first time. Practice on as many people as you can, and try to remember every aspect of the process that has been laid out for you here. By practicing this routine, you can eventually develop an ability to subtly induce positive transformation in virtually any willing volunteer you happen to meet.

READY, AIM, FIRE (A TRANSFORMATIONAL MEDITATION)

With Scott Grossberg

Now that we have opened our mind enough to see how suggestion (and therefore any hypnotic technique) can be applied with far more depth than expected, let us see what can happen if we turn that process on ourselves.

READY...

As our western-culture brains are taught to think the way we do, it becomes harder to realize just how much control and flexibility we have that allows us to shape our own reality and existence while living in balance with our surroundings. One must be careful, however, since it is easy to fall into the trap of learning only a diluted version of something without understanding the complete picture. When this happens, it can collapse everything into having too basic a meaning. When one comes into possession of the short answer to something, (for instance, "It's just a trick"), it becomes easy to short cut to that meaning, and thus, one may never end up understanding its true or complete meaning.

The meaning of all things constantly changes. It can only be fully determined and measured equally in relationship with the environmental moment during which it was being defined. The meaning of any or all things cannot be fully described unless the moment has already happened in time, at which the conditions of that moment must become part of the meaning as it is being defined. This can get complicated, but this is something one must be aware of, if one is attempting to shape their own reality. Everything in every moment is a microcosm in itself, and there is profound wisdom at every turn. The key is to understand that *one can shape this microcosm*, and all it takes is mental focus and discipline, to maintain a flow of positive energy into whichever system is being focused on.

In hypnotherapy, one quickly learns about how powerful the mind is with its ability to make complete changes in one's mental health, habits, state of mind and even create positive physiological transformations both for the better of oneself, as well as the worse. One can hypnotize oneself to feel something that can't rationally be felt. One can be hypnotized into thinking that foods that are bad for you, are good for you. One can be hypnotized into seeing things that aren't actually there (positive hallucinations). One can be hypnotized into not seeing things that are actually there (negative hallucinations). Most importantly, however, with just some commitment, one can be hypnotized into changes for the better in not much more than an instant.

My friend, Scott Grossberg, is known as an instant transformation and motivational coach. He claims that he can show people how to find what they truly desire in life and help them expand their abundance so that they experience success without getting bogged down in unnecessary details. He's a Fortune 100 advisor, a certified hypnotherapist, and an expert on NLP and persuasion. On top of that, he's an attorney, an entrepreneur and a really nice guy.

What Scott is about to share with you, are some extremely powerful and deeply moving thoughts. It will be important for you to read through the entire handling before you actually put it to use. This will enable you to understand the effectiveness and strength of one's visualization through self-hypnotic induction. Regard this offering with the respect it deserves, and you will find this dynamic meditation highly effective.

You will have to exercise the utmost of responsibility and care for yourself. For some, who have already-existing mental conditions that may see this as problematic in any way, it is suggested that approval from a physician or mental health care professional be granted before attempting this exercise.

Now, let us learn what it is like to be limitless . . .

Whether you call it self-hypnosis, an overactive imagination, living in a dream world or even delusion, the possibility that someone can completely go on a guided imagery journey of their own making and thus obtain life-changing skills and beliefs has fascinated people for ages. The following method will provide you with not only a way to create a powerful self-induction but aid you in creating your own superpower of mind control. You do not have to have any training at all in hypnosis to use this. However, for those who are overachievers, it is suggested that you study suggestibility, conversational hypnosis, and neuro-linguistic programming (NLP) just so you learn how it is possible to tweak these ideas for you to meet your own needs, wants, and desires.

AIM...

Scott created this amazing guided meditation, after having

participated in one of the legendary Tony Robbins' famous firewalks. The Grand Master of firewalking, Tolly Burkin, originally taught Tony. From personal experience, Scott says, "I can tell you that very little else you will encounter in life elicits such an intense and intimate response." Tony Robbins, of course, is not the only one to offer firewalks. In fact, some of the most name-recognized companies in the world use firewalks to incentivize and invigorate their executive staff. You may have already met someone who has participated in a similar training session.

For those who have never experienced a real firewalk, such a demonstration and participation is a powerful transformative experience commonly used for building a person's self-confidence and erasing negative emotions. Real firewalks are historically a rite of passage and can be life-changing on a very deep level. It is an event that allows us to face one of our deepest fears — fire — but then emerge with a new sense of accomplishment and personal power. As such, again, please treat this particular routine (and yourself) with respect.

Grossberg has continued to love the concept of the firewalk as a symbol of empowerment. He admits that it is hard for him to love the idea of paying lots of money and traveling great distances to get himself to another true firewalking experience. So during his own transformational seminars, Scott doesn't offer real firewalks. Dealing with the legalities and insurance issues are a nightmare for stuff like that (Scott would know, as he is an attorney). Quite creatively, he developed the following self-hypnosis guided imagery handling that permits him to create the same emancipating atmosphere of such an event without all the rigorous pre-event requirements and inherent risks of dealing with the injury-inducing, flaming coals that are necessary to include for the real-life experience.

You will want to conduct this in a room which permits you to safely walk between five to eight average steps, in a straight line, of course, adjusting the length of your "imagined fire pit" in the scripting so that you can safely walk while your eyes are closed.

FIRE...

With your eyes open, begin by simply standing up and walking across the room you are in. Please make certain that there is nothing in your path that can cause you to trip or stumble. Now walk back to the place from where you started. Notice that you are safe and comfortable. Notice your breathing and make certain you are taking deep cleansing breaths.

Take a moment and remember that firewalking is a rite of passage; a ritual that moves you from wherever you are now, to a place of greater confidence, strength, and courage. Those are the things you will be bringing back with you once this handling is complete.

It is also a test of one's own willpower and trust in oneself. You can use this session as a way to bring yourself freedom from doubt. In fact, if ever you find yourself in any kind of doubt, just a few minutes through this meditation will transform your confidence, your ability to stay in control and peace of mind. Throughout this session, you want to feel super-charged and yet super-calm.

Remain standing.

And now . . . you can either have someone else read the following to you or you can record it and then play it back to yourself, as you . . .

"Close your eyes. That's right. Relax and take a deep breath. Notice the way you feel. Notice the sounds around you, and notice the sensations of your body. You must stay standing at all times. If, at any time, you need to open your eyes to keep your balance or to attend to something important, you can completely feel free to do so.

"Now, bring your attention to the muscles of your eyelids. Notice how heavy they feel, making you feel completely relaxed and feeling great. Tell yourself that those muscles in your eyelids no longer need to work. And once you've told yourself that your eyelids no longer work, you will find that, in fact, you can go ahead and test them, only to find that, well, they really don't work. That's right. And the more you might try to open those eyelids, the more you find yourself just simply drifting deeper and deeper asleep. Staying awake enough to hear my voice, but certainly drifting, comfortably aware of everything inside you, as well as whatever things you might notice on the other side of those heavy, heavy, eyelids."

NOTE: The above induction is essentially the powerful beginning of the classic Dave Elman induction. Elman, the author of *Hypnotherapy*

(1970, Westwood Publishing), was one of the pioneers in modern hypnotherapy and its practical applications. Since his famous techniques proved to be such quick and highly effective induction methods, they have quickly spread to being used by stage hypnotists as well. As you can see, when put to action, it can also work equally as fast and efficiently for self-hypnosis. Once you practice this method, you will find that you can instantly reach a state of relaxation and high suggestibility simply by closing your eyes and reminding yourself that your eyelids just no longer work.

"Now, imagine the sound you hear when a hamburger or hot dog is placed on a red-hot skillet. Go ahead. Hear the sizzle. Hear all the sounds of cooking taking place. Now, shift your attention and imagine the extreme heat that you have felt in the past coming off an iron or after grabbing, by accident, the metal handle of a frying pan that had been left on a hot stove for too long.

"Perhaps you might even remember badly burning your feet while walking on the sun-baked sand at the beach. That is the type of heat you will be walking across in a moment. That's what you will be walking through.

"And when you walk over the fire and come out to the other side without any injury at all, you will instantly realize the complete confidence and self-assurance that lives within you. In fact, it always has, but see for yourself how it brings out a true warrior spirit within you.

"In a moment, you will be walking on fire... without injury, without pain, and without fear. You will know that once you do this, you will be forever changed. You will be powerful. You will be able to accomplish anything. You would like that, wouldn't you?

"Before you take your walk, think about the things that led up to your being here in front of this burning fire. Breathe deep. Feel how it feels just a little warm in your lungs as you continue to breathe. Now as you exhale, exhale hard, and imagine how it interacts with the fire in your mind. In your mind's eye, see a big, huge, roaring bonfire in front of you. Did you know that the word 'bonfire' actually came from the words 'Bone Fire?' That's right. This fire is so large and so intense, it can burn bones!

"It is the middle of the day and you can feel the heat and see the smoke rising into the air before you. In fact, your eyes feel like squinting just from the combination of the heat and smoke drying them out. You smell smoky, burning wood. Hear the crackling of the flames as they engulf the woodchips, turning them to searing, red and white-hot coals. Hear the popping of the wood. See the reds, and oranges, and yellows of the fire. Then see the coals that are forming and how they are glowing red and white-hot.

"Now you notice, next to the bonfire, a large empty pit that has been dug. It is about 10-feet long, about a foot deep, and about 2-feet wide. Later on, after all the burning hot coals have been formed, they will be poured into this pit for you to walk across.

"Turn back, now, to your bonfire. Before we leave this place, you are going to give yourself a gift. Something you will keep with you forever. It will be a personal and private gift and you don't have to share it with anyone else.

"Imagine that a piece of paper appears in your hand. Look at the paper now, and as you do so, a wish that you have suddenly appears written there. Take a moment and really concentrate on the wish and ask yourself 'What if this came true?' How would you feel? How would your life be better? How would you move forward towards your own success?

"Take another moment and look at the wish written on your slip of paper. This is your own personal, powerful, and profound wish. It's no one else's wish. It is just your wish.

"Fold the paper in half and walk over to the raging bonfire and throw the paper into the flames. That's right. Good. Watch the paper burn and be devoured by the fire; knowing that the energy and spirit of your wish is now being carried upward on the tongues of those flames and into the sky on the wings of its smoke. Your wish is now being carried off into the universe to fulfill its destiny.

"Really feel how powerful this ritual has made you. Step back from the bonfire and open your eyes. Really open them. Take a moment and notice how you're feeling. Are you excited or inspired? Are you feeling creative or encouraged? Perhaps you're feeling fully empowered or full of accomplishment.

"If you are wearing shoes, take them off and place them safely out of the way now.

"Go back to your starting point in the room. In a moment, you're going to close your eyes, again. And this time — you'll find yourself drifting quickly, and suddenly feeling ten times more relaxed as your were before. BUT . . . you are still standing with no problems. Agreed?

"Okay then. Go ahead. Close your eyes, again . . . feel what it's like to drift and remain standing. Remaining balanced.

"Yet you feel far more relaxed than you were before. Feeling quite good all over. In fact, better than you have ever felt before in your life.

"Notice now that it is night time. You are standing under a beautiful, clear, dark sky. The moon and the stars are shining down on you. You are at peace. More at peace than you ever remember being. There is almost a glow about you... however, now you notice that this glow is coming from a large bed of glowing, hot, burning coals on the ground, right there in front of you.

"Shift your attention to that pit which you saw earlier, next to the big bonfire. Only this time, it is not empty— it is filled with burning, hot coals. It stretches out in front of you 10 feet to the other side. As you look across the fire pit, feel the heat... Feel it as it radiates against your skin and your arms and your face. It is almost as if your face is on fire— the coals are so hot. And, against the darkness of the night, you can truly see the amazing glow of the fire. The flames seem to come alive and dance atop the coals— calling you to come to them.

"Hold the palms of your hands out in front of you now. That's right. Feel the heat. Feel the warmth. Perfect.

"Now in the past, you believed that fire could burn you and that it was something to be afraid of. In the past, you believed fire was something to run away from, but not any more. Not right now. While you are standing here with your eyes closed— just for these few moments— those beliefs are now no longer with you, those beliefs are now in the past— they are a million miles away and don't belong to you any more.

"Today, the fire before you, the coals before you, the heat before you is just like all the other challenges in your life — something to walk through and to come out on the other side a winner.

"Today, right now, right this instant you have the incredible power to accomplish anything. Right this instant you have the power to walk across the hot coals before you without pain, without injury, without fear.

"Now, in a moment, you are going to walk across the bed of coals. You are not going to dawdle. You are not going to hesitate. Only as quickly as you are ready to do so, you will march — you will walk – across the coals, as if hurrying to meet a lover you have not seen for a long time. You will walk quickly as if you are late for an appointment that will save your life. You will not hesitate. You will not falter. You will not dawdle.

"Now keep breathing deeply. Keep your head up. Do not look down. Focus only on your breathing and your intent. Focus on getting to the other side; knowing that as you walk across the bed of coals, you are conquering your own fears. As you walk across the bed of coals you realize you are taking control of your own life, your own decisions.

"NOW, walk across to the other side, quickly, without hesitation, that's right, feeling good all over, better than you've ever felt before.

"And, when you've reached the other side . . .

"STOP. Feel the rush of cold, refreshing, invigorating water as it is poured over your feet. As the water is poured over your feet, you are amazed to realize that you have just crossed over a bed of fire. You have just done what others would say was impossible. You have just achieved the incredible.

"How do you feel?

"Do you feel truly alive?

"Do you feel powerful?

"In your mind's eye, turn back around and look back over the bed of coals you have just conquered. That's right. Look. That bed of fire represents all the fears, all the challenges and all the obstacles you *used* to have in your life. That bed of fire is what used to keep you from taking the next step towards your own greatness.

"Take a moment and think about the triumph you have just accomplished. You are a winner. You are a success. Nothing can stop you now. Bask in the glow of what you have completed, knowing that you will carry this experience with you for the rest of your life.

"Now in a moment, you're going to count backwards from 5 to 1, and when you reach 1 you will open your eyes. In fact, go ahead and slowly start counting backwards now, as you feel yourself naturally shifting back to your present-time awareness. As you reach 1, open your eyes and notice that you are, once again, wide awake, feeling good all over, back to normal.

"You will clearly remember everything that you have done and everything you experienced. Most importantly, you will remember how you used this time to conquer your fears and anything that you feel has ever held you back. How you used this time to find your own personal power to accomplish anything.

"Anytime in the future, should you ever be faced with any doubt, hesitation or fear, all you need to do is remember what you accomplished here and your memory of this moment will instantly snap back to these feelings that you will remember having felt after you crossed that bed of fire. Remember, *here,* all the feelings and sensations that you have just gone through.

"Now . . . WAKE UP . . . to a life of abundance!"

"Feel free to take a few deep cleansing breaths as you come up from the subconscious dream-state, and take your time before feeling free to get up and move around to establish for your conscious-self, what it now feels like to be in your new and improved state of mind."

Once you are up and about, and while the experience is still fresh in your mind, this is a good time to journalize what you experienced in order to reinforce your expressions of victory, confidence and courage. You always want to end your journey with affirmations of success and encouragement.

What you have just experienced is exactly the intention of the real

Anthony Robbins firewalk that comes channeled to you directly from Scott Grossberg's personal experience having gone through the actual ritual with Tony Robbins, himself.

Self-hypnosis can not only be highly effective as a meditation for oneself, but this particular exercise can be recited, as provided, to others (or even large groups of people), in order to let them experience it themselves. Make sure (when doing this with others) that you choose your subjects wisely and return them all to a completely normal waking state without any injuries or distress.

For those readers who are more of a skeptical mindset, all of this might seem like just an elaborate affirmation exercise designed to simply "make you feel better about yourself." Make no mistake. Although on the surface it does serve the purpose of self-affirmation, making such quick assumptions to a process would be to deny the process its fair shake. To be clear, the purpose of the ritual is not to simply re-affirm oneself with positive thinking. It is to use the focus of one's positive thinking to magnify the transformation of circumstance to its favor. In this exercise, one shapes not just oneself, but one's greater reality, using mental visualization and heartfelt conviction.

THE PSYCHO-ACTIVE RITUAL

It is one of the goals of the shaman to create shared experiences with his people that show both one's mortality and one's connection to virtue. Scientifically, this is very curious, because a crossroads is found wherein one is given the choice to either be interested in "what is deluding me or interfering with my senses?" or "what is the most relevant thing to be interpreting?" Interesting here, is the notion that in some cultures, particularly dominant in western scientific methods, the idea of understanding reality as only through the five senses, is still a domineering characteristic.

As I sat on a recent panel discussion, I listened as each of the brain scientists spoke very intelligently and respectfully (I must add) about our sense of perception, and how we can be fooled by our senses in many subtle ways. What I found interesting was how the neuro-scientists seemed more interested in how each brain-sense was being activated to perceive something that may not be congruent to what is actually taking place. Oddly, however, they seemed less interested in going any deeper, satisfied with the idea that because the mystery has a neuro-scientific explanation, it needed no further understanding. Anything deeper from there might seem (to them) as just variables of conjecture regarding the same explanation.

In some cultures, like Buddhism and Sino-Indian philosophies, Mind or Thought is considered a "sense," but this idea is one of great debate, even to this day, in science. It is my belief, as well as others, that the notion of a sense of thought or mind is the reality of our interpretation as we process all our senses. Therefore, our senses, which can now scientifically be seen as numbering anywhere between, 5 and upwards of 20 (including the sense of rhythm, thermoception, equilibrioception, proprioception, sense of potential harm, and a host of others), still do not necessarily include *thought* as a sense, but rather, as the interpretation of all senses.

To a shaman or traditional healer, the idea of something as theatrically expressive as rhythm, movement, gesture, dance or even a special effect or symbol, if applied within a ritual in order to manifest transformative change (in oneself, but possibly in other people and organic systems too), will have a startlingly powerful effect and show amazing results just by its own application to a *ceremony*. This would be true, if for any other reason, that by your doing the ritual over time, your mind will become inspired with new ways to manifest its virtues. Just keep doing the ritual. Sound familiar? If you try the idea of a daily ritual to act upon whatever you want to strive for, so long as the ritual is mentally anchored and dressed with actions, words, and thoughts that vibrate with an energy that you find sacred and important, (and you are sensitive, insightful, and take good notes), you will notice some really uncanny things happen in favor of whatever ritual you create.

The bottom line is that one can create their own psychoactive ritual made up of nothing but pure mental energy, through the persistence of thought, self-reflection and contemplative interpretation by the use of exercising a personally sacred symbolism. I personally like to create these moments around stretching, yoga, exercise, meditation, playing a musical instrument or even while just getting from point A to point B. It can be as simple as having a symbolic picture that you look at while brushing your teeth. Even simple stuff like that, turned into a ritual, will tend to manifest improvements. I would even suggest that your rituals remain simple, so long as the symbolism is strong. This way, you have no excuse but to try it, because it is wasting no extra time for you and only a tiny little extra bit of energy. See just how little extra energy that you put into something can create massive results and unexpected blessings. The important thing to remember here is that one cannot expect anything from zero energy. It must first be accepted by you as a form of energy, so a little extra dressing is best applied in the form of thought and symbolism.

Although the length of time it takes before one might expect to see favorable results is usually pretty surprising (sometimes within 24 hours), the idea of creating a ritual should not necessarily be to have an intended end or consequence. It should merely be a moment of reflection in which you allow a channel to open up between yourself and the inspiration given to you by your familiar spirits or ancestors. Performing the ritual gives you that one micro-moment of putting your energy out there in your own special way. For something that logically appears more like "stone soup" than anything else, a personally pure and sacred ritual that you become accustomed to making a part of your life is actually all you need to create miraculous changes in health, relationships and personal transformations.

HEARTSONG

With Jerome Finley

October 28, 2014 was one week ago, as of my writing this. I had performed for a group of mostly physicians and neuro-scientists for the largest general science association in the world, The American Association of the Advancement of Science. That evening, the main subject would be on "Illusion and Delusion," and what I was asked to perform were bits from my repertoire which represented different ways of how our various senses may challenge our brain processes. This was essentially a performance given just prior to the panel discussion that I mentioned in the last section.

It was during this performance, that I was able to try for the first time, something that I had been meaning to try, but just never had the right time to do it. Here was my chance. The original idea comes from my friend, Jerome Finley. Incidentally, he told me a story of how this concept was taught to him as a 4000 year old technique, by a Quechua shaman and medicine man that he worked with during a "sacred plant ritual." For a young guy, Jerome really gets around. Group rituals are different from personal rituals in that usually the purpose of the group ritual is to partake in a meaningful experience that creates a connected bond between yourself and the individuals around you.

Since part of presenting this demonstration required that one knows how to take one's own pulse, and pretty much everyone in my audience that evening were physicians, I felt that this was a perfect group to try it out on for the first time. Jerome is an amazing teacher and an expert practitioner in many traditional healing techniques and sacred rituals the world over. With a completely sold-out theater, I was about to include into my repertoire Jerome's idea for the first time,. He had been telling me to try this and how interesting it was. Here was my chance.

What resulted from my trying this in front of such a discerning group of scientists was really quite scary and astonishing at the same time. It was scary because I really had no idea what to expect. Scientists, or any analytical person, for that matter, are considered very much a "wild card" for a performer like me. After I tried it, however, I could really see why Jerome had been so excited about it for so long...

This was an interesting exercise as it introduced the notion of a group dynamic that automatically challenges our senses, but does so in a very clever way. In fact, in my opinion, this is a perfect example of something that illustrates how there can be a "trick" or "effect" that is a device used specifically as ritual-garnish, yet for those who take part in the experience, a part of the soul feels touched, and is left stronger, more powerful and feels more meaningful than one would expect it to, even if the device behind the ritual is somewhat understood.

In most shamanic cultures, if any trickery is used as a part of the ceremony that may embody an element of amazement, it might more so be used as a "stepping stone," because those who truly desire to have the experience of something divine, will become acutely aware of its potential for manifestation. When it happens, however, you will know it, because you will become aware of a genuine act of grace. The shaman medicine people, themselves, will never take the credit for the work of their gods or spirit ancestors.

They are practitioners of the "old ways", and are the revered "reminders," that we be on the lookout for the truly divine as it is being summoned. Even the *tricks* that may be performed during their ceremonies (if any, at all), are seen as but "reminders" as well.

In the example I am about to explain, I don't believe that it is any form of deception necessarily that creates the meaningful connection that is felt, but it's the overall experience and what one's mind and soul feels as they journey in this direction with everyone who is present. Admittedly, although I did do this at my show for neuro-scientists as my first time trying it, it actually was not until the following week, as I was then able to accordingly adjust the parts that I felt needed improvement, before I was doing it with any sense of polish.. As I continued trying it out a few more times for less-formal audiences, I found what I believe is the perfect formula of ensuring its effectiveness. Of course, you will need to know what to say:

"We are about to go through a simple exercise as an experiment to see how well we can control and synchronize our beating hearts, our sense of self, brainwave patterns, and pulse rates. You may even begin to fulfill a personal dream of something you've always wanted to have happen.

"Just follow my simple instructions and notice how you FEEL after this exercise is finished.

"I want you all, at this point, to get a read on your own pulse. Go ahead and right now see if you can find that spot on your wrist, where you can feel the rhythmic pulse of your circulatory system at work. In a moment, I'm going to have you begin to tap your foot, so that everyone around you can hear the speed of your pulse. Try to concentrate on just the beat of your own pulse. Wait for me to say go, but then start tapping your foot each time, as you feel it.

"First we'll try some individuals... who has a good read on their pulse? Would you mind showing us by tapping your foot so we can hear the rhythm? Is anyone else showing a faster or slower pattern than our first contestant?" (Try a couple more people). "As you can see, everyone's pulse is slightly different from one another's. So let's try this...

"When I say, 'Go!' I want everyone who can feel their pulse, to

293

concentrate on their individual pulse and begin sounding it off by simply tapping their foot... Ready? On your mark, get set... Go!

(Wait about 20 to 25 seconds to emphasize the chaotic sound. So long as it continues to sound pretty chaotic, simply stop them from continuing. If they automatically begin to synchronize at the start, feel free to take credit, then you can end the demonstration early. However, so long as everything feels random...)

"Ok, everyone, please stop. That was... pandemonium. That was basically quite what you would expect, with everyone's pulse just off on its own course doing its own thing... The sound of chaos.

"Now, I've always wondered if those things that appear completely random are actually just a part of a complex pattern. So let's now strive to reach a deeper place within ourselves. Everyone close your eyes for a moment... And imagine yourselves floating in space, taking a few slow deep breaths...

"In the middle of our chest, beneath our breastbone, is an area that I call your *spiritual heart*. It is from here our deepest fulfillment of happiness arises. It is the source of the love and divine wisdom that we are all searching for in life; it is the only place where unhappiness can be instantly transformed into happiness. It is said that through it, we can reconnect with higher consciousnesses, and form deep and lasting bonds with the people, places and things around us.

"Take a deep breath and imagine your spiritual heart as well as all of your energetic heart-centers opening up, expanding, contracting, but then radiating beautiful iridescent rays of light that bubble outwards making a connection with everyone in this group deeply and completely.

"Take another deep breath, and as you inhale, go ahead and make a wish that you would like to fulfill... then as you exhale big, open your eyes. I hope everyone feels somewhat energized and refreshed. Okay, before we all start to get too comfortable in how we are feeling individually, let's take note of how connected we became just now, as a group. If I could please ask that everyone now find your pulses again... Get ready to start tapping your foot to the sound of your pulse... and just notice how this time it will slowly transform into a unified 'heartbeat...'

"Ready? On your mark, get set... Go!"

You will now simply stand or sit where you are and while checking your own pulse, tapping your own foot to its rhythm. Patiently tap to your own pulse, and wait a good 45 seconds, or about six long breaths. By this time, you should be starting to hear what sounds like a synchronizing heartbeat made by the pulsing rhythm of most everyone in your audience. All you need to do at this point is emphasize the heartbeat that you can hear, by either pounding your own chest to that rhythm clapping your hands, or tapping your foot slightly louder than everyone else, to the beat that you can hear is being developed. If on a microphone, just lightly tap the microphone to the "heartbeat" that you hear. All this does is emphasize how a synchronized pattern can be heard. The audience will hear it too, as it will actually be obvious.

"Can you hear the heartbeat? That, ladies and gentlemen, is the rhythm of our pulses, right now, beating as one single heartbeat. As you can see, by just refining our conscious energy, we all found a way to 'rhythmically' connect with one another! Okay, now everyone can stop tapping and be still for a moment. Close your eyes, take a deep breath and exhale fast and hard through your mouths to balance out your yin and yang energies... Now open your eyes. How do you feel? Everyone say 'GREAT!' Didn't I tell you how great you'd feel? But wouldn't it be something if, one day, we could connect everyone in the world by the beat of their own hearts?"

Thank your audience with a smile and be on your way. You just created a tiny little miracle.

Many people, during the reception that followed our AAAS panel discussion, approached to tell me how moved they were to have participated in this exercise. The position that I took, on the panel, was to offer a slightly different perspective than the scientists. I proposed that, perhaps, the experience of illusions (or delusions, for that matter) is just a process to more easily experience an alternative reality for the purpose of self-inquiry. In other words, any reason to believe an experience that isn't actually real nonetheless *feels real* may have an alternative meaning to the individual's reality than just the farce. Like a mirror...

This way, whatever is being interpreted makes its own purposeful connection, or communicates, to a deeper place in our unconscious that may guide us in an ultimately significant way. This transforms the wisdom used in the decisions we make, and brings more awareness to the well-timed connections we discover. Perhaps whatever we interpret in our own reality is more significant to our existence than any revelation of it as a deception. This is assuming, of course, that one is truly moved by the experience that was witnessed. Sometimes, clever optical illusions, like tromp-l'oeil paintings, are designed to be discovered as illusions, and are a reminder to us of how things aren't always as they appear. But could it be that another way of looking at tromp-lóeil includes an affect that it has on reality itself beyond the trick of its illusion?

We rely upon the human brain and how it works naturally to seemingly "hear" and experience connections, in this case, what sounds exactly like our individual hearts (or pulses) beating in perfect alignment and total synchronicity with the group as a single organism. Furthermore, the meditation, visualization and suggestions, will relax and connect, in mind and heart, all the people around you. Thus, all the audience members (as a collective) enter a light and relaxing meditative state that instantly helps to lower their heart rate, draw their attention inward, and make them more susceptible to our focused suggestions.

It will actually be hard to do this and not be lulled into a soft, meditative state of being directly affected by the sounds, rhythm, heartbeats and pulses of the people around you. We become naturally relaxed and easily hypnotized into following the more obvious group patterns and will even sometimes enter another pattern completely that often has nothing to do with our pulses. Natural syncopation occurs automatically just by being present within the whole group's beat, tone and tempo.

It is actually quite amazing at how it does seem as if one's own pulse takes on an aspect of the "heartbeat" that is heard. Finally, as soon as the "synchronized beat" makes itself the most apparent, you simply lead the way by emphasizing the beat to the group with your own louder beats. Doing this helps to lead your audience directly into syncopation. Once fully established, applaud them for their success.

I believe that this is an amazingly effective group demonstration that can lead to any feeling of personal connectivity between as few as two, and as many as hundreds of people. Heartsong is a perfect example, in my opinion, of how the emotional feeling and impression that is left from having participated in such a ritual will trump the scientific explanation of how or why it works.

Remember, this moment is not the *miracle*. This moment is the *reminder*. Be aware, and you will see the real miracle, soon enough...

MARY, MARY, QUITE CONTRARY

With Dr. Richard Restak

I was reading an article that my brain scientist friend, Dr. Richard Restak, just published in *The American Scholar*, Autumn 2014, on the subject of Delusions. Therefore, just in case, none of my prior offerings in this chapter seemed to do anything for your love of a fear-factor, you can try this one on for size. Excerpt from the article:

The following is a 10-minute experiment designed by Giovanni Caputo, a psychologist at the University of Urbino in Italy. It will enable you to experience a discomfiture that can lead to the onset of a delusion. (You may prefer to read the following description rather than carry out the experiment.)

Set out two chairs about two feet apart in a dimly lit room. Place a large mirror on one chair and sit on the other so that you can stare at your reflection in the near darkness. "After about one minute of mirror-gazing, most people begin to perceive a sense of unsettling distortion in their reflected face," according to Caputo. "The eyes start to move or shine, the mouth opens, or the nose becomes very large. If you continue to gaze, very big changes occur, until completely new faces appear." The participants in Caputo's experiment reported perceiving strange faces—often unknown, human or animal, living or dead, along with "fantastical and monstrous beings." Strong emotional responses accompanied these apparitions.

Some people felt that the "other" in the mirror watched them with an enigmatic, even threatening expression that created anxiety and dread in the viewers. Dynamic deformations of the new faces ("pulsations or shrinking") resulted in "an overall sense of inquietude for things out of control."

What, it seems, Giovanni Caputo has recreated here, is a simple and basic delusion-inducing ritual that appears somewhat influenced by what youngsters would call, *Bloody Mary*, and what certain ceremonial mediums would call *scrying*.

In the childhood game, Bloody Mary is usually done during slumber parties, at summer camp, or during Halloween. Basically the spirit of "Mary," (who is usually given a tragic story like she was murdered along with her child by being stabbed by a shard from a broken mirror), is summoned by taunting her, usually by spinning around 13 times, while reciting the words "Bloody Mary" with each full rotation, and then staring straight into the mirror with teasing intent, and whispering the words, "I was the one who murdered your child!" At this, the face of "Bloody Mary" allegedly will come out of the mirror and try to drag you into it with her. Though I was first introduced to the game by fifth grade summer camp, I never liked playing Bloody Mary as a child, and avoided it completely in my youth, choosing rather to listen to the bloodcurdling screams come from a distant cabin. One girl had to get sent home the next day. Another girl wet herself. Instinctively, even as skeptical a person as I was back then, I never felt that it was ever a good idea to taunt the dead, even if I had no reason to believe it was real.

In reality, however, the purpose of such an exercise is to illicit screams from frightened girls in the dark by creating an intensified altered-reality made by staring into a mirror (after spinning) and simultaneously staring fixedly into it while a single candle burns directly in front of it to illuminate one's face in the mirror. It is unlikely that anyone, least likely of all, Mary, will actually try to pull you into the mirror while trying this. There is, however, a very good chance that one will see one's face change or morph into someone or something that doesn't appear to any longer be oneself. It is usually as something like this happens that one is given such a fright, that it will jolt one completely out of one's own wits.

The reason for this has far less to do with something that really happens, and much more to do with the combination of being prepared for a fright, put in near darkness, and spinning around before staring intently into the mirror. Such combinations for frightening youngsters will vary from region to region, just as the story of Bloody Mary will change slightly with each telling, but in most cases, the ritual, the story, and the subsequent visual effects that follow will be similar. Essentially, our sight is prone to be challenged when there is insufficient light. Whereas nocturnal animals are all highly equipped with eyesight that can adjust so that it can still see with far less light, humans will always need lamps and man-made light sources, even though some do live nocturnal lives.

When we are put in front of a mirror in a dark room with only one candle burning, so that we are staring fixedly at a single point on one's nose or forehead, the lack of light will cause the eyes to blur slightly. If one does this after spinning around 13 times, certainly one's eyes will already be distracted with dizziness. This essentially forces the brain to conjure up what it is seeing by "filling in the blanks" (or unknown visuals), and making them into something. However, because these images are imagined, a feedback loop can sometimes form within our thoughts and an image that doesn't actually exist in reality is suddenly automatically conjured by the mind. The basic idea is that if one decides to taunt a horrific image to appear in the mirror, a horrific image may certainly appear.

What is interesting to me about this game, is that the mind does morph (in many ways) what it might perceive in the reflection of a mirror. Certainly, the mirror (and in general, the entire concept of "reflections") is one of man's oldest and most ancient oracular tools. The wicked queen in the children's fable of *Snow White*, would stare into her magic mirror and recite the now infamous incantation, "Mirror, mirror on the wall, who is the fairest one of all?" Michel de Nostradame, better known as the great seer, Nostradamus, and famous for his prognostications written in his book *Les Propheties* (1555), was said to scry into the reflections off the surface of a bowl of water in darkness and solitude with "fire light." The ideas of the reflection as being an image that brings forth new insights, predicts the future, tells people advice to find their true love or other hidden clairvoyant secrets, are obviously not just ideas from fairy tales, nor the writings of a madman, however...

Reflecting pools have been built to reflect the images of the most revered monuments, especially in the United States, as indicated by the Washington Monument, the US Capitol, the Lincoln Memorial, The World War II Memorial, and most recently, in Manhattan, the very moving 9/11 Memorial, which makes us reflect on all of those who were victim to the most tragic day so far in 21st century American history. Whether it is considered so or not, the magic symbolism of *the reflection* essentially imparts the same symbolic meaning as the divine duality, the masculine and feminine, the sun and the moon, the yin and yang. In *The Secret Teachings of All Ages* (1928) by Manly P. Hall, a 33rd degree freemason, who also authored, *The Lost Keys of Freemasonry* (1923), wrote of the symbolic importance of "the law of two's" as symbolized by the two identical tall bronze pillars that one would have to pass in between to get inside King Solomon's Temple. The two columns were named Boaz (meaning "strength") and Jachin (meaning to "establish" or "build").

The pillars symbolized the eternal duality of the number 2, and of course, all of its deeper meanings. Likewise, the alternating black and white checkerboard floor-pattern (seen pictured with it) symbolically represents the same, as Solomon's Temple, was built to be seen as a sacred code of magical and mathematical properties for the masons. The correspondences of alternating and opposing energies, is one of the greatest secrets of both science and magic.

A deep contemplative understanding of this "Law of Two's" is the key to realizing how to establish the strongest and most precise operations. So interestingly, what tribal shaman, many hypnotherapists, and Thelemitic ceremonial magicians all have come to understand about the "symbolic reflection" is that there is also a deeper way of working with this duality. This method, as is similar to the game, Bloody Mary, will tend to produce the initial effect of a metamorphosis, seen either in one's reflected face or surroundings. Rather than being frightened and loosing focus from this exercise by being jolted out of your skin, simply expect this to happen as a part of the process produced purely from your inner mind. Know that the idea is to just allow yourself the ability to interpret such reflections in a way that you feel is coming from a greater spirit within you.

Anything that is perceived as a suggestion or inspiration, through its reflection, can be correctly determined by first understanding its potential opposite (as a warning), but then also understanding how to intuitively or symbolically interpret the reflected image itself. In my personal opinion and experience, it is best to try to fully understand the opposite pairs of any one thing which one sees, as that is the nature of duality, and what one is getting in the reflection is ultimately the range of what one can expect, along with a glimpse of what might be (or what might not be) the best course of action. That which is also reflected, can become a symbol of something that gives you its energy and wisdom. Therefore, if you are focusing on the reflection of yourself, the answers and inspirations that come to you, will be coming from the *symbol of yourself*. If one is meditating on the reflecting pool that reflects the great Taj Majal, in India, you are reflecting on its symbol and thus everything that it represents (including its duality) which has the ability to give you wisdom.

The famous Elizabethan mathematician, astrologer, and ceremonial magician, John Dee, used scrying devices from crystal balls to highly polished mirrors made from obsidian, a glassy black stone "made from volcanic fire," as scrying mirrors that allowed him to consult with what he claimed to believe were "all-seeing angels." Is it possible that, somewhere in all this history, we may discover secret clues that lead us to understand more about the measurements between truth, reality, action, inaction, imbalance and manifestation?

It is actually possible to write an entire book just about this alone, so this is where I allow you to continue your explorations on your own, as I will now come back to why I started this conversation with you. We were talking about the neuro-sciences.

I find Caputo's Mirror Experiment to be a fascinating one, especially in the realms of the neurosciences because it brings up so many interesting ideas for future experiments using the same conditions. By shifting the intentions and observational experiences of the subjects and experimental parameters, what more may we one day discover?

During the scientific panel discussion that I mentioned earlier, we spoke of this phenomenon. I remember taking mental note that it seemed as if the fascination of most scientists, and in this case, even neuroscientists, regarding such illusion or delusion phenomena, is to just break down the components of how it is able to challenge the senses and make us perceive a different reality. What I mentioned that I was most curious about (regarding such interpretations), on the other hand, was why such things, as a symbolic reflection, will cause us to experience these deep and internal aspects within ourselves? Could there be a way of seeing greater significant meaning from our interpretations as opposed to feeling like you are safer to disbelieve what you are experiencing is being communicated to you?

After mentioning something like this to the other neuroscientists during that program, I remember feeling as if there might have been a chance that I had gone off-topic. No one really seemed that interested in "going there." I don't actually see what I am talking about here as completely immeasurable, however, since what we are talking about is still observable in so many different ways.

In the end, I look forward to hearing about future experiments in this realm. I believe that there is a lot going on here that can start bridging science, philosophy, and language with the magic of how we interact with consciousness. Meanwhile, I will watch, "in reflection," and try to see what happens.

20Q 2.0

This brings us to the state of mind that I put myself in when confronted with a mind-reading situation. As *The Man Who Knows*, everyone wants me to tell him or her what he or she is thinking. I have become somewhat accustomed to being the human "try-it-yourself" test. It was actually the reason why I wrote my first book, *Picture Your ESP!* and also the reason why this last chapter was written for you to read right now. You won't have to believe me if you can test and prove it for yourself.

First, one needs to be completely open minded, and admittedly, I have been put in more than my share of situations where I am confronted by either an abject charlatan, or someone so deep in their own ideas that everything that comes out of their mouths, sounds completely (and sometimes, amusingly) unintelligible. Simply open-minded, is best and preferred.

When one's inner mind becomes completely entangled with the larger realms of consciousness, one does internally see and feel an openness that allows one to experience a mental expanse so wide and infinite... to some, it will feel as if one is falling slowly out of one's mind. You will see both sides of a coin as it spins inside itself, folding and unfolding in space/time geometry. Things, like thoughts, can be summoned to come up sideways from other dimensions. Some people call this an opening of one's "third eye." If you are careful, you can catch yourself during this state of mind with what I can only describe as a "mental trust fall." The experience can be short, but it can also be prolonged. Short experiences will bring about lucid feelings through which you can quickly summon a sense of inspiration, symbolic feelings, or just an energy that may equate to something that is happening in the moment. Longer experiences will set off a chain reaction that will awaken you energetically and physically, keep your mind humming with the most direct answers for making decisions. It can also be likened to surfing, as some waves are smaller, but those who catch the real big waves, will get a prolonged experience of feeling something eternal.

What I am about to explain actually came from a third eye experience. As far as using one's third eye in conjunction with an understanding of my role as your storyteller, it is important that, for all who read and contemplate this with intrigue, just where I am coming from. It is about simply this:

I enjoy playing with ideas regarding the potential of our thoughts.

There really isn't any deeper reason than that. Sometimes "playing" is the best way to open us up to understanding natural laws and principles. It is how we did it as children. It is how spontaneous inspiration can be found. It is the basis of all good social conduct. All of that is sprung from a playful motivation. Allow yourself to be playful with the way you naturally *think*.

As for my on-stage presentations, there are many techniques and principles that I am applying in order to get my main points across. They are also my *signature trade secrets*. By reading this book, however, you are getting a sense of my psyche. What you have been shown in this book's final pages, are real ways that you can try and test for yourself with an assortment of unusual awareness skills . Each of the experiments, tests and games that are offered in this section really do work with practice and dedication. If you find one concept isn't quite as much to your taste as another that only means that you are beginning to define yourself within the experiments that are offered.

There is also a good chance that you may not feel an affinity with a section because you are just not fully "tuned-in" to the idea as of yet. My choice in these matters has always been to mark it as something that I will just come back to, rather than feel like it just doesn't work at all. As I am confident that what I am offering are systems that do show uncanny affects that are interesting and worth noting, I hope you will continue to try even the ones that you feel are not working for you, from time to time, just to see if improvements can be made.

Mind reading is elusive. Our minds flash from one thought to the next, and most of the time, this is happening unconsciously. However, just as in everything, the more you show an interest and explore a subject matter, the more you learn and the better you understand it. Only one golfer in history has ever gotten a hole-in-one on her very first try, and most golfers play for many years before they are able to. It is interesting, however, that so many players are able to do it at all, since the odds of getting a hole-in-one is about one in 40,000. That would quite realistically mean that, to get a hole-in-one at any point in your life, you would have successfully demonstrated an ability to change and transform your reality far beyond the laws of chance.

Yet in 2009, Unni Haskell successfully aced a hole-in-one on her very first time ever playing the game of golf on a golf course. She did it at Cypress Springs, in St Petersburg, FL, at age sixty-two! So, as we can see, there are also incredible exceptions. The true essence of how we are able to do such remarkably improbable things in our lives, however, is through the very simple human exercise of always striving to better ourselves at the things we focus our attention on.

Oftentimes I will have people who know me, or who have heard of me, randomly challenge me, usually because of one of three reasons. To see if:

1) I am really a mind reader.

2) They can validate their disbelief by saying something to catch me off guard.

3) I will figure out some way to blow their minds like what they once saw me or some other mentalist do on TV.

I am always ready for them. Now, you can be too...

"The only thing you need to do is open your mind, try not to block me, and answer honestly any questions I may ask you, okay? The idea here is to work together so that an open line of connection might be established. It isn't going to be about fooling you or 'blowing your mind.' We are just going to see if we can establish a connection."

The above script should be rehearsed and understood well, so that you know how to lay out the basic rules of what needs to happen. It ensures that your participant must not try to *psychically block you*, but rather, give feedback to any impressions as they come. The exercise is to try to establish potential thought-related entanglement within a system that will either be smooth or clunky depending on your ability to test yourself on the spot. On the days that you are smooth though, it allows you to get to the *essential thought* in a very fast and fluid manner.

For the most part, anything they feel emotionally attached to can be thought of. If they want to be challenging by thinking of something that they won't give any clues of, I handle it in one way, and if they ask me for meaningful advice, I handle it more as an energetic demonstration with wisdom that I try to summon from any deeper spirit within me. If your participant wants to tell you something, let them tell you what they want to tell you. As their guide, you must be patient and *listen carefully* to what they are saying. This is your time to connect with them and care about where they are coming from.

Once they have told you everything that they need to, you should have been given enough time to entangle with their present spirit and their situation. All that I have done was put a clever methodical order and loose script to map out an overarching process. This allows you to test yourself against someone who challenges you as well as gauge responses while joking and forming genuine connection to your volunteer. It will start you off in a direction that you will find, with practice, gives you an opportunity to "root yourself into an intuitive spirit...

"Are you thinking of Sex again? I'm just joking... You WERE thinking of Money though... or something that costs money (Ha ha)... Ok, what you are thinking of actually involves something you have some form of emotional investment in... That is what I am getting... does it involve a possible relationship of some sort? Is it a little about money and a possible direction for your life?"

Obviously, this first line should be delivered casually and lightheartedly. You will, in one swoop, have mentioned the most obvious things that most adults of most any culture would be thinking of. Also, if it is one of those things, usually it becomes clear which one it is by just using simple observation combined with some good old-fashioned *psychic guesswork*. The more slowly and casually you can read the signals on their face as you say each of the significant things, starting with "Sex," then moving sequentially through "Money," then "Relationship," and then "Of Some Sort," followed by "Direction of Life." Divining is just dividing and deciding, remember? If it's none of the above, start by saying, *"Are you absolutely sure NONE of it relates to any of what I just said? It really has nothing to do with ANY relationship that you have had or might end up having?"* If I'm going to miss, the first thing I want to know is if they are *positively certain* that I missed. Usually they will also give me some sort of clue here as to what it is, by their expression and response.

Almost everything relates to the things mentioned in your first statement... If they are convinced it does not, then what they are thinking of is obscure. Don't let that phase you.

For those times that they are adamant that none of what you mentioned had anything to do with what they are thinking of, you need to let them know that these ideas must have then popped into your head for *some reason*. Perhaps it is because they *need to pay more attention to those things that you just mentioned*. So make sure to have them make a mental note of that. The first things you mentioned are frankly things that we must *always* keep in the forefront of our hearts and minds.

"Wait... are you thinking of a 'symbol or a specific thing' in particular or are you thinking of word that is describing something? Like a completely random item, that might be a date, or personal security info, Does it have a color, symbol, or shape attached to it?"

By scripting your path in a similar manner that I am showing you, you should, in most cases, have the subject of their thoughts narrowed down by now. Essentially, you are looking for their eyes to register a "hit" as you recite slowly and deliberately through your lines. You don't need to recite the entire paragraph. You can stop reciting after they acknowledge for you which direction they are thinking, as it will most likely be in that direction. This will get you *halfway* to the finish line. Technically, from a psychic's perspective, your challenger ought to be happy that you could even get that close.

You should be already getting credit for having determined any of what you have already said, up to that point. However, if you can get any closer from here, you will be given extraordinary credit. This part will take *some real intuitive decision-making*. It won't necessarily be a "bulls eye" either, but you can come impressively close. Considering that they could have thought of anything at all and not tell you what it is, it will be as close to really reading someone's mind as you can do without direct conscious entanglement.

This will, however, give you the experience of how quickly the mind can hone-in on the information we are looking for, by just combining our organized thoughts with our intuition. Being that you need to be somewhat intuitive as well, you can now use that energy in trying to *discern or divine* what aspect of the subject matter is being concentrated on. Because of the manner in which you recited your impressions, remember, that they will have told you something general about what it is that they are thinking about. They will even confirm for you if what they are thinking of is an object or a symbol. They will let you know if there was any aspect of what they were thinking of that describes something specific... They will also register confusion if any of your statements don't match up. They will let you know if what they are thinking of might be used for security information, like a pin number, a birthday, or social security number. They will also confirm for you if what they are thinking of pertains to something with a color, shape, symbol (it could be a car, a movie, a type of food, a song, a sports team or a video game... so the recited statements can quickly narrow your choices)

If you were found to be correct after reciting your first round of statements, you will have most likely developed more of an idea of what remaining statements would be most relevant to make.. By the time you are finished with your *leading statement*, you have now given yourself an easy multiple-choice test of four general areas that might be what your spectator is thinking of. The chances will be strongest that your volunteer is either thinking of (1) *a relationship of some kind,* (2) *an injury or health concern,* (3) *a career project task, or* (4) *something quirky and specific.* If you can correctly determine this multiple choice, you will have gotten yourself off to a good start and now you only need to be intuitive a few more times before nailing it. .

Let us say that your participant indicates that it's a *"relationship of some sort."* Depending on their expression, how they respond to your statement may determine what kind of "relationship" they are talking about. Remember, if you saw their face first contort, then relax as you said "Of Some Sort," it could be their grandmother's necklace. If it does become clear that it is a relationship, you now need to decide if it is a human or non-human relationship, and that will usually be evident in how they react as you wisely use the wording *"relationship of some sort."* They might also be thinking of their pet. Once you have determined that it is a human relationship, you can move to determining:

1) Male vs. Female.

2) Lover, Friend or Family member (older vs. younger). Might

also be a Role Model (athlete, musician, leader in field, etc).

3) Religious or Philosophical relationship. (it could be Jesus)

4) Appearance: Young vs. Old, Dark vs. Light Eye/Hair Color, Short vs. Tall, Thin vs. Heavy).

5) Aspects of the Name (Long or Short / Common vs. Uncommon) Go by birth name or nickname?

The above five determinations must all be at least contemplated and are worth mentioning casually, using memes like "might it involve" and/or "could it be connected to," or "this is what I am getting..." in order to keep everything rather vague until you find your direction. Furthermore, with practice, the system becomes extremely dynamic. You can continue to zero-in, more and more, adding descriptions and characteristics, just like a real psychic might.

Again, these subjects are mapped-out to attempt to find the quickest path to whatever would be considered a *perceived mental target*. Remember also, that as you intuitively run down this list, you simply need to get to your target as quickly as possible, so once you know what it is, you can either continue to zero-in, or give them a spontaneous intuitive reading of their future based on simply adding up all the information that came to you. Whatever you want to determine as symbolic can be used to give a short reading, or one can use any psychic oracle reading system that one feels most comfortable with (tarot cards, ESP symbols, palmistry, runes, astrology charts, etc). Taking people up on their challenges to read their minds will quickly teach you how to read other people's thoughts with all your senses firing.

Now, if right after your first statements of a "Relationship," you notice that you are being taken in that direction, it might still be a non-human relationship they are thinking of. You can now just ask how close you are, and usually they will offer some assistance. Most relationships you will encounter will be about two people. However, if it is determined that it is an animal, one can determine first between (a) Pet vs. Animal Totem Spirit, followed by (b) Dog vs. Cat or other Animal (c) Large vs. Small and (d) Appearance vs. Personality. So the sequential order, by which you zero-in on the thought, has been mapped in an efficient manner in order to (usually) get you in close enough to establish a "hit," but not necessarily directly on target.

If it is non-living, one first determines between (a) Common vs. Expensive and/or Valuable, (b) Location vs. Activity, (c) Food/Drink, Music and Sports (multiple choice). Getting a facial read on all of the above (in that sequential order) helps to "crack the code" of which direction (out of the three choices) one will need to move from there. It can be stated like this:

"This is something, like an item of some sort, or of something happening somewhere? Does it involve something expensive, or something of worth? I feel that this has something to do with either a location or an activity... around food, excitement, maybe music?"

Now, you will only need to follow one of the three directions in order to arrive into target range (a, b, or c, below).

a) Common vs. Valuable usually denotes an item, when the remaining subjects do not appear to strike a chord. It leads to contemplations and impressions between Possession vs. Non Possession (something desired). Depending on what you end up with there, your most common possibilities will end up being (1) something wearable, (2) ring, (3) watch, (4) something printed, (5) motorized or electric vehicle or machine, (6) art, (7) "things that make other things," (8) chair/furniture and (9) computer or new technology.

b) Location, Music, and Activity, is a multiple choice that also breaks down into its own categories. Location (if not in the U.S.A.) will lead to Tropical, Exotic, Islands, Africa, Middle East, Asia, Europe, Cold Climate. Music could be a concert, musical instrument, a musician, DJ, band, song or piece of music. Activity most likely points to a sports or live social event, thrill seeking adventure, or conference/gathering.

c) Food & Drink will mostly break down into, (1) a Restaurant or Gathering Spot, (2) Pizza, (3) Latin, (4) Burgers, (5) Sushi/Asian (6) Fruits/Vegetables, (7) Breakfast, (8) Italian (9) Alcoholic or Non-alcoholic beverage (10) Sweets/ Desserts.

The manner in which one approaches mentioning the categorical dichotomies listed above will definitely take some practice in order to be fluent, and with a good memory system (See *Presidential Memory* at the end of Part I). Since it is a pretty intuitive system as it is, it is actually quite easy to practice and get better. It's not about getting it right all the time. It's about being fearless, knowing your role as the mind reader, and playing off your mistakes so that they are used as significant signposts for further interpretation.

Of course, as in all of the tests I like to create, this demonstration is best played and (especially practiced) as a *game,* which is not designed to do anything but show how people can be connected in ways that are beyond what one would expect. Obviously, it should appear to your spectators as if you are simply calling out potential correlations to their thoughts without an underlying method. So long as you remember even the most general order that they are to be stated, it is a simple matter to just find creative and dramatic ways of acting as if you are inspired as you list each category. The dichotomies are there so if you choose the correct one of the two, ordinarily (with only a few common-sense exceptions) you won't have to mention the other. However, if you mention the wrong one of the two, no need to panic. Simply toggle quickly over as if you had a "transmission mishap," or as if the other thought simply just meant something else, and continue to form your impressions. As you speak, just watch their faces and try to gauge yourself against the feedback you receive from your own intuition as well as interpreting their facial reactions.

Since each scripted impression that you make is designed to give you information that will zero-in on a thought, while giving off the appearance that "impressions" are coming to you spontaneously, you are now gifted with a power to (under certain conditions) literally read minds at most any given time. Remember, it is always best that whatever is thought of, must be something meaningful to the challenger. It can't just be "anything."

Please use this secret (as well as the others hidden in this book) to help spread positive and friendly intentions, and *never* to take advantage of others. If there is anything to believe about deceptive magic it is this: learning these demonstrations all possess really bad karmic effects if or whenever used with ill intention. If you have noticed how extraordinarily the other demonstrations mentioned in this book *do work,* just know that using more formulaic approaches in an improper manner will have its own consequences. Respect these constantly fluctuating dualities of how we manifest genuine circumstance, and you will find a limitless universe to explore at your disposal.

Alain Nu, The Man Who Knows™

EPILOGUE

GAME OVER;
BEGIN EXPLORING

When I think about all the things that we have imagined throughout history that came true, everything from putting a man on the moon to realizing Star Trek "tricorder" technology (that interacts with your smart phones and allows you to scan the chemical makeup of virtually anything in front of you— really), it becomes far easier to grasp how we are a species of animal who is constantly as well as literally shaping and transforming our reality. Although it's easy to see that we do this as we make connections (like adding one plus one and so on), we must now ask ourselves if that is the only way that we are learning, growing and evolving? Are we only making connections in this "one-foot-in-front-of-the-other" three-dimensional manner, or is it possible that our complex neuro-electric connections within our brains allow us to function our learning (or KNOWING) from other dimensions as well?

In the spirit of "as above; so below," we can see communities of people, as well as even individual human beings, shaping and transforming reality and existence. If *only* a three-dimensional learning process takes place, it would make it much harder to figure out how people like Johann Sebastian Bach, Nicola Tesla, Leonardo Da Vinci, or any of the others, were able to function so far above and beyond the creative thinking processes of the average person. Do we all simply take advantage of other people's inventions and just blindly adopt them into our lives (microwave ovens, cell phones, mini-pad computers, 24 hour internet connectivity, etc...) as they come? Many of us do. In fact, we actually have to, in order to stay on the "cutting edge," since the technological landscape changes very quickly from year to year.

As we learn more and more, we also discover newer needs that give birth to newer inventions. Like an intense colony of ants that inhabit this planet on a larger scale, we work as a team of inventors who carve our way through time and knowledge. As soon as one takes an idea as far as one can, there is always another who will *carry and shape that idea forward through time* in technological, aesthetic, purposeful, and conceptual ways.

Thus, we continue on, expanding our minds into the universe of our future, past and present. However, when one becomes truly inspired, one finds oneself overcome suddenly with a powerful drive to make a contribution that furthers our exploration, understanding or knowledge in an important way. Suddenly, there is a certain feeling of possession that takes place from within which feels as if some kind of energy is being channeled from elsewhere. Where is that inspiration coming from?

Did Bach write all the masterful scores of music that he wrote in his short lifetime simply because he happened to be in the right place at the right time? Did Buckminster Fuller discover the geodesic dome by accident? Was Nicola Tesla just a silly foreigner with impractical ideas, (like Edison enjoyed suggesting)? If I were an alien, looking down on our planet from outer space, I might be observing more how the planet appears to be an expression (and at the mercy and influence) of human cultures and communities, which can then be seen as an expression of each individual. This can then, in turn, be seen as expression of their own inner universe within each separate mind, and so on. We are all able to shape and transform our realities in ways that make it meaningful, joyful, exciting and challenging and it all can begin in our mind, right now.

My aim, throughout this book, was to share with you my personal journey that ultimately led me to becoming *The Man Who Knows*, (which was not my idea at all, but a crazy branding scheme that my manager had surprise-dropped on me when we first met). Nonetheless, I think I have made it quite plain to see that, indeed, I am not an ordinary thinker. Rather, I hope you feel that I have tried to be as rationally minded (as well as open-minded) as I can about these mysterious, mystical and paranormal subjects. I am curious enough to experiment in an open way of interacting with a "source," or "spirit" or "inner wisdom" which may be called upon to offer help or guidance. I am curious to try and make sense of a world which many people are just beginning to notice is starting to make less and less sense (just watch the news on TV), and finding it more and more frustrating, exhausting, depleting, or too stressful to hold everything together.

I like to think of this book as a place for you to explore; to "mysteriously empower yourself" while contemplating the many mysterious powers that you always wondered about. Might we ever discover a hidden mystical understanding that functions on a deeper level within us? Might there be an untapped resource that we all have which allows us to build upon our own mental powers? The experiments and games included in this book might actually reveal some clues that help us along our way to such self-mastery. Most of these can be done impromptu, although most will also take study and practice to fully master.

You can always simply refer to this book. You can always make it fun, yet at the same time, treat it like an experiment. Since I wanted to be completely inclusive of all things from the mysterious to the paranormal, I touched upon all kinds of fascinating and much debated topics, from spontaneous healing, to the power of positive thinking, transcendental meditation's affect on crime reduction, and even ghostly manifestations.

We covered telepathy, telekinesis, precognition, and interactive consciousness games. We lightly touched upon the subjects of qi gong, the yin and yang, the seven chakras, hypnosis, NLP, pendulums, ESP symbols and the controversial Law of Attraction. We learned about some state of the art "consciousness controlled" computer programs, games and machines that are available to consumers today. We even talked about machines that communicate with spirits, the psychic impressions of a UFO expert, and a UFO encounter with the world's most renowned celebrity metal-bender. I hope from reading this, I have awakened an interest within you, which may blossom into your own direction of research, development, and understanding.

Before I allow you to stop reading, however, I would like to mention, as *The Man Who Knows*, that I know you did try one or two of the tricks from the first chapter, and that they didn't go quite as planned. What you most likely assumed was that the trick was designed to work by itself. Yes, I also know that you know what it was that went wrong, but that's not completely the point. What you didn't know was that in order for *any* of the demonstrations shown in this book to work, it takes you having to put your *spirit* into it. So you see, there is a spirit after all! This is the difference between something that works and something that doesn't. Once you have internalized full control of the principles that you were given, and you feel you can apply these principles as tools within your interactions with people, you will find your margin for error will greatly diminish.

"Practice makes perfect" is another way of saying, "if you just do the ritual, your desired transformation will take place." Sometimes it takes more practice than other times. Sometimes it just works. But if your intention is for something to work, it will work. Think about what Uri Geller said in my interview with him. He doesn't make things work because he is special and blessed with special powers, necessarily, (even though that UFO incident might push him over the edge); his message is that he makes things work because he is so positive that it will work. He is, in fact, positive about everything. The simple message here is to keep your mind as open as possible while staying aware of your surroundings, in control of your body in space, what it is being subjected to, and how the universe is responding to you. You will be surprised at how much control you find you can have over what appears to be pure circumstance.

Creating the appropriate energy to exercise the rituals you will use towards personal transformation will also become important. We discussed earlier, a list of criteria for creating personal rituals whose purpose is to connect your inner spirit with a potential collective consciousness. The following example is a simple visualization and breathing ritual that you can use to help motivate yourself:

Close your eyes and imagine your spirit-energy being generated by setting the duality of 'heart' and 'mind' in motion. This duality is a powerful one. It will spin extraordinarily fast, and has the ability to cause reality to shift into its direction. The idea is that such a vibrant energy will cause a tipping point to flow in the direction of your intention, whatever it might be, no matter.

Breathe deep, imagining the energy building inside you while visualizing the way you feel when you are the most focused and aware and how powerful you are when you can feel that awareness and drive within you, bursting to say something important, meaningful, or to make a statement of expression. This is the most important thing to you right now. This is the thing that you have been meaning to say and now is your chance for you to express it.

Breathe deep again, and as you exhale, allow yourself to imagine everything that represents what you want for yourself in the future to instantly become a part of the reality around you, while opening your eyes. This empowered feeling within you has now manifested itself into existence. Know now that your present creative spirit has become that much easier to access having revitalized your energy in this way. Look around you. You are in full control.

As an experiment, try the above visualization exercise, (and then re-read and re-learn whichever demonstration you tried from Part I, which didn't originally work). If you then try it on someone else, I bet you will do much better the second time, especially if you take the time to try the above ritual before re-reading. You see, mentalism really does involve mind-power, just not in the same way as one might expect!

Speaking of which, I also know that you have hardly tried any of the demonstrations yet in the last section. But, yes, some of that stuff does take some real commitment and personal study. One might now see that it is not quite as easy to do this stuff as one might have originally thought. I believe that one of the lessons learned here is that virtually anything is possible if you put your mind and your heart to it. Just apply a little discipline. Create visualizations and rituals that empower you. After that, you won't need to do anything else but the ritual.

It might all boil down to this:

We find wisdom in all things from ancient to present, even in what is imagined. Learning is something we must love to do, because learning is the fastest way to knowing.

We can then use such wisdoms to implement rituals and mental patterns that nourish one's spirit while experimenting on circumstance and balancing personal energy.

Discipline, awareness and careful monitoring of one's food, water, breathing, movement, and body/mind, gives us the ultimate control of our spirit.

We have an open mind to accept the universe around us as an amazing and infinite multidimensional source of knowledge and divine energy. These are all really *basic ancient wisdoms*, but they can lead you to some interesting breakthroughs as well as a continued personal discovery and growth. They may also simplify your life. After all, you now know that you can nourish not only your body but your mind and spirit as well. By nourishing yourself in all of these ways, and in all of the ways our planet provides for us to do so, you are giving back to the people and creatures around you and re-nourishing our planet in turn. It is, of course, just as important that one stays away from those things that poison our selves, our bodies, our minds and our spirits.

Having a *state of mind* that is open, aware and constantly learning will bring more energy, balance, and even surprising fortune into your life. Now you will have more control than ever over complex issues to direct your life, and to shape your reality, transforming it in positively meaningful, joyous, mystical and even entertainingly mysterious ways.

Go be.

ABOUT THE AUTHOR

Alain Nu,

The Man Who Knows, formed his lifelong passion for mysterious and unknown realms in his early childhood. Growing up in San Francisco in the late 1960's to 1970, Alain was exposed at an early age to the world of fortunetellers, street performers and other practitioners of the "mystery arts." Like many children, his mind was agile and creative. He was fascinated by paleontology and became an avid and knowledgeable young rock collector.

Largely shunned by his peers for somehow being "different," he turned his natural desire to connect with others inwards. With two hard-working parents and little outside community, he befriended neighborhood animals and regularly "walked" with a pack of free-running dogs that seemed to flock to his magnetic energy. This experience of friendship beyond species had a definite impact on his belief that a "force" of sorts connects all living things in the universe.

His parent's decision to move to Washington, DC, cemented his destiny through a process of personal struggle and triumph. At the time, being the only Asian student in his new school, the other students now ostracized him to an even greater degree than before. Operating completely outside social cliques and other mainstays of childhood to adolescent life, he spent his time honing his skills in magic and esoteric studies.

As a youth, his interest in the unknown manifested in anything he could research, and/or get away with — basement séances, UFO clubs, and playfully testing he and his friends' psychic ability with playing cards. He asked his father, who worked at the *Library of*

319

Congress, to bring home hard-to-find books on magic, strange phenomena, and parapsychology, so he could learn as much as possible about these topics. He became close friends with and worked for Mark Chorvinsky (now deceased), who was the publisher/editor of *Strange Magazine*, which covered many topics of the weird and unexplained. Connecting with this new world of people consumed with a passion for pursuing the unknown on so many different levels brought Alain's personal sense of the importance of these topics to a new level. Eventually, Alain's interest turned towards the field of "mentalism"—parlor demonstrations of ESP, mind reading and telekinesis.

The path on which he found himself seemed to be his only true calling, and Alain came to the moment of decision on which his entire future depended. To Alain, there was no question that he was already doing exactly what he needed to do. Against tremendous odds, he built a career that eventually brought him to headline at Caesars Palace in Las Vegas and star in four of his own hour-long television specials: *"The Mysterious World of Alain Nu"* which aired on TLC and international television. His endless creativity and high standard of excellence over many years earned him several awards, along with the deep respect and admiration of his peers.

Always trying to keep up with the latest studies on the brain and consciousness, Alain's interest was piqued by recent findings linking quantum physics and serious parapsychological research. Invigorated by the implications of these parallel fields of study, Alain's role became clearer than ever: To develop programs that introduce ordinary people to their own extraordinary abilities.

Determined to seek his own path as "The Man Who Knows," Alain has intrigued Washington society with his incredible programs of wonder along with the message of furthering one's openness to the marvels of human interconnectivity. Presenting at universities, corporations and association events, Alain gained a wide reputation for entertaining very sophisticated audiences with his uncanny demonstrations that blur the line between science and the mysteries of unexplained phenomena.

"To watch him is to throw out all the rules of physics. Time and space are malleable in Nu's deft hands, said Eric Brace of *The Washington Post*. Mike Weatherford, entertainment columnist for the *Las Vegas Review Journal*, noted, "He did things that I had never seen before." And *Showbiz Magazine* added: "Alain Nu is seriously mental."

Always contemplating the fine line between fact and fiction, Alain Nu continues to challenge the mind to explore how we are all strangely connected through a mysterious energy. His audiences all share a common sense of awe, exclaiming: "I don't know how to explain that;" "No way, no way;" and "I don't believe in magic. But, I saw it happen. And, I believe what I saw."

Alain Nu is "the modest explorer, the gracious and kind tour guide leading the audience into investigations and ultimately mysterious realms," says Donn Murphy, Ph.D., Executive Director of *The National Theatre*. "It works beautifully... with electric energy, enormous imagination and warm appeal."

In his one-man, touring stage show *Invisible Connections*, Alain Nu utilizes these untold powers to foretell our actions, reveal our unspoken thoughts and create seemingly impossible phenomena. "Nothing is impossible as long as you know how to adjust your perception," says Alain Nu. "Think about it. With just our thoughts and words as tools of visualization, we have the beginnings of untold power."

"I feel that each of us has a super hidden potential that is real," he says. "I'm hoping to show people that their own intention to develop such powers can, indeed, be practiced!" says Nu.

Alain Nu's amazing live programs, are still offered worldwide, and incorporate elements of probability, psychology, suggestion, professional techniques or just plain "good timing." He is a consummate public speaker and entertainer. However, taking this all one step further, Alain is quite certain that there is *something more*.

How does he know this? "I feel that each of us has a super hidden potential that is real," he says. " I'm hoping to show people that their own intention to develop such powers can indeed be practiced!" says Nu.

Learn more about Alain Nu at TheManWhoKnows.TV.

INDEX

Committee for Scientific
Claims of the Paranormal,
99
Committee for Skeptical
Inquiry, 230
Confucius, 192, 209, 210, 211,
264
Congressional Medal of
Honor, 119
Consciousness and the Source
of Reality: The PEAR
Odyssey, 169
Cowell, Simon, 161
CSICOP. *See* Committee for
Scientific Claims of the
Paranormal
Csikszentmihalyi, Mihaly, 118
Curry, Adam, 170

Da Vinci, Leonardo, 313
Daily Mirror, 155
Dallas, TX, 128
David Lynch Foundation, 78
Dawkins, Richard, 98, 99
De Niro, Robert, 160
Dee, John, 301
DeGeneres, Ellen, 72
DeMolay, 96-98, 134
DeMolay, Jacques, 97, 98
Denny & Lee, 105, 107, 125
Dowsing, 151, 254
Duc, Minh, 125
Duke University, 262
Dunne, Brenda, 92, 93, 168,
169
Dunninger, The Great, 7
Dyment, Doug, 263

Eastwood, Clint, 72
Eddington, Sir Arthur, 60
Elman,Dave, 283
Erickson, Milton, 272, 276, 277

ESP, 7, 11, 171, 237, 246, 262,
263, 264, 266, 308, 315, 320
Evason, Jeff and Tessa, 148

Feng Sheng, 201-204
Finley, Jerome, 149, 291-297
Fleming, Chris, 140-148
Follies and Fallacies in Medicine,
56
Fox, James, 109
Fuller, Buckminster, 314
Fulves, Karl, 18
Gallagher, Barbara, 132
Gardener, Martin, 18
Geller, Uri, ix, 7, 153-164, 228,
316
Gellerism, 153, 155
George Institute for Global
Health, 68
Gibo, Aiko, 132
Gödel Escher Bach an Eternal
Golden Braid, 61
Gorakshashatakam, 195
Granit, Ragnar, 60
Green, Perry Joseph, 229
Griffin, Merv, 159
Grinder, John, 272
Grossberg, Scott, 279-289

Haddock, Frank Channing,
229
Hall, Manly P., 299
Haney, Denny, 105, 125
Hardyman, Will, 130
Hartline, Haldan Keffer, 60
Harvard School of Medicine,
56, 58, 64
Harvard University, 60
Haskell, Unni, 304
Haunted America, 132
Haunted Times Magazine/Radio,
143